Lost
Chicago

DAVID

GARRARD

LOWE

A CENTURY OF PROGRESS

I WILL

1833   1933

COME!
CHICAGO
WORLD'S FAIR

Lost Chicago

DAVID GARRARD LOWE

Watson-Guptill Publications / New York

For My Father, Who First Took Me to
Henrici's and the Union Stock Yards,
and My Uncle, Who Won the American Derby
with Windy City

Copyright © 2000 by David Garrard Lowe

Revised and enlarged edition published by
Watson-Guptill Publications
a division of BPI Communications
770 Broadway, New York, NY 10003

First edition published 1975 by Houghton Mifflin Company,
Boston, ISBN 0-395-20726-6

Library of Congress Catalog Card Number: 00-107305

ISBN: 0-8230-2871-2

Manufactured in the United States of America

First printing, 2000

1 2 3 4 5 6 7 8 9 / 07 06 05 04 03 02 01 00

Editor: Sylvia Warren
Designer: Derek Bacchus
Production Manager: Ellen Greene

Cover photograph: Detail of the soaring rotunda of
Henry Ives Cobb's Federal Building, built between 1895 and
1905, and wantonly destroyed in the mid-1960s.

The typeface used in this book is Adobe Garamond.

: ACKNOWLEDGMENTS :

This new, revised edition of *Lost Chicago* was made possible in part by a grant from the Graham Foundation for Advanced Studies in the Fine Arts, Richard Solomon, director.

I would like to begin by thanking Sally Forbes. Her wide-ranging knowledge of photographic research, her extraordinary experience in magazine and book publishing, and her taste were essential to the completion of this book. I would also like to thank her for her unflagging encouragement and her sound good sense.

The creation of the new edition of *Lost Chicago* was facilitated in important ways by Edward Morris Bakwin, who shared with me his profound knowledge of Chicago and provided me with invaluable books on the city. Richard H. Brown searched out publications for me, ascertained facts, and supplied welcome cheer.

The research for the text and for the illustrations for this volume was wonderfully helped by a host of friends and acquaintances. I would like to mention in particular Anna F. Weaver, Joseph R. DuciBella, Mr. and Mrs. Harlow Niles Higinbotham, Mr. and Mrs. Edward Byron Smith, Jr., Mr. and Mrs. Frederick Selch, Gregory Selch, John A. Holabird, Jr., Zurich Esposito, Margot Gayle, Barton Faist, James M. Wells, David W. Dunlap, Mr. and Mrs. Richard DuBrul, Melody Walker O'Brien, Lloyd Barber, Judith C. York, and Celia Hilliard.

No list of acknowledgements would be complete for this book without mention of those connected to a number of august Chicago institutions who showed me great consideration when I was pursuing my research. Among them, Lynn Osmond, president of the Chicago Architecture Foundation; Timothy Samuelson, curator of architecture at the Chicago Historical Society; Kathy S. Cottong, director of the Arts Club; Alice Tucker, executive director of The Casino; Richard R. Seidel, historiographer of the Episcopal Diocese of Chicago; Joe Cataio of the Moody Bible Institute Library; and Jay Satterfield and Daniel Meyer, Special Collections, the Regenstein Library of the University of Chicago.

I would like to thank the staff of the Chicago Historical Society; the Newberry library; the Theatre Historical Society of America; the Woman's Athletic Club; and the Arlington Heights Public Library.

In cities other than Chicago, the research for the book was aided by a number of highly knowledgeable individuals. In Paris I was helped by Madame Melle Comminges of the Roger-Viollet archives. In Montreal at the Centre Canadien d'Architecture, Madame Maria Antonella Pelizzari was invaluable. While I was working in the Prints and Photographs Division of the Library of Congress in Washington, Sam Daniel helped to direct my quest. In New York Janet Parks of the Avery Architecture and Fine Arts Library of Columbia University was, as always, a most knowing guide. I would also like to thank Mark Peil of the New York Society Library.

I would like to acknowledge the special help of James H. Burke, John Cadenhead, Elspeth Hart, Francis P. King, Suzanne McDonough, and the director of the World Monuments Watch Program, Kristin Sechler.

Finally, I wish to thank Noah Lukeman, who understood the need for a new edition of *Lost Chicago* and never ceased to encourage it, and my editor at Watson-Guptill, Sylvia Warren, whose keen interest, painstaking work, and good judgment added immeasurably to the quality of this book.

I SOMETIMES FEEL that my Chicago is like an immense picture puzzle, a picture puzzle from which the pieces are removed one by one—the Chicago Stock Exchange, the Arts Club, the Northwestern Railway Station—until, at last, there will be nothing left of the city I knew. When I published *Lost Chicago* in 1975, I naively hoped that I had said all that needed to be said on the destruction of the metropolis's architectural patrimony, hoped that the book would be a veritable paper Great Wall of China which would keep the barbarians out of my Celestial City.

Alas, since then a quarter of a century has passed and more and more irreplaceable pieces of Chicago have been removed from the pictorial board. Some, like the 900 Michigan Building, were architectural masterpieces; others, like the Cliff Dwellers Club atop Orchestra Hall, reverberated with memories of a notable past. When my publisher inquired whether there was enough material to justify an updating and revision of *Lost Chicago,* I was forced to answer, with a kind of savage sadness, yes. This volume is the result. Included between its covers are newly-discovered illustrations of earlier losses and photographs of more recent ones; new, expanded captions for almost every illustration; revisions of the text where research and wisdom indicated that they were needed; and a final chapter which carries the book up to the present. Here are the magnificent concrete and spiritual ghosts of the Windy City: the Marbro Theatre, upon whose vast silver screen Marilyn Monroe sang of the symbiotic relationship between girls and diamonds; the Stop & Shop, through whose doors strayed the pungent scent of freshly-roasted coffee promising Araby within; and the Chicago Stadium, where in 1932, FDR was like a bright candle in the Great Depression's Stygian darkness.

In the "Overture" to the *Swann's Way* portion of his great novel, *À la Recherche du Temps Perdu (Remembrance of Things Past)*, Marcel Proust wrote:

> But when from a long-distant past nothing subsists, after the people
> are dead, after the things are broken and scattered, taste and smell alone,
> more fragile but more enduring, more unsubstantial, more persistent,
> more faithful, remain poised a long time, like souls, remembering,
> waiting, hoping amid the ruins of all the rest; and bear unflinchingly, in
> the tiny and almost impalpable drop of their essence, the vast structure
> of recollection.

Proust's remembrance of things past was refreshed when, as an adult, he tasted again a madeleine, a little cake like the ones he had been given as a child. I hope, though words and pictures cannot physically reconstruct the structures which have been destroyed, that this new edition of *Lost Chicago,* will, Like Marcel Proust's madeleine, be a means of assuring that at least they will not be forgotten.

David Garrard Lowe
June, 2000

CHICAGO was always, for me, a magical city. When I was very young, in the 1940s, the magic took the simple form of shopping with an aunt on State Street, luncheon beside the fountain of Marshall Field's Narcissus Room, and a tour of that perpetually wondrous Xanadu, Field's toy department. On very special occasions, I might be permitted to select a gift for myself, a stagecoach with four galloping horses or a PT boat which fired wooden projectiles. Sometimes, in the afternoon, we entered the exotic fantasy of the Oriental Theatre, and there amid the curious chinoiserie of its auditorium I sat entranced while, on the stage, the Mills Brothers sang "Paper Doll." Of all the city's richly varied movie palaces, the Oriental held first place in my heart, though it had stiff competition from the Paradise out west on Crawford Avenue, where Lorado Taft's statue of Apollo in his chariot raced tirelessly across a star-filled sky.

Later, Chicago's magic was enhanced by visits with my father to Henrici's on Randolph Street; amidst its Edwardian opulence of exuberantly carved wood, waving palms, and enormous paintings in gleaming golden frames, I was first introduced to such old-fashioned delicacies as finnan haddie and pêche melba. If we were going to the theater, perhaps the Garrick almost across the street which my father continued to call by its original name, the Schiller, I might be told of that long-past glorious time when Chicago had boasted dozens of legitimate theaters and Sarah Bernhardt had announced that she preferred it to New York.

Both my father and my grandfather had worked in the Union Stock Yards, and no place was more magical than that vast congregation of bleating, grunting, lowing animals. The pens stretched for as far as the eye could see, the freight trains out of the West seemed endless, and the packing houses were entire towns unto themselves. Often I heard stories of the years when Nelson Morris, Gustavus Swift, and Philip D. Armour ruled the Yards, true princes of the blood.

But Chicago still had princely aspects in the late 1940s and the early '50s. There was the elegance of American Derby Day at Washington Park, conjuring up memories of that earlier Washington Park with its smart processions of broughams, landaus, and victorias. There was the sophisticated excitement of the arrival of the *Twentieth Century Limited* at the La Salle Street Station and the Hollywood-tinged glamour of the departure of the *Chief* and the *Super Chief* from the Dearborn. There was the sense of power, the summoning of the ghosts of Lincoln, William Jennings Bryan, and Franklin D. Roosevelt, during national political conventions. None was more dramatic than the one in 1952 when the lobbies of the Congress and the Blackstone and the Stevens—as we still called the Conrad Hilton—were jammed with delegates passionately split between Dwight Eisenhower and the hero of the heartland, Robert Alphonso Taft. There was the lingering '30s chic of the Chez Paree, with its dance bands and headliners such as Lena Horne. And always, at night, there was the shimmering fantasy of the Wrigley Building dominating Michigan Avenue, and, behind it, the Lindbergh Beacon atop the Palmolive Building, which gave to the Loop the sense of a perpetual premiere.

Indeed, the supreme magic of Chicago was always the sheer physical presence of the city, the unequaled splendor of its architecture. For me, growing up was coincidental with becoming aware of that architecture. As the names of its builders entered my consciousness—Le Baron Jenney, Dankmar Adler, Louis Sullivan, John Wellborn Root, Daniel Burnham, Henry Ives Cobb, Martin Holabird, Frank Lloyd Wright— I began to look about with interest and wonder and love. A walk through Chicago became a kind of pilgrimage to their creations: Adler & Sullivan's Auditorium and their Stock Exchange, Cobb's Potter Palmer castle and Federal Building, Burnham's Mecca, Wright's Francis Apartments, Holabird & Root's Diana Court. These were, in a very real sense, Chicago's true shrines, for here one felt that man had expressed his better nature, that he had, in some mysterious way, been in touch with a force greater than himself.

After college, when I moved away, every trip back to Chicago was a revelation of monuments fallen: the Mecca, the Palmer castle, the Garrick Theatre, the Federal Building, the long bar of the Auditorium, the Stock Exchange, Diana Court. Even lesser landmarks, the places that had given the city its special personality, were not spared: the Paradise Theatre, Henrici's, the Chez Paree, the Lindbergh Beacon, and, unbelievably, the Stock Yards themselves. Their owners had not saved them. City commissions had not saved them. They were an incomparable heritage mindlessly squandered, pieces of gold minted by the fathers and thrown away by the sons. I could not save them in their concrete form, but I was determined that somehow I would preserve their spirit. I would do it in the one way I could, by writing a book that would reveal them and their architectural predecessors in all their glory. Perhaps, by showing the splendor which has been lost, I might, in some small way, help to preserve that splendor not yet departed.

David Garrard Lowe
1975

North Lake Shore Drive, 1941. Photograph taken from the Palmolive building by Andreas Feininger.

TABLE OF CONTENTS

Chicago river

Jefferson park

CHICAGO TRIBUNE

BULETIN

Madison Street

Chicago river from Clark St Bridge

West Side from Lake Street Bridge

The Island

IN THE BEGINNING there was only the great lake on the east and, to the west, the billowing sea of grass. Between them, a kind of island, the future site of Chicago was a damp place in which grew countless wild onions. Any understanding of the city, its grain elevators and packing houses, its rail yards and mail order business, its tall towers with their broad windows set to catch the morning sun, and its low earth-hugging prairie houses, must first take this into account.

Chicago is in the midst of sea-lanes as surely as Britain is. This fact has made everything else possible. The level sea of grass and water about it gave impetus to its architects to raise unchallenged mountains from whose tops they could sight across a continent and to build pattern-shattering houses, as sheltering as cottages on the edge of a stormy ocean. For Chicago is not inland. Springfield, Massachusetts, is inland; Harrisburg, Pennsylvania, is inland; Chicago is not. To the New Englanders and New Yorkers who journeyed out in the nineteenth century it seemed inland; seemed so because they had traveled across western New York and Ohio and Michigan and Indiana to get there. But it cannot be called inland unless one considers Naples on the Tyrrhenian and Venice on the Adriatic Sea inland. Those who have witnessed the twelve-foot breakers crashing along the lake and beheld the waves of snow on the great plain stretching limitless to the Arctic know that it is a city on an island between two seas.

There are places that have the good fortune to have their beginnings attended by romance. Rome, with its legend of Romulus and Remus, and New York, with its purchase by Peter Minuit for the equivalent of $24, are two. Philadelphia's beginnings are without romance, as are Washington's. Chicago's are rife with it. The very words most commonly associated with the city's birth, *coureurs de bois,* are redolent of the splash of a paddle upon a crystal lake, of men in buckskin, of afternoon shadows slanting through a virgin wood. Among the Europeans who came to this continent, the French were the first to see the site of Chicago. They did not discover it; it was not lost. For centuries Miamis and Illinois and Potawatomis and Ottawas and Chippewas had roamed over it, gathering there to trade pelts for corn, feathers for flint. And it was the Indians who named this ground of meeting and passage. They called it "Chi-ca-gou," the Place of the Wild Onion.

The recorded history of Chicago begins with two extraordinary Frenchmen, Jacques Marquette, a Jesuit priest from Laon in Picardy, and Louis Jolliet, native of Quebec, fur trader, discoverer, seeker after copper. In 1673, on their way back to Green Bay following their exploration of the Mississippi, Marquette and Jolliet crossed the Chicago portage. They found the countryside along the Illinois River rich and full of promise. Father Marquette wrote in his diary:

OPPOSITE: *Wood engraving of Chicago from Appleton's* Picturesque America, *1872–74.*

BELOW: *This map of 1703, drawn by Louis Armand de Lorn d'Arce, Baron de La Hontan, gives a fairly accurate picture of the region at the beginning of the eighteenth century. At this time "Chicago" was spelled in a variety of ways.*

> We have seen nothing like this river that we enter, as regards its fertility
> of soil, its prairies and woods; its cattle, elk, deer, wildcats, bustards,
> swans, ducks, parroquets, and even beaver.

This was variety enough to attract any hunter of animals, but Marquette was a hunter of souls, and the next winter, in December of 1674, he returned to Chicago to preach the gospel to the Indians, thus becoming the city's patron, its first romantic legend, its Romulus. Marquette built a shelter, "une cabannez," which in the patois of the *coureurs de bois* meant either a tent or a wigwam. Most likely it was a hut made in the French fashion of upright poles sunk in the ground, chinked and plastered over with clay and roofed with other poles over which was laid bark or hides.

For almost a hundred years after this, during the long reign of Louis XIV and of his great-grandson, Louis XV, the country of the Illinois would be ruled from Versailles; its loss to the English would later be an important factor in the decision of Louis XV's grandson, Louis XVI, to help the American colonies in their revolution. It was a part of that vibrant French world which stretched from the Strait of Belle Isle on Canada's far Atlantic coast, through Quebec and Montreal, and down the Mississippi past Dubuque and St. Louis to New Orleans.

Other Frenchmen came after Marquette: priests and hunters and traders and trappers. But it is Robert Cavelier, Sieur de La Salle, who is remembered above all. It was La Salle who claimed what became Louisiana for the French, pushed for the establishment of a great city at the mouth of the Father of Waters, built a fort at Starved Rock overlooking the Illinois River. And it was La Salle who, sometime around 1681, began using the word Chi-ca-gou to indicate specifically the site of the present city rather than the whole region.

The French era in Chicago ended in 1759 with the defeat of Montcalm by Wolfe upon Quebec's Plains of Abraham. But the influence of the French did not end. Inspecting the territory in 1766, an English officer, Captain Harry Gordon, reported back to his superior, General Thomas Gage, that the French were carrying on trade "all around . . . by Land and Water." Once the American Revolution had begun, this was a situation which the British could not tolerate. A prime object of their suspicion was Jean Baptiste Point Sable, a native of Santo Domingo, born of a French father and a black slave mother, who was described as "a handsome negro (well educated and settled in Eschecagou), but much in the French interest." Point Sable was not only handsome and educated, he was a highly successful trader possessing a mill, numerous outbuildings, in addition to a dwelling built in the manner of those found in all the French settlements of the mid-American continent—logs of modest diameter set upright, fastened at their top with a horizontal timber, and the whole structure surrounded by a porch. In 1779 he was arrested by the British and sent to Mackinac Island for the duration. Point Sable's house really marks the beginning of permanent settlement in Chicago. After the Revolution, he would return and then, at the end of the eighteenth century, sell his house to a French trader named Le Mai, who would in turn sell it to John Kinzie, who bore the first important non-Gallic name in the city's history.

But before that, before names such as Kinzie with all its connotations of the Yankee world of serious sabbaths and steady industry could come to Chicago, there had to be a revolution. Chicago's early days are marked by the influence of unseen battles in distant places. The Plains of Abraham had made it British; now Yorktown made it American. President Washington, aware of its strategic location at the head of the water routes leading into the heart of the continent, wanted to build a fort there. But it was the Louisiana Purchase of 1803 that made the fort a necessity. In July of that year, Captain John Whistler, under orders from General Henry Dearborn of the War Department,

came to Chicago to build it. Years later, in London, the painter James McNeill Whistler was asked by a Chicagoan if he had ever been to the city. "No," Whistler replied, "but my grandfather founded the place."

Captain Whistler built Fort Dearborn near what is now Michigan Avenue on the south side of the Chicago River. It was constructed in the American style, with the logs laid horizontally one on top of another, locked at the corners by notches and the spaces between chinked with a mixture of clay, straw, and moss. It was an impressive structure. There were storehouses, a powder magazine, a blockhouse, quarters for a modest garrison of some seventy officers and men. It was the beginning of civic architecture in Chicago, the first public building, the core of the future city. In an attempt to wean the rich trade with the Indians away from the British, there was also a government factory, or trading house. And now, mingling with those named Bourbonne and Ouilmette (which transmogrified to Wilmette would give its bearer a kind of immortality), appeared men called Hayward and Varnum and Irwin, men who came overland from the former English colonies of the Atlantic seaboard rather than down the lakes from Montreal and Quebec. None was more typical of these than John Kinzie, who arrived in the spring of 1804. Establishing himself opposite the fort on the north bank of the river, he was soon trading with the Indians, equipping trappers, supplying the garrison, and doing a considerable business in articles of silver he himself made. Within five years of the construction of Fort Dearborn, the population of Chicago, not counting the garrison, had reached the impressive total of forty souls.

For the first eight or nine years after the fort was built all went smoothly, almost dully. The whole surrounding country was still prairie, with the quiet routine of the settlement broken only by the fur traders who headed out to the beaver country in autumn and came back with their pelts in the spring. Now and then there would be the supreme excitement of a wolf hunt when one of the numerous packs sloped too near. Chicago seemed destined to grow gradually outward, ring upon ring, like a maturing tree, like Louisville or St.

The construction of the first Fort Dearborn in 1803 by Captain John Whistler marked the true founding of the city of Chicago. The center of the parade ground is now on the southwest corner of the Michigan Avenue bridge. The fort was burned the night of August 15, 1812, following the massacre of 52 settlers and soldiers.

Louis or Indianapolis. But that was never the style of the Place of the Wild Onion. It had always had a flare for the dramatic, an undeniable rendezvous with history.

In Europe, Napoleon and the English were engaged in a vast, titanic struggle for control of the continent, and, in a sense, for control of the world. The United States had watched the battles—Marengo, Trafalgar, Austerlitz—from the sidelines, but there was no doubt where the nation's sympathies lay. There was a profound sense of gratitude for French help in the Revolution, a still-bitter hatred of the English, and a strong sentiment for annexing Canada. In 1812 President Madison finally declared war on England. It was not a wise move. The British won victory after victory and encouraged the Indians, with promises of a return of their western lands, to attack American settlements. Chicago was particularly vulnerable, and word came on August 9, 1812, to evacuate Fort Dearborn. Plans were made as quickly as possible, but by the time the evacuation began on the fifteenth, there were some 500 Potawatomi warriors in the vicinity. It was a tiny procession that left the stockade: the garrison of fifty-five regulars, a militia company of twelve citizens, and, loaded into two wagons pulled by oxen, nine women and eighteen children. They counted on their consistently friendly relations with the Indians to protect them.

The column had not proceeded more than a mile and a half when the warriors attacked. "The troops behaved most gallantly. They were but a handful," Margaret Helm, one of the women, wrote later. "In the meantime a horrible scene was enacted. One young savage, climbing into the baggage-wagon containing the children of the white families tomahawked nearly all of them." When the battle was over, twenty-six regulars, all of the militia, two women, and twelve children were dead. Of those captured, some were tortured to death on the shore of Lake Michigan; others perished as captives. A few eventually escaped—among them the Kinzies. There, on that bright August morning, between the great lake and the sea of grass, was born the legend of the Fort Dearborn massacre.

After plundering the fort, the Indians set it afire, and soon only the damaged powder magazine remained to proclaim the United States' western empire. Now only a few French-Canadian traders or British-paid Indian war parties on their way to attack American settlements passed the still-unburied bodies of the slain. It was a precarious moment in the history of Chicago. The region might well have remained British, or perhaps no new settlement, no fresh growth of village, would have sprung up at the portage. But the peace treaty of 1815 once more returned the site to the United States and the importance of the island between the two seas was not forgotten. In 1816 the order went out from Washington to build a new Fort Dearborn. There was one feature of the second fort that could be called an attempt at serious architecture, and this was its two-story porches. These verandahs with their slender wooden columns were a rustic echo of the splendid Federal style which had swept all before it along the Atlantic seaboard. These columns were Chicago's first feeble stirrings of architectural consciousness, its primitive copy of the elegant pilasters with which Samuel McIntire was adorning the houses of Salem's Chestnut Street.

The same year that the second fort was built, John Kinzie returned with his family and took up residence in his old cabin. Other survivors returned too, such as the Ouilmettes; and new ones came. There was fiddle-playing Mark Beaubien, who, by building two inns, the Eagle Exchange, near what is now the northeast corner of Randolph and Market Streets, and the Sauganash, at the corner of Lake and Market, became the godfather of Chicago's grand hotels. There were also more and more Yankees, among them Gurdon S. Hubbard, a native of Windsor, Vermont, who was an agent for John Jacob Astor's American Fur Company. In time he would become one of the town's first packers and would make a fortune in real estate. But Hubbard has another claim to remembrance, for he was the man who cleared a trail from Danville, Illinois, north to Chicago. It was first called Hubbard's Trail, then State Road, and later still, State Street.

There were already, for the observant, prophetic signs pointing toward the urban magnificence which the words "State Street," "Michigan Avenue," and "Lake Shore Drive" would one day connote. Illinois had been admitted to the Union in 1818, and Chicago's trade with the region's growing population was booming. There was even talk of a canal linking the Great Lakes with the Mississippi, which would make the Place of the Wild Onion the key to unlocking the riches of the North American continent. No one saw these signs more clearly than the pioneer geologist Henry Schoolcraft:

> The country around Chicago is the most fertile and beautiful that can be imagined . . . to the ordinary advantages of an agricultural marketing town, it must, hereafter, add that of a depot, for inland commerce, between the northern and southern sections of the Union, and a great thoroughfare for strangers, merchants and travelers.

Detail of map from the French era of America's heartland. This is believed to be the map that Louis Jolliet drew in 1674, the year after he and Jacques Marquette crossed the Chicago portage. The Illinois River is here called the Outrelaize.

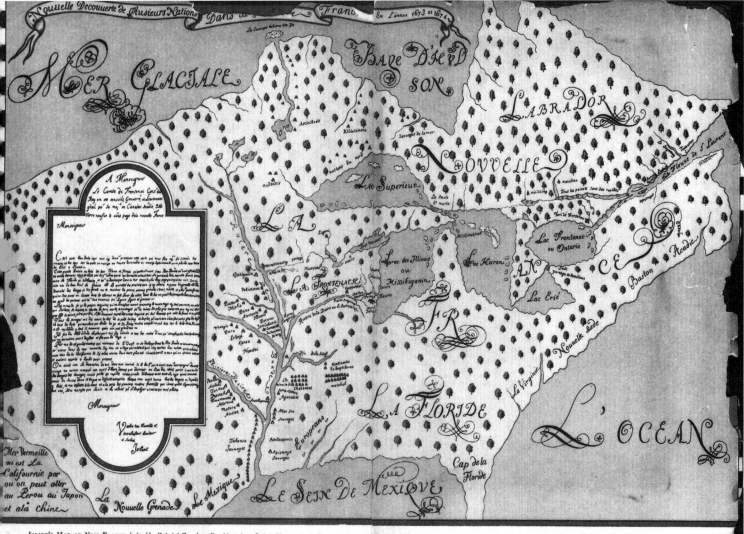

JOLIET'S MAP OF NEW FRANCE (1674).—Gabriel Gravier, *President de ta Societe Normande de Geographie,* who first published a *fac simile* of the original map in the French Geographical Review of February, 1880, believes this to be J map, drawn by him at Montreal directly after his return from his Mississippi voyage. It was dedicated to Frontenac, then Governor of New France, and the names, *Buade,* given to the Mississip; *Outrelaize,* to the Illinois, and *La Frontena* ritory between the Wisconsin and Illinois rivers—all complimentary to Canadian authorities—indicate that it was the on resented to Frontenac. Joliet's later maps are dedicated to C in them the Mississippi is named in bearing similar names to the above is mentioned by Parkman (Appendix of the Great West 10)

—||| BUILDINGS FOR A CITY |||—

HENRY JAMES, writing to his brother William, expressed the excitement he felt on being in Rome: "In the course of four or five hours I traversed almost the whole of Rome and got a glimpse of everything—the Forum, the Coliseum (stupendissimo!), the Pantheon, the Capitol . . ." The great public buildings of a city should indeed stir us, for they are the true treasuries of a people's experience. Here famous men and women acted and spoke; here took place those events that affected the course of a nation's history. The survival of such buildings helps us, in a very real way, to draw near those people and those events. It is a dead imagination that is not quickened by being told: "Lincoln spoke here" or "This was the scene of Clarence Darrow's last trial." Chicago has been prodigal in its destruction of its civic structures. The sacking of the first Fort Dearborn and the fire of 1871 robbed the city of much of its historical architectural heritage, but later public buildings have been casually obliterated with scarcely a pause to consider their significance.

ABOVE: *Chicago's first Court House was erected at the northeast corner of Clark and Randolph streets in 1835. The courtroom was on the first floor, with city offices in the basement. Behind the Court House is the jail.*

OPPOSITE, TOP: *The growing self-assurance of Chicago is reflected in the handsome second Cook County Court House and City Hall, designed in 1853 by the city's first architect, John Van Osdel. This 1855 daguerreotype shows the Montgomery and Emmett Guards drawn up to hear a Fourth of July oration by Mayor John Wentworth. The structure occupied the center of the block bounded by La Salle, Clark, Randolph, and Washington streets, still the site of Chicago's government buildings. It was here that Abraham Lincoln's body lay in state, and it was the Court House bell which sounded the alarm for the Great Chicago Fire until the building itself was consumed in the holocaust.*

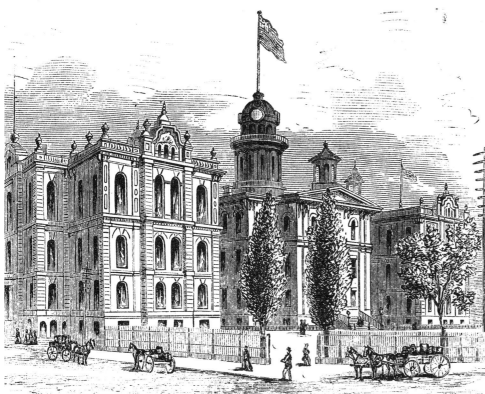

LEFT: *In 1858, the Court House was given an Italianate third floor and a more elaborate cupola. Shortly before the Great Fire impressive wings were added to the structure.*

After the fire, Chicago sought to assert its recovery by raising a city hall to rival the costly municipal edifices being built in Philadelphia and elsewhere. In terms of both lavishness and size, Chicago's City and County Building was second to none. The work principally of James J. Egan, the county architect, the vast structure took nearly a dozen years to build and did not open until 1885. Many were impressed by it. "The heart and center of Chicago is the huge pile of masonry which reminds the visitor by its polished granite pillars and general massive and somber grandeur of the cathedrals and palaces of St. Petersburg," the English writer William T. Stead observed in If Christ Came to Chicago! The city's aldermen defended the building's $5 million cost by saying that it had been built for the ages. Egan's confection was pulled down in 1906–08.

"... and we expect to be the financial center, and presently the political center, too — Chicago plus New York and Washington," Henry B. Fuller, in his novel, The Cliff-Dwellers.

In the last decade of the nineteenth century, Chicago felt itself to be a second capital of the United States, and it was not unusual to hear serious proposals to move the government to the Windy City. In keeping with its acknowledged importance, the federal authorities decided to honor Chicago with a building which would be its administrative center for the Midwest.

Henry Ives Cobb's (1859-1931) Federal Building brilliantly personified the city's civic pride. Constructed between 1895 and 1905, it filled the block bounded by Adams, Jackson, Dearborn, and Clark streets. In one of its courtrooms, Judge Kenesaw Mountain Landis fined the Standard Oil Company $29 million for restraint of trade; in another, Al Capone was sentenced for income tax evasion. The structure, which also housed the United States Post Office, was an awesome feet of engineering. The complex of eight stories, basement, and a dome set 16 stories above the pavement was supported by wooden piles driven to hardpan some 72 feet below street level. In the preparation of the foundations Cobb was assisted by General William S. Smith.

9

ABOVE: *The Federal Building's 300-foot-high octagonal rotunda was one of America's supreme interiors. Inspired by the monuments of Imperial Rome, the rotunda was crowned by a dome 100 feet in diameter, larger than that of the Capitol in Washington. The Federal Building was at once Henry Ives Cobb's triumph in Chicago and his swan song. Born in Brookline Massachusetts, he had studied at the Massachusetts Institute of Technology and worked for Peabody & Stearns. In 1882 Cobb moved to Chicago, and among his many important commissions were seventeen buildings for the University of Chicago constructed between 1892 and 1899, which became models of the Collegiate Gothic style in the United States, and the ruggedly handsome Romanesque Revival Newberry Library, completed in 1893.*

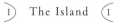

The Federal Building's dazzling Beaux Arts interior of polished granite, white and golden Siena marble, mosaics, and gilded bronze cost more than $2,000,000. This magnificent edifice, the most notable example of civic architecture in Chicago, was wantonly demolished in 1965–66.

BELOW: *The Chicago Historical Society, organized in 1856, dedicated the first building constructed specifically for it, in 1868. Located at the corner of Dearborn and Ontario streets, the Society's Palladian-inspired style of attached pilasters and elaborate cornice above a rusticated base clearly echoed the style of such prestigious eastern institutions as the Boston Athenaeum. The elegant building, along with most of its irreplaceable collection of thousands of bound volumes, pamphlets, maps, and letters relating to the early history of Chicago and the Midwest, was consumed in the Great Fire.*

Chicago's early interest in painting resulted in the Art Institute on Michigan Avenue (at right in the photograph above), *one of the most successful Romanesque designs by the internationally known architects Daniel Burnham and John Wellborn Root. After its opening in 1885, it was the scene of trail-blazing exhibitions of the work of the French Impressionists. When the Art Institute moved across Michigan Avenue in the 1890s, its old home became the august Chicago Club. The building collapsed in 1929 during remodeling. The building on the left—still standing today— is the Fine Arts, by Solon S. Beman; it was the focus of the city's creative life, where Little Theatre began in America and where, before the First World War, Margaret Anderson published* The Little Review.

The new home of the Art Institute of Chicago, which opened for the 1893 Columbian Exposition, was the work of the Boston firm of Shepley, Rutan & Coolidge. Its entrance hall, seen here in 1894, had a light well, now covered, which provided natural light for the viewing of the Institute's collection of plaster casts from the 1893 Fair, including Daniel Chester French's seated version of his "Republic," the standing version of which presided over the exposition's Grand Basin. This priceless collection was allowed to deteriorate in the years after the Second World War.

It would be difficult to imagine a more self-assured evocation of the eighteenth-century palaces of Paris than the United States Appellate Court which stood on North Lake Shore Drive near Scott Street. From the office of Holabird & Root, the building was constructed between 1921 and 1923. The renderer for the project, Gilbert Hall, had just returned from Paris and longed to bring some Gallic charm to the shores of Lake Michigan. His balanced composition of a pillared entrance with flanking pavilions beneath a mansard roof flawlessly accomplished his purpose. The original client for the structure was the Illinois Life Insurance Company, controlled by the Stevens family which built the LaSalle and the Stevens, now the Conrad Hilton, hotels. When, during the depression, the life insurance company fell on hard times, the United States government purchased its palace. Chicago lost a rare interpretation of French eighteenth-century architecture when the Appellate Court was demolished in the 1960s.

In the days before the federal income tax, the United States government was financed for the most part by custom duties on imported goods. Chicago's fortress-like custom house—also known as the U.S. Appraiser's Office—at the northwest corner of Sherman and Harrison streets, was built in 1891 from designs by Freret & Klewer. Its bold rustication, arched windows, and corner turrets owed much to the buildings of Henry Hobson Richardson. This fine federal castle was swept away in 1950.

Time of the Temple

THE 1830s MARKED an important phase in the development of Chicago, for in that decade the once-modest village moved swiftly toward cityhood. In 1830 Chicago was plotted and surveyed, and the following year it was designated the seat of the new Cook County, a name honoring Illinois's first attorney general, one Daniel P. Cook, who most likely never set foot in the place which would confer upon him his only lasting fame. Soon a post office was established, a lighthouse and sawmill built, and the first bridge—consisting of floating logs—was stretched across the Chicago River at what is now Randolph Street. In 1833 Chicago was incorporated as a town. Charles Joseph Latrobe, a celebrated English visitor to America in these years, saw Chicago in the 1830s and recorded in his *Rambler in North America:* "I have been in many odd assemblages of my species, but in few, if any, of an equally singular character as with that in the midst of which we spent a week at Chicago. . . ." It seems that they were already doing things on Hubbard's Trail that they didn't do on Broadway.

The village was teeming with fur traders, land speculators, new immigrants, gamblers, horse thieves, Indians, and soldiers. The last two, however, were about to depart the scene. During 1831 and 1832, the settlers had been frightened by reports of Indian outrages, mostly the work of the Sauk and Fox tribes led by the powerful chief Black Hawk. After Black Hawk's defeat, the United States government decided to expel all Indians from the fertile, long-coveted region stretching from the southern half of Lake Michigan to the Mississippi. So in 1835, the Potawatomi, some 5000 in number, gathered in Chicago for the last time to receive their government annuities, bid farewell to their old hunting grounds, and depart for their new homes in the West. The early Chicago historian John Dean Caton was present, and has left a vivid account of that melancholy goodbye:

> They assembled at the council-house, near where the Lake House now stands, on the north side of the river. All were entirely naked, except for a strip of cloth around the loins. Their bodies were covered all over with a great variety of brilliant paints . . . The long, coarse, black hair was gathered into scalp-locks on the tops of their heads, and decorated with a profusion of hawk's and eagle's feathers . . . They advanced, not with a regular march, but a continued dance.

With its raison d'être gone, Fort Dearborn was evacuated in 1836, and slipped into dereliction until its last vestiges disappeared in the Great Fire. Its site is marked by brass strips embedded in the street on the west side of Michigan Avenue near the southern approach of the Michigan Avenue Bridge.

The astonishing growth of Chicago just forty years after the construction of the second Fort Dearborn is revealed in this photograph of 1858 looking southeast from the corner of Washington and La Salle streets. The church is the First Baptist, built in 1853; the architect is unknown. In 1864, it was purchased by the Second Baptist congregation and moved across the river to the corner of Monroe and Morgan streets, where it survived well into the twentieth century. Behind the church can be seen a row of Greek Revival houses of the type that gave to early Chicago the air of a New England village.

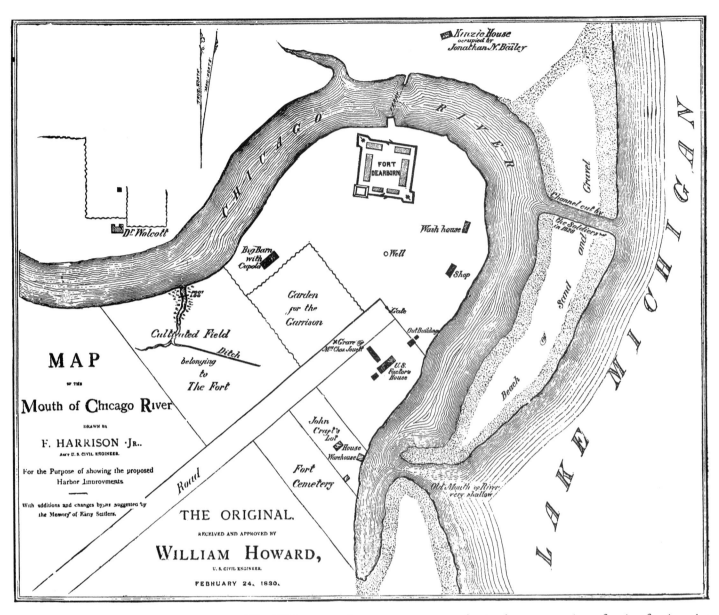

MAP

of the

Mouth of Chicago River

DRAWN BY

F. HARRISON ·JR..

Ass'T U. S. CIVIL ENGINEER.

For the Purpose of showing the proposed
Harbor Improvments

With additions and changes by us suggested by
the Memory of Early Settlers.

THE ORIGINAL.

RECEIVED AND APPROVED BY

WILLIAM HOWARD,

U. S. CIVIL ENGINEER.

FEBRUARY 24, 1830.

Chicago as it appeared at the beginning of the 1830s. The map was commissioned by the United States government so that plans could be made for improving the city's harbor.

The 1830s were a fortunate moment to begin the construction of a city, for America had embraced a new architecture. If the first century and a half of Chicago's history can be termed the period of the cabin and the fort, the next twenty-five years may be called the time of the temple. After the Federal style, with its reflection of the work of the brothers Adam, its avid admiration of the formal squares and crescents of English cities such as Bath and London, America had found another model: Greece. There were both aesthetic and political reasons for this change. In the first place, the War of 1812, with the burning of the President's house and the Capitol, had stirred up violent anti-British sentiment in the United States. Second, the Greek War of Independence of the 1820s against the Turks had deeply aroused Americans who identified with ancient Greece's republican traditions. In a thousand villages with names such as Athens and Corinth and Sparta, the citizens of the new republic paid tribute to the old.

Aesthetically, the tradition began with a book, *The Antiquities of Athens,* by two Englishmen, James Stuart and Nicholas Revett, the first volume of which was published in London in 1762. By 1770 a copy had found its way to the Library Company of Philadelphia, where it was subsequently studied by Benjamin Latrobe, the second architect of the Capitol, who introduced the Greek Revival style into the United States, and other architects of the nation's early years such as William Strickland, Thomas U. Walter, and Robert Mills. It was not long before illustrated manuals by builders such as John Haviland, Asher Benjamin, and John Hall had made it possible for any competent carpenter to produce structures with all the trappings of Greek temples: fluted and plain columns, capitals of every order, pediments, pilasters, fasciae, and metopes. And soon the style, in stone or adapted to brick and wood, swept the country from Montpelier, Vermont, to Frankfort, Kentucky.

It was an ideal style for a city only a day or two by schooner away from the seemingly inexhaustible Michigan forests of white pine, one of the finest woods in the world. Here were millions of growing columns, perfectly straight, selling for a mere $20 per thousand board feet. Brick was used for the larger buildings, but for the great bulk of Chicago's new structures, pine was the marble.

The special glory of the Greek Revival style, as practiced in the United States, was that it was readily adaptable to almost every need. When it came to domestic architecture, it stretched to any size, from modest story-and-a-half cottages with pilasters at the corners and simple Greek-type moldings, to columned mansions such as one built in 1836 by Virginian Archibald Clybourne, Chicago's first constable. Undoubtedly one of the supreme examples of domestic Greek Revival architecture was the house that Eli B. Williams, registrar of the United States Land Office, erected at the southeast corner of Monroe and Wabash. With its splendid portico of six Doric columns and its fine proportions, the Williams house was a temple worthy of the classical towns of New York and New England.

The style served just as well for churches and schools, shops and offices, hotels and public buildings. Thus it was inevitable that Chicago's first Court House, built in 1835 at the corner of the Public Square at Clark and Randolph streets, should have been a temple-like rectangular brick building ennobled by a free-standing portico of four wooden Doric columns. The Greek Revival was evident in the Saloon Building at the southwest corner of Lake and Clark streets, the Faneuil Hall of the early city, where, in 1837, the young Stephen A. Douglas captured Chicago's collective heart. It was in the manner of the three-story Bank of Illinois on the corner of South Water and La Salle streets and of the Lake House, the first hotel in town to boast a French chef and a printed menu.

Chicago had need of a vast variety of buildings, for the 1830s were boom times in the old Northwest. It was a period of one of the greatest migrations in the history of mankind, a migration which ranks with the movement of the Huns into Europe and of the German tribes south into Italy and Spain. At the beginning of the decade the population of Chicago numbered 100; by the end it was more than 4000. The key factor in the city's spectacular growth was the completion, in 1825, of the Erie Canal, linking the Great Lakes with the sea and making it possible for the traveler to move by water from the Atlantic coast to Illinois, Minnesota, and Wisconsin. Suddenly, from being almost deserted, the Chicago lake front became a forest of masts, and by 1843 the city was clearing some 700 vessels a year.

Indeed, Chicago was so packed with newcomers, with Yankee settlers, with business-men, with laborers who had come to work on the canal that was being built to link Lake Michigan and the Mississippi, with speculators and passers-through that it was almost impossible to shelter them. If licensing had been in effect, half the dwellings in town would have qualified as boardinghouses. In 1835 more than 80 percent of the population of Chicago had been there less than a year. Charles Butler, a New York real estate broker and railroad promoter, was astonished by what he saw: "Emigrants were coming in almost every day in wagons of various forms and in many instances families were living in their covered wagons while arrangements were made for putting up shelter for them. It was no uncommon thing for a house such as would answer the purpose for the time being to be put up in a few days."

This need to erect a house in a few days resulted in the first example of that extraordinary inventiveness which Chicago was to display throughout the last two thirds of the nineteenth century. No city in the East had grown as rapidly as this, and wooden buildings had continued to be "framed" with heavy, slow, expensive post construction, just as they had been in medieval England. A chance to break away from this tedious and wasteful method was made possible by the circular steam-driven saw, which permitted lumber to be cut into much smaller units, into two-by-fours and two-by-twelves and one-by-tens. Man was thus ready for one of those seminal inventions as important as the arch and the dome. Using these new cuts, Chicago builders began putting up light, strong, and inexpensive "balloon frames." The invention was not only important in itself, but it revealed a new cast of mind, the mind of the prairie, a mind not looking back across the sea to castles and cathedrals, but looking forward to a new world. Here we now stood, in our own land.

One man, more than any other, symbolizes the boomtown of the '30s. William Butler Ogden's introduction to Chicago certainly did not portend a love affair. When he came out in 1835 from his native New York State it was to attempt to save the family fortune from what he considered the rash investment of a rich brother-in-law. The rash investment was a 182-acre tract close to the river on the north side. Anxious to salvage what he could of the $100,000 purchase price, Ogden ordered the entire parcel auctioned off at once. But then something surprising happened. The $100,000 had been retrieved by the time only a third of the land had been sold. Ogden halted the auction and decided to take a closer look at this curious collection of human beings gathered on Lake Michigan's western shore.

Ogden not only looked, he fell in love with Chicago. And his passion was not blind. Within two years the newcomer had made a fortune in real estate, and when, in 1837, Chicago was chartered as a city, William Ogden became its first mayor. Here was a new type of Chicagoan totally different from the voyageurs and the traders, the Kinzies and the Ouilmettes. Here was a man on a new scale, a businessman with a vision. That vision was to make the city the hub of the heartland, to bring every farm in the Midwest, every ear of corn, every grain of wheat, every hog and steer, within easy reach. But that would take time. Before then, he would give Chicago a very special gift: its first architect.

Ogden had met John Van Osdel in New York, and after he became mayor he sent for him to build a house worthy of this new civic dignity. Van Osdel arrived, not only with the plans for Chicago's first architect-designed dwelling, but with the necessary windows, stair rails, and trimmings as well. The architect of William Ogden's house was the supreme builder of Greek Revival Chicago. He was also one of those completely sympathetic people: an editor of the *American Mechanic,* which later became the *Scientific American,* a dedicated Garrisonian Abolitionist, and a man of great social charm. From his office on Clark Street flowed an almost endless stream of houses, hotels, and public buildings. He was responsible for the new Court House, the dedication of which was marked by a proud procession half a mile in length that included all the grandees of the burgeoning city: the military and fire companies, members of the Mechanics Institute, the political clubs, the Free Masons and the Odd Fellows. Three stories in height, crowned by a tall cupola, the Court House cost more than $100,000 but the good citizens felt that it was worth it, for the edifice was a proclamation that Chicago must now be taken seriously.

Of all of Van Osdel's buildings of this period, however, none is more significant than the emperor of early Chicago hostelries, the Tremont House, which he constructed in 1850 on the southeast corner of Lake and Dearborn streets. The first Tremont House, built in the 1830s, had been a simple wooden structure, not very different from the city's old inns where accommodations had often been merely a mat on the floor. Van Osdel's hotel changed all that forever. "The Tremont House has precedence of all others," the paper *Gem of the Prairie* boasted in January 1851. "It is one of the chief ornaments of the city. . . . The

John M. Van Osdel (1811–1892) arrived in Chicago in 1835 and made history by opening the city's first professional architect's office in 1841.

house is five and a half stories high and its internal arrangements, including furniture and decorations, are all in the highest style of art, and of the class denominated princely." The significant word here is "princely," for Chicago was already intent upon creating hotels where every man was a king; it is but a step from the Tremont's marble mantels and rosewood furniture to the crystal-filled ballrooms of the great hotels of the post-fire years. In the Tremont's public rooms the early Chambers of Commerce met, business was transacted in its lobby, and, in time, history would be made from its balconies.

Van Osdel was as capable of turning out a playhouse as a hotel or a court house, and in 1851 he built a splendid one for John B. Rice, the father of the Chicago theater. The settlement already had a not inconsiderable history of entertainment. In its very first year as a city, Harry Isherwood, a member of the theatrical firm of Isherwood and McKenzie, came from the East and put on plays in the old Sauganash Hotel. Soon the city had a real playhouse, a room 30 feet wide and 80 feet long, located on Dearborn Street and proudly calling itself the Chicago Theatre. There, in 1838, a troupe headed by Joseph Jefferson, Sr., came to delight one and all with *She Stoops to Conquer, The Magpie and the Maid,* and something called *The Turn Out, or the Enraged Politician.* Among the players was a nine-year-old boy, Joseph Jefferson, Jr., who was to become nationally famous in the role of Rip Van Winkle. Jefferson vividly recalled his first impression of the city:

> . . . off we go ashore and walk through the busy little town, busy even then, people hurrying to and fro, frame buildings going up, board side-walks going down, new hotels, new churches, new theaters, everything new. Saw and hammer—saw! saw! bang!!—look out for the drays!— bright and muddy streets, gaudy-colored calicos, blue and red flannels and striped ticking hanging outside the drygoods store, bar-rooms, real-estate offices, attorneys-at-law. . . .

The theater, he remembered, had a drop curtain with "a medallion of Shakespeare, suffering from a severe pain in his stomach, over the center, with 'One touch of nature makes the whole world kin' written under him."

Delight in diversion was characteristic of Chicago from its infancy. At a period when the Midwest was being thickly settled with communities dedicated to high-mindedness rather than to high-living—Oberlin in Ohio, New Harmony in Indiana, Bishop Hill in Illinois—Chicago came down strongly on the side of having a good time. It was a city where, in the 1840s and '50s, a "grocery" meant an establishment that sold liquor as well as foodstuffs, and many of them managed to find room for a roulette wheel as well. Of course there were those who objected to all this frivolity. But when, on April 21, 1855, a number of persons were put on trial for violating Sunday closing laws, a riot ensued in which several policemen were injured. That same year a referendum was held on the question of prohibiting the sale of liquor. The citizens made it emphatically clear where they stood—or staggered. The results: for the prohibition, 2784; against, 4093.

Yet the city's churches prospered too. When Father John St. Cyr arrived in 1833 to minister to Chicago's thirty-six Catholic families, he took one look at the log cabin which was to be his chapel and decided to build something more impressive. What he got was better, though by no stretch of the imagination could it be called splendid. St. Mary's, on the corner of State and Lake streets, was an unplastered rough-board structure 36 feet long and 24 feet wide, in which a simple table served as the altar. Its total cost was $400. The next year the Presbyterians and Baptists built churches. It was left to the Episcopalians, though, to construct Chicago's first important church building. They had staked out a parish in the midst of the wealthy residential sections of the North Side, with no less a personage for senior warden than John H. Kinzie, son of the trader who had settled beside

Fort Dearborn. When, in 1837, they consecrated their new St. James Church on the corner of Cass and Illinois streets, it was clear that they had chosen their location astutely. A faintly Gothic building, St. James had the distinction of being the first brick church in town; it also had the first tower as well as the first organ.

If men such as William Ogden were settling in this new city on the island between the lake and the prairie, if actors readily found audiences there, if the population was approaching 20,000, if its large hotels were filled, if domes and towers were rising above the cottonwoods, it was because of commerce. And if commerce was increasing at a fantastic rate, it was because of the island's extraordinary location. No one saw this more clearly than Margaret Fuller, the trancendentalist friend of Emerson and Hawthorne, who arrived in 1843:

> There can be no two places in the world more completely thoroughfares
> than this place and Buffalo. They are the two correspondent valves that
> open and shut all the time, as the life-blood rushes from east to west,
> and back again from west to east.

The first artery of this gigantic circulatory system was the Erie Canal; the second was the Illinois and Michigan Canal—linking the lakes with the tributaries of the Mississippi and thus with the Gulf of Mexico. One hears time and again of the Suez and Panama canals, but this canal, first prophesied by Jolliet, had effects as profound as either of those. Now it was possible to go by water from New York to New Orleans, and Chicago was the system's heart. The position of the island had been assured when it was a portage; it was now a port; it would one day, for the same reasons, become a harbor for trains. Men noticed the island's favored location, and men, extraordinary men, built Chicago, such men as built no other American city. One can easily write a book called "Makers of Chicago," but it would be difficult to write a "Makers of New York" or "Makers of Boston." And now one of the giants appeared.

In 1832 in the Blue Ridge Mountains of Virginia, a young inventor had brought forth a clumsy contraption of wood and iron pulled by four horses. That ungainly contrivance could do something unheard of, something as revolutionary as James Hargreaves' spinning jenny or Eli Whitney's cotton gin: it could cut six acres of wheat in less time than it took six men to do it by hand. Cyrus McCormick began offering his machines for sale, and canny Scot that he was, he noticed that more and more of his orders came from the new lands of the West, from Illinois, Iowa, and Indiana. Virginia was inconveniently far from these markets and, looking for a better location for the factory he hoped to build, McCormick decided upon Chicago. There, in the autumn of 1847, in partnership with Charles M. Gray, who already had a reputation for his fine grain cradles and scythes, and with backing from the ever-alert William Ogden, Cyrus McCormick began the manufacture of his reapers.

If Eli Whitney is credited with the creation of the cotton kingdom, then it is not too much to say that Cyrus McCormick created the kingdom of wheat, for the Old Northwest was, in the 1840s and '50s, a one-crop region, and wheat was that one crop. Chicago, almost exclusively, was its port of exit. In 1843, the city had sent 700,000 bushels to the eastern markets; by 1847, when McCormick's reapers had begun to make an impact, it sent 2 million.

Carl Sandburg was one day to stamp Chicago indelibly as the "Stacker of Wheat" and the "Hog Butcher for the World." Now, in the Greek Revival city of the '40s and '50s, the foundations of the second of these vast enterprises were also laid. The slaughtering of livestock was nothing new for the city. Gurdon Hubbard had begun it in the '20s, and there had been Mark and John Noble, and Archibald Clybourne, official butcher to the

soldiers at Fort Dearborn, and George Dole, who in 1833 had slaughtered a number of cattle, packed the beef in barrels, and shipped it to Detroit. But all of this was on a small scale, comparable to Chicago's agricultural-implement manufacturing before the advent of Cyrus McCormick. It took a man with a special genius to make it into a great enterprise. That man, Nelson Morris, who arrived in 1852 as a boy of fifteen, represented a new addition to the lifeblood of the city.

He was from Germany, from Fulda in Franconia, and somehow in the villages where he and his father bought and sold cattle, he had heard of Chicago—a name already synonymous with opportunity. The hopeful dream of millions in the nineteenth century drew him to this new land.

Alone, at the age of twelve, Morris arrived in Philadelphia, almost penniless and with little formal education. But it was not of the East he had heard, but of the West, and slowly over a period of three years he worked his way there, one month as a farm laborer, the next as a charcoal burner, earning his passage on the Erie Canal to Buffalo and on a Great Lakes freighter to Michigan City, Indiana, and then walking the rest of the way to Chicago. His long journey had tutored him well in English, and he got a job with John B. Sherman, who had founded the city's first stockyards at Ogden Avenue and Madison Street. His salary was $5 a month, but he knew cattle and soon had a reputation as the smartest buyer in the yards. Before long he had his own packing company. Morris pioneered the idea of using "everything but the squeal" to make margarine and buttons and glue and fertilizer and isinglass, pioneered the idea of refrigerator boxcars, pioneered the idea of assembly-line production. Again, as it was with McCormick's harvester works, it was the location of the island that made it all possible. Here the cattle could be driven overland from the farms of the heartland and the ranches of the West, slaughtered, and then shipped by water to the markets of the East. At first it was land and water; later it would be the rails, but always everything was possible because of the invisible but compelling travel-lanes of the continent.

A drawing of a typical dwelling in the French settlements of America's heartland. The first shelter Jean Baptiste Point Sable constructed on the site of Chicago in the eighteenth century most likely resembled this in some aspects, particularly in the vertical placement of the logs forming the walls.

⊣‖ RESIDENCES ‖⊢

NIGEL NICOLSON, the English writer, makes an interesting argument for preserving old houses in the introduction to his Great Houses of Britain: "Apart from emphasizing the architectural inventiveness of the British, these houses also illustrate how our ancestors lived and, to some extent, how they thought." The systematic destruction over the past fifty years of America's old residences—great houses, modest dwellings, and apartment buildings—has been one of the major factors in the architectural impoverishment of our cities. This vandalism has also created an almost insuperable barrier to a full understanding of our nation's past.

⋮ GREAT HOUSES ⋮

ABOVE: *One of the first residences in Chicago to qualify as a great house was the one constructed in 1843 at the southeast corner of Monroe and Wabash streets for Eli B. Williams, a local official. The work of Edward J. Burling, its Greek Doric columns rising up to an entablature without a pediment related it to the Greek Revival plantation houses of the South. The house survived for years as a fashionable restaurant called Maison d'Orée, but was eventually swallowed up by the commercial expansion of the Loop.*

OPPOSITE, TOP: *By the 1850s, fashionable Chicago builders had abandoned the Greek Revival for the various Victorian styles, one of the most popular of which was the Italianate characterized by tall arched windows and bold cornices decorated with brackets. Striking examples of this new taste were the large houses on Park Row off Michigan Avenue near 12th Street. Among the city's most fashionable enclaves, Park Row survived the fire and later shared the location with the new Illinois Central depot completed in 1892, until one by one the old houses were demolished in the expansion of the depot's parking lot.*

LEFT: *Before the Great Fire, Michigan Avenue was essentially a residential quarter. In this view looking north from Adams Street near the present Art Institute, it is possible to get a good idea of its old elegance. The house on the corner is that of Henry Hamilton Honoré, a Kentuckian who came to Chicago in 1855 and made a fortune in real estate, and whose daughter Bertha became Mrs. Potter Palmer. It was from this house that she was married. In the distance is the white marble mansion of William H. Browne, where President-elect and Mrs. Lincoln were entertained shortly before they left for Washington. All the houses on this block were destroyed in the fire. The People's Gas Building now occupies the site.*

Rich and secure, Chicago continued to build throughout the Civil War. Typical of the mansions of this period was the one Leander McCormick constructed on Rush Street on the North Side in 1863. The brother of the great Cyrus of reaper fame, Leander was also active in the family business and is credited with conceiving the idea of putting a seat on the harvester. The family is shown here on their front steps, with Leander, the bearded man on the right. Their pose is significant, for in her memoir "Long Ago," published in Caroline Kirkland's anthology, Chicago Yesterdays, *Mary Drummond recalled: "Another institution of our day was the custom of sitting on the front steps . . . for those of us who did not rejoice in porches and large grounds. . . ."*

The front parlor of the McCormick residence (with Robert Hall McCormick, Leander's son, in the doorway) accurately reveals the taste of a fashionable Chicago family of the time. The curved white marble fireplace, the expanse of mirror, the flowered carpet, and the elaborately carved furniture were all considered de rigueur. The McCormick house perished in the Great Fire.

After the fire, many wealthy Chicagoans who had lived on Michigan Avenue and other downtown streets that were turned over to commerce moved farther south. One of the places they went to was Aldine Square on Vincennes Avenue between 37th and 38th streets. It was the creation of the firm of Cudell and Blumenthal, headed by Adolph Cudell, a recent arrival from Aachen, Germany; its handsome uniform houses, facing a private park containing fine elms and an artificial lake, gave it a distinctly European feeling. No trace of either the houses or the bosky square now survives.

The other choice South Side location was Prairie Avenue. Two miles from downtown, paralleling the tracks of the Illinois Central, it was, in a real sense, the Fifth Avenue of the whole Midwest. But not all of Prairie Avenue. The novelist Arthur Meeker, who grew up there, makes that very clear in To Chicago with Love: ". . . it would be well to define what we meant by early Prairie Avenue. On this point my mother was adamant. Although it was one of the longest arteries in the city, she always maintained that only the first six blocks from 16th to 22nd streets comprised 'The Sunny Street that held the Sifted Few.'" The three-story mansion on the right at 1905 Prairie Avenue was designed for Chicago's "Merchant Prince," Marshall Field, by Richard Morris Hunt, architect to the Vanderbilts and the first American architect to attend Paris's École des Beaux-Arts. When it was completed in 1876, the mansion cost $250,000 and later was the first residence in the city with electric lights. Field lived in the red brick, stone-trimmed Empire style mansion from 1876 until his death in 1906. Field and his wife, Nannie, made their residence one of Chicago's supreme social centers. In January of 1886 to honor their two children, Marshall Field, Jr., and Ethel, who married Arthur Tree and then the British hero Admiral Beatty, the Fields gave one of the most famous parties in the history of the city. The theme of the ball was provided by Gilbert and Sullivan's popular operetta, The Mikado, and the 500 guests all came in exotic oriental costume.

LEFT: *The Junoesque lady attired as Cleopatra for a costume ball is Delia Spencer Caton, whom Marshall Field married after the death of his first wife. Delia Field died in 1937 and the mansion came into the possession of Marshall Field III. In 1937, the new Bauhaus, under the direction of L. Moholy-Nagy, made up of those who had fled Hitler's Germany, was established in this Beaux Arts palace. Despite its rich social and architectural history, the Marshall Field house was razed in 1955.*

ABOVE: *The library of the Marshall Field house was decorated in Renaissance style with a red and gold coffered ceiling. The room's focal point was the elaborate fireplace with a stained glass overmantel depicting one of the five muses in a languid aesthetic pose.*

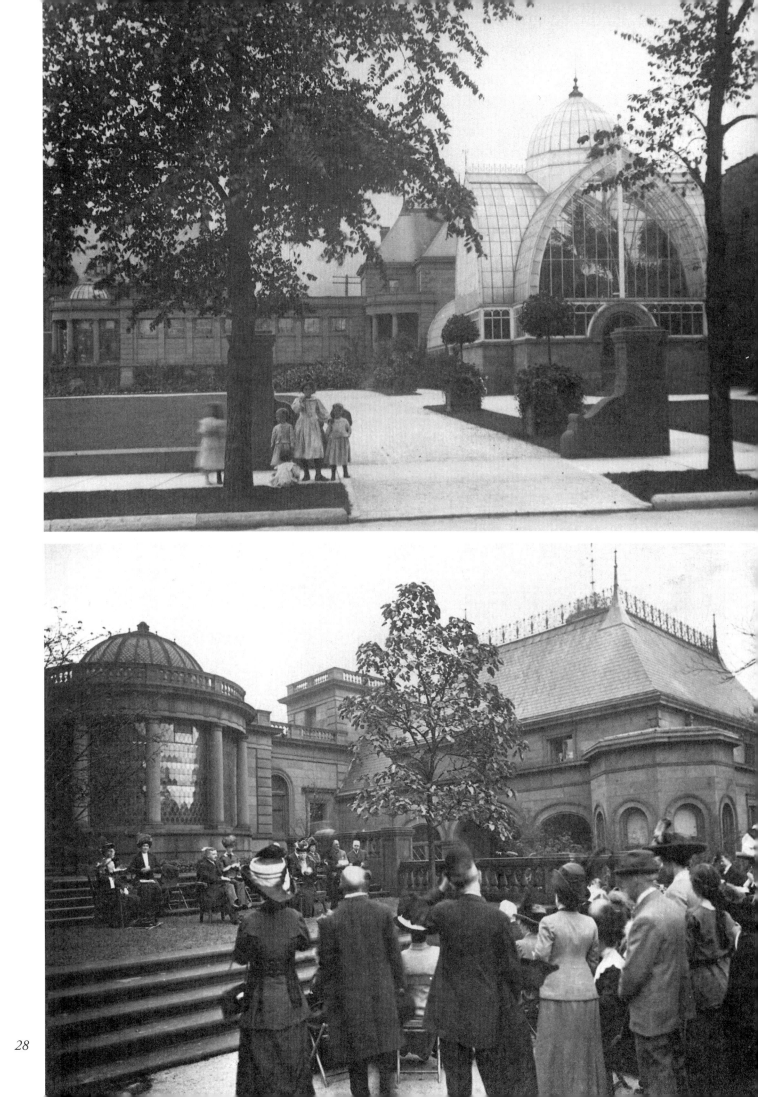

OPPOSITE, TOP: *Undoubtedly the grandest house on Prairie Avenue was that of George M. Pullman at 1429. A Second Empire brownstone chateau which Arthur Meeker described in his novel* Prairie Avenue *as being reminiscent "of the Grand Opera in Paris," the Pullman residence was originally constructed in 1873 by the Chicago contractor John M. Dunphy. In 1879 the sleeping car magnate had Solon S. Beman, the architect of the town of Pullman, add a large conservatory, the largest in any Chicago private residence.*

OPPOSITE, BOTTOM: *This 1912 photograph taken on the Pullman terrace shows the ceremony marking the centennial of the Fort Dearborn massacre. The massacre site was but yards away. George Pullman's palace was demolished in 1922.*

ABOVE: *This view of the entrance hall of the Pullman residence, taken from a family album, is a splendid example of the fine woodwork so dear to the hearts of nineteenth-century Chicagoans. It is a reflection of a time when a wave of immigration from Germany and Czechoslovakia had created an enormous reservoir of skilled cabinetmakers.*

One of Chicago's truly historic
houses stood at 2100 Prairie Avenue.
Indeed, its discovery was a key
incident in the life of one of
America's greatest architects, Louis
Henri Sullivan. As he relates in
The Autobiography of an Idea,
published in 1924: "When Louis
Sullivan was in his eighteenth year
. . . he had occasion one day to pass
in the neighborhood of Prairie

Avenue and Twenty-first Street.
There on the southwest corner of the
intersection, his eye was attracted
by a residence, nearing completion,
which seemed far better than the
average run of such structures. . . ."
    This was the first major
commission of Burnham & Root.
The house greatly pleased its owner,
John B. Sherman, a power in the
Union Stock Yards, and led to other

important projects for the young
architects, such as the Calumet Club.
It also resulted in the marriage,
in 1876, of Daniel Burnham to
Sherman's daughter, Margaret. The
house, along with most of its Prairie
Avenue neighbors, has disappeared,
leaving behind only Solon Beman's
Kimball mansion and Henry
Hobson Richardson's Glessner house
to manifest the street's departed glory.

It is not surprising that Robert Todd Lincoln, the only surviving child of the martyred President, should have selected Solon S. Beman, the architect of the town of Pullman, to design the house that he built in 1893 at the northeast corner of Scott Street and Lake Shore Drive.

Robert Lincoln was an attorney for the Pullman Company, then its president, and after 1906, the chairman of its board. The three-story house, a restrained brownstone mansion, aptly reflected the quiet, publicity-shy life Lincoln lived there with his wife and two daughters.

The Lincolns sold the house in 1911 and moved to Manchester, Vermont, where Robert lived until he died in 1926. The house he built, the only surviving Chicago landmark closely associated with the memory of Abraham Lincoln, was destroyed in 1959.

Those Chicagoans living north of the river before the fire generally rebuilt on their old property. The McCormicks had always been North Siders; indeed, at one time there were so many of the clan ensconced in the vicinity of Rush and Erie streets that the neighborhood was familiarly referred to as "McCormickville." The focus of this gathering was the sumptuous brownstone dwelling built for Cyrus Hall McCormick at 675 Rush Street, between 1875 and 1879. The architects were Cudell and Blumenthal, who took as their model the Pavilions de Marsan and de Flore that Hector Lefuel had recently completed for the Louvre.

The dining room and foyer, like all the McCormick interiors, were the work of the fashionable New York decorating firm L. Marcott & Company. Cyrus McCormick lived only five years in his grand house, but his widow, Nettie Fowler McCormick, died there in 1923 at the age of 88. Afterward it was the home of her son, Harold F. McCormick, after he divorced Edith Rockefeller, the daughter of the first John D., and married the Polish opera singer Ganna Walska. Following the Second World War, the house was emptied of the treasures Harold McCormick had gathered—antique furniture, paintings, tapestries, as well as a library of more than a million manuscript items relating to the McCormick family, which went to the State Historical Society of Wisconsin. In 1955 the residence was demolished.

ABOVE: *The William Borden mansion at the northwest corner of Lake Shore Drive and Bellevue Place was Chicago's preeminent example of a Richard Morris Hunt French Renaissance chateau. Borden, for whom it was built in 1884, was a lawyer and mining engineer who had made a fortune in Leadville, Colorado. The limestone residence, with its corner oriel window, dormers, and high roof, closely resembled the seminal* mansion Hunt had completed a year before on New York's Fifth Avenue for William K. Vanderbilt. This great house by a great architect was replaced by a banal apartment building in the early 1960s.

OPPOSITE: *The delightful mix of old mansions and new high-rise apartments which once gave North Lake Shore Drive visual vitality is brilliantly captured in this 1941 photograph taken from the Palmolive building by Andreas Feininger. On the near left, at 1000 Lake Shore Drive, is the Edith Rockefeller McCormick mansion, demolished in 1955. Just across Bellevue Place is a partial view of the William Borden chateau.*

The Farwells, brothers and partners in the dry-goods and real estate business, built their houses next to each other on Pearson Street, just north of the Water Tower. Charles B. Farwell's residence, on the left, was architecturally the more significant. The work of the Chicago firm of Treat & Foltz, it was a flamboyant, $100,000 example of the popular Queen Anne style and, when it was completed in 1882, was widely admired for its advanced steam-heating system, modern plumbing, and plate-glass windows. John V. Farwell's house, on the right, was destroyed for the widening of Michigan Avenue in the 1920s, but Charles's lingered into the '30s as a restaurant called Chez Louis. The entire site is now occupied by a commercial building.

If one could magically reconstruct any of Chicago's lost great houses, the first choice would have to be the castle designed in 1882 for the merchant, real estate tycoon, and hotelman Potter Palmer and his dazzling consort, Berthe Honoré. Though there might be confusion as to the style, suggestions ranging from "early Romanesque" to "Norman Gothic," which its architects, Henry Ives Cobb and Charles Sumner Frost, gave it, from the moment it rose on Lake Shore Drive between Banks and Schiller streets, there was no doubt that this mansion was the Windy City's Buckingham Palace. Rumors said that the castle had cost $700,000. During the 1893 Columbian Exposition, the mansion provided the perfect setting for Mrs. Palmer's receptions for Presidents Grant and McKinley, the Duke of Veragua, who was said to be a direct descendant of Columbus, and the

Infanta Eulalia of Spain. Mrs. Palmer continued to live in the mansion after her husband's death in 1902; after her death in 1918, her casket, under a blanket of orchids, lay in state in the Palmers' dream house. In 1950, the wrecker's ball reduced the Palmer castle, which would have made an ideal residence for Chicago's mayors, to dust.

The interiors of the Potter Palmer mansion were unabashedly eclectic. The central octagonal hall had Moorish touches, while the library beyond was described as "Flemish Renaissance."

No room in the Potter Palmer mansion was more famous than the 75-foot-long picture gallery, Mrs. Palmer's special creation. It was her voice which Henry B. Fuller gave to Susan Bates in his penetrating novel of Chicago society, With the Procession: "'Well, we might just stick our noses in the picture-gallery for a minute. . . . Some of these things are going to the Art Institute. . . .'" With the help of her friend, the painter Mary Cassatt, and Mr. Palmer's friend, the art dealer Sarah Hollowell, the Palmers filled the gallery with modern paintings by, among others, Renoir, Monet, Pissarro, and Degas. Many of these now grace the walls of the Art Institute.

A second-floor bedroom in the Palmer castle.

Among the architects who remained disciples of Louis Sullivan was George Maher. Arriving in Chicago in the 1870s, he was first associated with August Bauer, a one-time partner of Dankmar Adler. The huge granite house Maher built on Ridge Avenue in Evanston in 1901 for James A. Patten, a patron of Northwestern University, was a product of his determination to produce an American style. The imaginative use of the thistle motif in the glass and woodwork of the entrance hall to suggest the Pattens' Scots antecedents was an outgrowth of Maher's interest in the Chicago Arts and Crafts movement. His boldly innovative Patten house was demolished in 1958.

ABOVE: *The English manor house which Howard Van Doren Shaw designed for Edward Morris and his wife at 4800 South Drexel Boulevard in Hyde Park in 1910 reflected their families' unassailable positions in Chicago's social hierarchy. He was the son of Nelson Morris, one of the "Big Four" packers of the Stock Yards, and she was the daughter of Gustavus Swift. Family legend says that their clergyman, Jenkin Lloyd Jones, suggested that his nephew, Frank Lloyd Wright, be the architect for the new house the Morrises were planning, but that the young Wright abandoned all hope when Mr. Morris declared that he wanted a Gothic ballroom. The two young girls in this photograph are the Morrises' daughters: the elder, Ruth, became a noted pediatrician; the younger, Muriel, became a well-known psychiatrist and the probable model for Julia in the Lillian Hellman short story of that name.*

RIGHT: *The wrought-iron entrance gate of the Morris house.*

Two views of the library with its magnificent carved walnut paneling. The portrait above the bookshelves, of Helen Swift Morris, is by Sir James Shannon.

In her 1983 memoir Code Name, Mary *Muriel Gardiner* recalled the extravagent house and grounds: "When I was ten my parents built us a still larger house, in late Tudor style, which, with its gardens, garage, stables, and tennis court, occupied half a large city block. We had more than a dozen servants: a housekeeper, a cook, a laundress, my mother's maid, my father's valet, our nurse, a gardener, a coachman-chauffeur, two butlers, and several maids."

Howard Van Doren Shaw's evocation of Hampton Court, as well as its famous gardens by Rose Nichol, disappeared in the 1940s.

Conceived as a summer retreat for Byron Smith, a noted financier who founded the Northern Trust Company, Briar Hall stood on an 80-foot-high bluff in Lake Forest overlooking Lake Michigan. The orange brick and white terra-cotta-trimmed residence constructed in 1893–94 contained all the amenities expected by upper-class clients, including a library, butler's pantry, servants' rooms, and a trunk room. This gracious example of Holabird & Roche, working in the Colonial Revival manner, vanished in the 1950s.

Few architects have possessed a more perfect sense of scale than Chicago's master of the Beaux Arts tradition, David Adler. His first commission, in 1911, from an uncle, C. A. Stonehill, resulted in a delightful Louis XIII–style chateau in Glencoe, north of the city. The pink brick and white stone residence, which stood on a high knoll overlooking Lake Michigan, was demolished in 1962.

These charming houses were captured by an anonymous photographer in the early years. The photographs reveal a fact too often forgotten: the vast majority of newcomers who arrived in Chicago in the latter half of the nineteenth century from Europe and the older states of the East did not live in slums. Chicago was a town where a man who was willing to work could usually get a job, and the prairie west of the city was soon dotted with houses like these.

ABOVE: *With its peaked roof houses and church spires this 1934 view of the near South West Side, taken from approximately 18th Street and Damen Avenue, has a distinctly Middle European quality about it. Beginning in the 1870s, the district was, in fact, the destination for thousands of Bohemians, Germans, Poles, Slovaks, Lithuanians, and Croatians who created neighborhoods with names like "Pilsen." The twin-spired church is St. Paul's at 22nd Place and Hoyne Avenue, built in 1900 for* a German Catholic parish. The large industrial complex in the distance is the McCormick Reaper Works, later International Harvester. This important base of the near South West Side's economy ceased operation in the 1950s. The neighborhood is now predominantly Mexican.

OPPOSITE: *The Mecca, built on the South Side at State and 34th streets in 1891, was the result of the collaboration of Daniel Burnham and George Edbrooke,* a leading warehouse and store designer. Its two soaring courts— a glory of glass and iron—were a brilliant solution to the problem of public space in a city with Chicago's harsh winters. When the Mecca was a sought-after address by Chicago's society, the courts were carpeted and boasted elaborate fountains; later, when this part of Chicago was occupied by blacks, the building gave its name to the song "Mecca Flat Blues." The Mecca was destroyed in 1952 for the expansion of the Illinois Institute of Technology.

APARTMENTS

THIS PAGE: *The dining room and living room in Mr. and Mrs. Samuel Marx's apartment on Astor Street reflected the cutting-edge modernity of Chicago designers like John Wellborn Root and Andrew Rebori. Designed in 1938 by Mr. Marx, the architect responsible for the legendary original Pump Room in the Ambassador East Hotel, the apartment's glass block sideboard, Parson's table, and innovative lighting fixtures provided an ideal setting for the couple's dazzling art collection. The still life in the dining room is by Matisse; the one in the living room is by Braque.*

OPPOSITE: *The four-story Francis Apartments, on the South Side at 4304 Forestville Avenue, were an important example of Frank Lloyd Wright's early years. Designed in 1895, the rich ornament of the building's cream-colored terra-cotta and its wrought-iron gates dramatically reveal the influence of Wright's mentor, Louis Sullivan. Even though they had been designated a Chicago architectural landmark, the Francis Apartments were demolished in 1971.*

The Rails Reach Out

IT IS SYMBOLIC that Chicago's first railroad, the Galena & Chicago Union, was chartered a year before the city itself, for if there is any one factor responsible for Chicago's phenomenal growth it is the iron horse. That historic line put Galena first in its name, for Galena, an important river town, was then much larger than Chicago. This was, in fact, the beginning of the vast Chicago & North Western Railway, but it almost never got rolling. The year after the road was chartered a financial panic hit the country and it was the determination of one man, William Ogden, that saved it. But it took even a man with Ogden's vigor ten years to sell enough stock to make people realize that this was a serious undertaking, and it was not until September 1847 that the right of way was surveyed. It was Ogden who understood the importance of the railroad to the island that was Chicago, understood it as the Elizabethan sailors had understood the importance for England of the sea-lanes to the Americas.

The way some men have a passion for women and others for food, Ogden had a passion for transportation. As mayor he had found unlimited worlds to conquer: Chicago's streets were undoubtedly among the worst in America. After a heavy rain or during the spring thaw, wagons and beasts and unwary citizens often sank a foot or more into the town's rich mud. It was not unusual to see signs proclaiming NO BOTTOM HERE or SHORTEST ROAD TO CHINA in even the busiest thoroughfares.

The dire condition of the city's streets is vividly illustrated in a story told about "Long John" Wentworth, the tall, witty New Hampshire–born editor, promoter, and politician who eventually became the city's mayor. One day a friend spotted "Long John" struggling in the all-engulfing muck and asked if he could help. "No, thanks," shouted back Wentworth, "I've a horse under me." As mayor, Ogden constructed more than a hundred miles of improved streets, threw dozens of bridges across the city's deep gutters, and backed the building of plank toll roads out into the country in every direction.

All of this was but prologue to the energies he put into the development of railroads, an interest which would one day make him president of the vast Union Pacific. When the first ten miles of Galena & Chicago track had been laid, Ogden brought to the city, lashed to the deck of a sailing vessel, a small locomotive with an enormous stack which he christened *The Pioneer*. And pioneer it did, putting along at the spine-tingling speed of 20 miles an hour while pulling a string of open wagons filled with local notables. After that demonstration, Chicagoans never again had to be convinced of the practicality of railroads. The Galena & Chicago was soon returning a handsome profit; by 1850 it had been extended to Elgin, some 30 miles away.

Now the lines spun out, like the strands of a stupendous iron web centered on the

Architecturally, no other Chicago station approached Solon S. Beman's monumental Grand Central of 1890. Its Norman tower, soaring 247 feet at the southwest corner of Harrison and Wells streets, contained an 11,000-pound bell to warn travelers of the time, while its iron-and-glass train shed with a span of 156 feet was one of the marvels of nineteenth-century engineering. The station was originally conceived by the railroad promoter Henry Villard as part of his failed plan to extend his Northern Pacific Railway from St. Paul to Chicago. The property was acquired by the Baltimore & Ohio and was the departure point for its luxurious all-Pullman Capital Limited, the favored transport of Washington-bound Midwest politicians. Prominent Chicago architect Harry Weese called the 1971 razing of Grand Central an act of "wanton destruction."

*The Galena & Chicago Union
Railway Station, the first in the city,
was completed in 1848, near Kinzie
and Canal streets. In the days before
the telegraph, the line's president
often posted himself in the cupola
to spot incoming trains. When the
station opened, the line had only 10
miles of track, but by 1850 it had
reached west to Elgin, some 40 miles
from Chicago, and in the 1850s
began serving Rockford and Freeport
in northwestern Illinois. The line
never got to Galena. After the
erection of a new depot at Kinzie
and Wells streets, the old station
served as a railroad employees'
reading room until it vanished in
the 1880s.*

incipient metropolis at the foot of the lake: the Chicago & Rock Island; the Michigan Central; the Michigan Southern; the Pittsburgh, Fort Wayne & Chicago. None, though, could approach in importance the august Illinois Central. Construction of the new line began in December 1851 simultaneously at Chicago and Cairo, the city at the southern tip of the state where the Ohio flowed into the Mississippi. By 1856 Illinois Central trains were pulling into the heart of Chicago at Randolph Street, bringing with them the riches of the middle third of the continent and leaching business away from the city's chief rival, St. Louis. The names connected with the line read like a primer of American history. Daniel Webster, Stephen Douglas, and Henry Clay all had a hand in the legislation that led to its birth. George B. McClellan was its chief engineer, Abraham Lincoln a lawyer on its staff, Mark Twain a pilot on one of its steam packets. And it was an Illinois Central train, the *Cannon Ball,* which Casey Jones drove that fateful April morning in 1900.

By the middle '50s nearly 3000 miles of track touched Chicago, and 96 trains a day came and went over its 10 trunk and 11 branch lines. In these years more miles of railroad were constructed in Illinois than in any other state in the Union, and soon 10,000 miles of track connected Chicago with all the important commercial centers in the country. The Mississippi was bound to it at sixteen points; by the time of the Civil War, the city had 820 locomotives and 1500 cars in its yards, and passenger fares alone were annually bringing in $65 million.

In combination with Samuel F. B. Morse's new telegraph, the nerve center of Chicago could dispatch boxcars to carry corn and wheat and cattle and hogs and oats as they were needed, boxcars to carry McCormick's reapers, boxcars to carry shoes and glass and furniture. Chicago became the bowknot at the center of the country, from which the wealth-bringing ribbons of iron stretched east to the Atlantic, south to the Gulf, north to Canada, and eventually west to the Pacific. Ogden's dream had become a reality. Snow and mud were no longer problems; months were added each year to the commercial activity of the city. The journal *The Prairie Farmer* did not let the achievement go unsung:

Our horses now freed from the road-dragging toil,
We will keep on the fallows, and till well the soil,
And when we have leisure the city to greet,
With our ladies we'll then in the cars take a seat.
Now free from the dread of the mud and the slough,
Feeling sure that the rail-car will carry us through;
Then welcome the steam horse with sinews so strong,
Ourselves and our produce can now move along.

No American city was linked to the romance of the railroad the way Chicago was. It resembled the imperial European centers—Paris, for instance—where the stations, like the points of a gigantic compass, beckoned in all directions: Gare de L'Est, Gare du Nord, Gate de Lyon. In Chicago it was the Dearborn, the La Salle, the North Western. Here, in time, like the ocean liners of New York slipping their Hudson River berths, the superb trains would head out to Boston and Montreal, to Los Angeles and Seattle, those majestic trains—the *Broadway Limited,* the *Twentieth Century,* the *Panama Limited,* the *Chief* and the *Super Chief,* the *Overland,* the *Aristocrat,* the *Royal Palm,* the *Denver Zephyr,* the *City of New Orleans.* None carried the name of Chicago, for it was not their destination. Chicago was where they all began.

It was the railroad that made Chicago the capital of America's heartland, its attainable metropolis, its possible dream. The United States has had a handful of such cities— Boston for New England, San Francisco for the West Coast, New Orleans for the Gulf. They are the nation's most interesting cities, these provincial capitals. It was not of New York that the inhabitants of Peoria and Mattoon and Kokomo and Goshen and Cedar Rapids and Blooming Prairie thought when the cars went by at night, lit up, affording tantalizing glimpses of flashing silver and cut flowers and sparkling glasses of ice water. For nearly a century the trains would be a brilliant advertisement for Chicago, would draw to it like a moving magnet the young men and women of the farms and hamlets for a thousand miles around where the land was drained by the Wabash, the Skunk, the Maumee, and the Sangamon.

The railroads did something else too; they helped to change the way Chicago looked. The 1850s had witnessed the full flowering of the Greek Revival city, but the Greek Revival had its limitations. In the surviving pre-fire photographs, the style is shown working perfectly for the little State Street shops selling hoopskirts and washbasins and for real estate and law offices. But for all intents and purposes, these are the shops of a village, serving an area as limited in its way as the small Greek city-states which first bred the style. Chicago was no longer a city-state but the capital of an empire. The railroads made it possible for a company's central office to serve the needs of thousands of scattered villages. This demanded structures that could house the hundreds of white-collar workers who helped swell Chicago's population from 28,000 in 1850 to 100,000 ten years later. The Greek Revival did not readily expand to office building size.

This sudden change in the requirements of American business coincided with a revolutionary shift in taste. The reign of the Greek Revival had not been unchallenged. Americans had long been fascinated by the pseudo-Gothic structures which had begun to be built in England in the middle of the eighteenth century. In 1838, the American architect Alexander Jackson Davis had constructed a castle-like extravaganza, Lyndhurst, on the Hudson above New York City; in 1846, Richard Upjohn had made a dramatic Gothic statement with his Trinity Church at the head of Wall Street. If one could think of the Parthenon and Chartres at the same time, it was no great step to include also Egypt's Temple of Karnak, the Roman Forum, the palaces of Venice, or anything else that might strike one's fancy. And that is just what was happening in the world of fashion at this time. Now, instead of manuals on the Greek style alone, the builder could take his choice from a veritable department store of tastes. There were Andrew Jackson Downing's *Cottage Residences,* plumping for the Gothic; John Ruskin's *The Stones of Venice;* Viollet-le-Duc's *Dictionary of French Architecture from the Eleventh to the Sixteenth Centuries;* and Calvert Vaux's *Villas and Cottages* coming down on the side of the Italianate. For the architects of the period, it was a rich, tempting, and very dangerous mélange.

There was one more element in this astonishing change of scene and that was the rapid technological development of the period which readily permitted the construction of buildings of five and six and seven stories, allowed glass to be made in ever-larger sheets, and facilitated the carving of wood in a fantasticality of shapes. None, though, had a more profound effect than the complete cast-iron fronts that began arriving from New York in the 1840s. Painted white in imitation of marble, these precast *palazzi* came in any style the builder wanted: Classical, Italianate, or Gothic. They were turned out mile upon mile, with arches and columns and brackets and acanthus leaves enough to satisfy even the greediest client. Chicago, the city that had given the world the balloon frame, readily accepted all of these innovations and all these styles. They were evident in the new office buildings springing up close to one another on State, Dearborn, Clark, and La Salle streets. There they stood— Cobb's, Dickey's, Link's, Garrett's, Magies', the Honoré—splendid from their high, cast-iron first floors past their five ranks of crowded windows with ornamental lintels, up to their heavy bracketed cornices and flat galvanized iron roofs.

Nowhere, though, was the new taste—which has been termed variously Reign of Terror, Gingerbread, Victorian, and Parvenu—more evident than in domestic architecture. All the restrained features of the Greek Revival were quickly abandoned. The square or oblong shape of the house persisted for a time, but the classic cornice and the returns were lost almost at once. In their place came a heavy, overhanging cornice with scroll-sawn brackets. Next, corner pilasters disappeared and the verandahs, which replaced the columned porches, became ever more elaborate. Ceilings, as though expressing new wealth, rose higher and higher, while windows, their tops now arched, grew taller and thinner. Capping it all was a forest of elaborate chimneys, a mansard roof instead of the simple low gables of the past and, if the owner was rich enough, a cupola. This was the ideal of the villas rising in the new suburbs of Hyde Park and Kenwood, of Lake View and Evanston. It could be seen on fashionable Park Row just off Michigan Avenue and in the grand quarters of the North Side.

Even the pride of the city, the Court House, did not escape this revolution in taste. When Van Osdel had built it in the early 1850s, it was a fine, direct Greek Revival structure, but just before the Great Fire he added two vast wings and an enormous cupola and labeled the whole thing "French." If Van Osdel could follow fashion, so too could his greatest contemporary, Edward Burling, the architect who had built that jewel of the Greek Revival city, the splendid Eli B. Williams house. Now, at the southeast corner of Washington and La Salle streets, he designed in the French style a handsome building to house the Chamber of Commerce and the Board of Trade. Three stories high, it was constructed of the favorite material of the new city—limestone from the Lemont quarries in Cook County, called by its promoters "Athens marble." Burling's unfailing good taste is important in the history of Chicago. In 1871 he formed a partnership with Dankmar Adler and in a single year following The Great Fire, the firm designed more than 100 buildings. In 1879 Adler opened his own office and shortly afterward took in Louis Sullivan as a draftsman.

⊣║ THE AGE OF THE IRON HORSE ║⊢

"THAT'S MY MIDDLE WEST — not the wheat or the prairies or the lost Swede towns, but the thrilling returning trains of my youth," says the narrator of F. Scott Fitzgerald's *The Great Gatsby,* and then goes on to recall his Christmas passages through Chicago's "old dim Union Station." The Union was Fitzgerald's own transfer point on his way home to St. Paul, Minnesota, from Princeton, New Jersey. Chicago was a city permeated by the romance of the rails. Even a partial listing of the lines which served it rings like an American geography lesson: Pennsylvania; Baltimore & Ohio; Gulf, Mobile; Chicago, Burlington & Quincy; Norfolk & Western; Erie, Lackawanna; New York Central; The Soo; Atchison, Topeka & Santa Fe; Illinois Central.

Henry James too was struck by the number of railroads radiating from the metropolis of the Middle West. In a letter written from Chicago in March of 1905, the great novelist reveals his astonishment at both the city and its rail lines: "This Chicago is huge, infinite, . . . lying beside a colossal lake (Michigan) of hard pale green jade, and putting forth railway antennae of maddening complexity and gigantic length."

ABOVE: *Trains ready for departure at the Illinois Central's Randolph Street Station about 1890. With the formidable backing of Senator Stephen A. Douglas and former mayor "Long John" Wentworth, the Chicago City Council in 1852 permitted the Illinois Central to enter Chicago by way of a 300-foot-wide swath on the lakefront. The noise and smoke and burning cinders which resulted were a constant source of irritation to those trying to improve the lakefront. In 1919 the line agreed to ameliorate matters by electrifying its operations in Chicago, and the new electric trains were inaugurated on July 21, 1926.*

INSET: *The Chicago & North Western Station at Wells and Kinzie streets, completed in 1881, was a massive Queen Anne–style structure designed by W. W. Boyington. The North Western, which absorbed the Galena, was one of Chicago's supreme wheat shipping lines. Its nearly 900 miles of track carried the wheat of the heartland to a grain elevator on the north bank of the Chicago River whence it was shipped across the Great Lakes to the East and to Europe. The station, home to the crack San Francisco Overland and the Portland Rose, was abandoned in 1911 and the Merchandise Mart now occupies the site.*

ABOVE: *The Lake Shore & Michigan Southern & Rock Island Depot, erected in 1873 at Van Buren and Sherman streets. The Rock Island had made history in 1856 by constructing the first bridge across the Mississippi. The Second Empire–style depot was superseded in 1903 by the La Salle Street Station.*

LEFT: *Theodore Dreiser, in* A Book About Myself, *recalled: "[W]e would make our way to the great railway station at the end of Dearborn Street, where a tall clock-tower held a single yellow clock-face." The most picturesque of Chicago stations, the Dearborn, also known as the Polk Street Station, designed by Cyrus L. W. Eidlitz, was completed in 1885. Among the many lines it served was the Atchison, Topeka & Santa Fe. A fire in 1922 destroyed the upper part of the station's dramatic Flemish-style tower and its peaked roofs. The Dearborn is now a commercial galleria.*

55

With its entrance colonnade of tall
Doric columns, its pair of baroque
clock towers, and its fine stonework,
the North Western Railroad Station
at 406 West Madison Street was
a magnificent Beaux Arts edifice.
A 1911 work of Frost & Granger,
the architects of the Northern Trust
Company Building on La Salle Street,
it was truly a monumental Italian
Renaissance gateway to Chicago. The
Commission on Chicago Historical
and Architectural Landmarks voted,
in April of 1980, to designate the
station a landmark, but the head
of the City Planning Commission
refused to give the necessary approval.
The Chicago Tribune's Pulitzer
Prize–winning architecture critic,
Paul Gapp, labeled the claims of
those opposed to designation—that
the station would impede the neighborhood's redevelopment—"pure
balderdash." The North Western
Station was demolished in late 1981.

The gateway to the city from the
south was the Illinois Central Depot,
which served not only the Illinois
Central, but the New York Central's
southern routes as well. Built in
1892 by Bradford L. Gilbert, a New
York architect, the depot, east of
Michigan Avenue near 12th Street,
is seen here in a 1920 drawing. Next
to it are some of the old surviving
residences of Park Row. The familiar
landmark was razed in 1974.

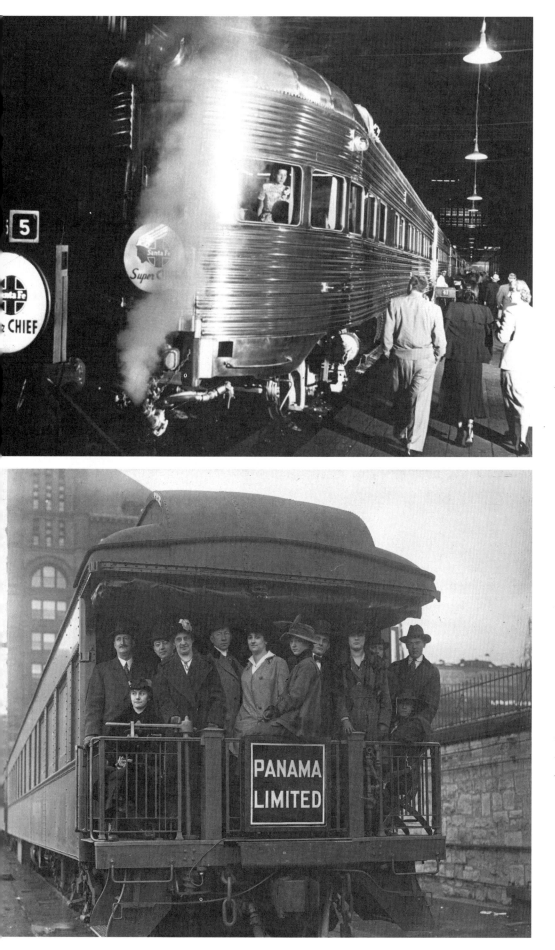

The Santa Fe's sleek Super Chief *at the Dearborn Station in the late 1940s, ready for its thirty-nine-and-a-half-hour run to Los Angeles. The* Super Chief *evolved from the* Chief, *an all-Pullman deluxe train inaugurated by the Santa Fe in 1926. The streamlined observation car was by Budd. Chicago press photographers gathered daily at the Dearborn Station to snap pictures of arriving Hollywood celebrities such as Greta Garbo, Bing Crosby, and Charlie Chaplin.*

The Panama Limited, *leaving the Illinois Central Station in 1916 with a load of passengers determined to enjoy themselves in the sunny south. The luxurious train received its name in 1911 when the Panama Canal, still under construction, was considered the wonder of the modern world. For its run to New Orleans, the* Panama Limited *boasted a barber shop, a mahogany-paneled library, a dining car offering such Louisiana delicacies as fresh Gulf shrimp, and a bar car with forty-two brands of bourbon.*

ABOVE: *The most glamorous of American trains, the New York Central's* The Twentieth Century Limited, *leaving La Salle Street Station in 1939 headed to New York's Grand Central. The all-Pullman, later all-drawing-room, train began its life in 1902 and quickly became the conveyance of choice for bankers, brokers, and Broadway stars and the setting for a 1934 film by Ben Hecht and Charles MacArthur. In case there should be a problem with the crack train's engine, the New York Central kept relief engines at the ready at strategic spots* along the line. Like most of America's magnificent trains, *The Twentieth Century rolled into oblivion in the 1960s. The La Salle Street Station disappeared in the 1990s.*

OPPOSITE, TOP: *The Twentieth Century's chief competitor for pure luxe was the Pennsylvania Railroad's* Broadway Limited, *also inaugurated in 1902. While the* Century *took a northerly route up the Hudson River, the* Broadway Limited *linked Chicago's Union Station and New York's Pennsylvania Station by way of Philadelphia and the Keystone* State. *Shown here is the elegantly modern observation car of the redesigned* Broadway Limited *in Chicago on its first run, July 7, 1938.*

OPPOSITE, BOTTOM: *The* Twentieth Century *achieved a rare sophistication with the streamlined Art Deco style which the distinguished industrial designer Henry Dreyfus gave to it in 1938. The Dreyfus-designed lounge car had both ashtrays and a photo mural of the* Chicago Tribune *tower.*

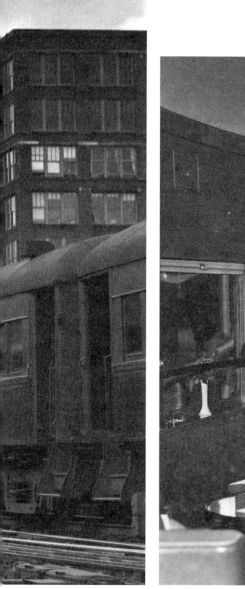

In 1880, on 4300 acres just south of Chicago, George M. Pullman began building America's first planned industrial community. By the time he had finished in 1894 Pullman contained not only workers' housing and a vast sleeping-car plant, but a library, hotel, theater, school, hospital, market, and church. The administra-tion building and factory, like all the structures in the town, were designed by Solon S. Beman. They faced Lake Vista, a three-acre artificial lake from whose center a tall column of water shot into the air, propelled by the awesome Corliss Engine that Pullman had brought back from the Philadelphia Centennial Exposition of 1876. Beman's powerful octagonal water tower has been demolished, and Lake Vista and its curved drive disappeared with the extension of Cottage Grove Avenue. The adminis-tration building, which survived like the royal palace of a kingdom without a king, was seriously damaged by fire in 1999.

OPPOSITE, TOP: *Pullman was as famous for its dining cars as for its sleepers. This photograph, taken in the 1920s, captures the appointments which were the company's hallmarks: the spotless napery, the heavy silver, the courteous white-coated waiter. Beneath its offering of ham, the dining car menu invariably carried the phrase, "The Best Ham What Am," the motto of Morris & Company, the Chicago meatpacker which had the monopoly on supplying that part of the pig to Pullman.*

OPPOSITE, BOTTOM LEFT: *The* Santa Barbara, *built by Pullman for the Southern Pacific in 1887, gloried in seats upholstered in red mohair and cabinetwork of mahogany, oak, and satinwood. Light was provided by kerosene lamps and heat by coal stoves.*

OPPOSITE, BOTTOM RIGHT: *Among the most sumptuous of the private cars of the Gilded Age was the one which the Pullman Company fashioned in 1897 for*

the Mexican political leader, Porfirio Díaz. The Louis XV–style interior exemplified Belle Epoch lavishness.

ABOVE: *View of the Pullman Car Works in March of 1956 showing the production of new, lightweight railway cars for the New York Central System. The Pullman factory, which closed in 1958, was heavily damaged by fire in 1998, and despite the factory's historical significance, its future is uncertain.*

Queen of the Lakes

CHICAGO HAD NEED of all its new offices and houses and public buildings, for now still more infusions swelled its population. On a single summer day in 1857, 3400 foreign immigrants arrived on the Michigan Central Railroad. To the French and the Yankees were added Scandinavians and Belgians and Slavs; English and Irish poured in on the Black Ball packets from Liverpool, and Germans on the ships operated by the Chicago bankers Henry and Elias Greenebaum out of Bremen and Hamburg. Soon Chicago, with only 46 percent of its population native-born, was more cosmopolitan than New York.

The Irish were the first of the new wave to settle in significantly large numbers; driven by the consequences of the Great Potato Famine of 1845–49, they came by the thousands from Waterford and Cork and Limerick. For the most part unskilled, they crowded into the neighborhood south and west of the stockyards known as "Back-of-the-Yards" and into Bridgeport, east of the Yards, where their political allegiance caused them to be termed "unwashed Dimmycrats." The Irish became the soldiers of the Democratic party organization and would supply the city with the stuff of its political legends: "Bathhouse John" Coughlin, "Hinky Dink" Kenna, Pat Nash, Ed Kelly, Martin Kennelly, and Richard J. Daley. In a city where the first church had been Roman Catholic and where men were generally judged by what they could do rather than who their fathers were the Irish found advancement easier than in the eastern states. The NO IRISH NEED APPLY sign, with which the Boston Brahmins attempted to protect their social and economic hegemony, was unknown in Chicago.

The Irish Catholics were not the only oppressed group who found Chicago a haven. The city's first Jews had arrived in 1841, and six years later a synagogue, Kehilath Anshe Mayriv, the Congregation of the Men of the West, was established. Anti-Semitism seems to have been rare in the city. Abraham Kohn was clerk of the Common Council in the 1860s, and men such as the packer Nelson Morris, department store executive Leon Mandel, the Florsheims of shoe fame, the Regensteiners of the window envelope, Moses Bensinger of the Brunswick sporting goods company, Philip Block of Inland Steel, Governor Henry Horner, and Julius Rosenwald of Sears, Roebuck would play an important part in the city's life.

The great majority of the Jews who came to Chicago in these years were from Germany, and it was the Germans of all faiths who, of the newly arrived groups, made the most profound impact on the city. There were Germans in Chicago as early as the 1830s, but it was the combination of the failure of the liberal revolutions of 1848 and disastrous economic conditions in the Rhineland that drove them to America in great numbers. By the late 1840s the Common Council found it necessary to have

"Whenever the traffic of the city growing so magically upon its banks had burst its bounds, the river was spanned by a red-wooden turn-bridge. . . . To stand on the Rush Street Bridge at nightfall was . . . a joy indeed to the lover of ships."—Hobart Chatfield-Taylor, Chicago.

The city remained a major port throughout the nineteenth century, its waterways—the Great Lakes to the north and east and the Mississippi system to the south and west—making it a kind of American Suez. This view, looking east from the Rush Street Bridge around 1869, makes it clear why first-time visitors were startled to see, in the heart of the continent, a scene reminiscent of the wharves of New York and Boston.

German-speaking tax collectors in some sections of the city and most large shops soon had at least one German-speaking clerk. In 1850, more than 17 percent of the population was German-born, and the foundations of a German city within the city had been laid. They were the first ethnic group, for instance, to settle on the Near North Side and in 1846 constructed St. Paul's Evangelical Lutheran Church and St. Joseph's Roman Catholic Church. The Germans rapidly moved northward to Lincoln Park, and the Germania Club on North Clark Street was an important center of Chicago's German-speaking population. Generally literate and skilled, the Germans quickly established their own cultural institutions: churches, schools, hospitals, theaters, and, above all, musical organizations such as those that made the Saengerfests in Wright's Grove nationally famous. In 1851, the *Illinois Staats-Zeitung,* one of the most illustrious foreign language newspapers in the United States, began publication. It was the Germans, too, in the trade union movement and later in the Socialist party, who made many of the most eloquent appeals for economic justice in Chicago.

The Germans also had an indelible impact on the city's architecture. There can be no doubt that this vast Rhinelander migration contributed a great deal to the love of rough stone walls, heavy arches, and towers which became a hallmark of Chicago and other midwestern centers. The city was soon rich with German-born architects: Edward Baumann, Cord Gottig, August Bauer, and Otto Matz, who as the first official architect for the Illinois Central Railroad designed its terminal at the foot of South Water Street.

The meeting places of the city's disparate elements, of recent immigrants and cattle kings, of wheat speculators and lumbermen, were the new mammoth hotels. Nothing more clearly symbolizes the booming metropolis of the late '50s and '60s. The Chicago hotel was, almost without exception, built to serve the railways. To find its equivalent, it is necessary to look abroad to the great caravansaries such as London's Charing Cross and the Grosvenor at Victoria Station. The note of grandeur had first been set by the second Tremont House, but it soon had keen competition from a dozen other equally opulent hostelries. There was the Briggs House, a vaguely Gothic structure on the northeast corner of Randolph and Wells, whose dining room offered such delights as roast prairie chicken and Glace Jenny Lind. There were the handsome Clarendon, the proper Adams House, the St. James, the Burlington, and the sumptuous Richmond House, at the corner of South Water Street and Michigan Avenue, where in September 1860 Albert Edward, the Prince of Wales, stayed. Queen Victoria's nineteen-year-old son became tongue-tied when he stepped out onto one of the hotel's balconies to face an assembled throng of enthusiastic Chicagoans, but blunt old John Wentworth had a remedy for that. "Say something to 'em, sonny," the mayor said, genially slapping the future Edward VII on the back. The prince, who was on a tour of Canada and the United States, was fascinated by the 160,000 population boomtown with its mix of wooden shanties standing next to brick and stone structures that would not have been out of place in London or Paris and was astonished to see a wooden house on rollers being moved down a street. The highlight of the royal visit, though, was a rail trip to the village of Dwight some 90 miles west of Chicago, where the prince and his entourage stayed in a small private residence and shot prairie chickens. One day Albert Edward bagged twenty-three.

Horace Greeley, the hopelessly peripatetic editor of the New York *Tribune,* had won the city's heart in 1858 by declaring that Chicago could boast at least half a dozen hotels that were better than anything New York could claim prior to the opening of the Astor. And that was before the two masterworks of the supreme architect of the Chicago hotel, William Boyington, had been built. The first of these, the huge Sherman House at the corner of Clark and Randolph, rose up in six stories of finely cut Athens marble, could accommodate 300 guests, and always had an orchestra playing in its grand dining room.

But Boyington's chef-d'oeuvre was the opulent Grand Pacific, whose roof was put on just before the Great Fire. Turning for inspiration to the extensions of the Louvre just completed for Napoleon III by Louis Visconti and Hector Martin Lefuel, Boyington created an edifice which would be a model for Chicago hotels for years to come. In a daring display of prodigality, he brought together Doric, Ionic, and Corinthian columns, balconies, domes, pavilions, a forest of chimneys, and caryatids to compose a building which had, in the words of a contemporary guide to the city, not one, but "four grand entrances." Here was indeed a palace for the people.

It was no easy task to reach these magnificent hostelries, for if the city's head and shoulders were of Athens marble, its feet were still of mud. Though Mayor Ogden had tried valiantly to improve the quagmire streets, Chicago's swampy, water-logged soil defied all solutions. Finally, in desperation, the City Council in 1856 ordered all grades to be raised to a height that would insure proper drainage. This was a costly proposition, for it was quickly estimated that the ordinance would force the lifting of street levels from four to seven feet. But there was no alternative. With the use of mud dredged from the bed of the Chicago River, the streets rose like the levees along the lower Mississippi. The Court House square was the first to be raised, leaving the buildings surrounding it set in sunken gardens, with their second stories now at street level. Once more Chicago's ingenuity was called on. Vacant lots were quickly filled in and houses built at the new level; ground floors were buried, turned into instant basements, and new floors added on top of the old. This worked well enough for residences, but it scarcely filled the bill when it came to five- and six-story office buildings and hotels.

The new challenge coincided with the arrival of another of those men whom destiny brought to Chicago at the right time. It had been that way with the organization of the packing industry, with the reaper, and now it was George Pullman's turn. The son of a Brockton, New York, mechanic, Pullman had been a cabinetmaker and house mover. He arrived in Chicago just as the ordinance raising the grade went into effect, and he found a city in which the owners of large downtown buildings were frantic from fear of losing their grand first floors with their high rents to the new level. None were more disturbed than the proprietors of the palatial Tremont House. Pullman walked around the building and then went inside and asked for the manager. "I can raise your hotel without breaking a single pane of window glass or stopping your business for a day," he told the astonished man. The owners of the Tremont were skeptical, but they were also desperate, and they had little choice but to give this brash young newcomer a chance. Placing twelve hundred men with large jackscrews around the perimeter of the hotel, Pullman ordered each one to move his screw half-a-turn, a fraction of an inch, on his command. Slowly, almost imperceptibly, the five-story brick building rose into the air until it was at the level of the new grade; then a new foundation was placed under it. The attendant publicity created Pullman's first fortune, and he was soon levitating entire blocks. The nation watched in astonishment as Chicago miraculously pulled itself out of the primordial muck.

But destiny had not brought George Pullman to Chicago to be merely a lifter of buildings. His twin trade of cabinetmaking and house moving had sparked an idea more wondrous than that. Pullman knew that Chicago was the port from which the trains sailed out in all directions. He knew, also, that it was the city that set the standards for hotel comfort and luxury. Pullman wanted to wed those two things; to put the Sherman and the Tremont and the Richmond on wheels and send them out across the prairie. In 1859 he asked the Chicago & Alton Railroad for permission to make over some of its day coaches into sleeping cars with rows of upper and lower berths. The line replied that the idea was expensive nonsense: no passenger would pay extra to sleep on a train. But Pullman did not give up. Taking over an abandoned repair shop, he called into play his skill as a cabinetmaker to create the most beautiful railway car in the world. Of splendidly carved black walnut, its ceiling handsomely frescoed, its floors carpeted, Pullman's "Palace Car" boasted two drawing rooms, the most modern lavatories, and sumptuously upholstered seats which converted into beds. He spent $18,000 of his own money on the car, and, like Ogden with his first locomotive, he christened it *The Pioneer*. The press hailed *The Pioneer* as a marvel, but again the railroad men said that it was too expensive, as well as too high for their bridges and too wide for their station platforms. Like a sorcerer who had conjured up something out of its time, George Pullman carefully put away his splendid creation. It would wait, gleaming and glorious, until 1865, when an awesome occasion would call it forth.

If Chicago was not ready for Pullman's sleeping car, it was unstinting in praise of what his jackscrews had done for the city. With the major buildings lifted a full story into the air and set upon new foundations, the downtown streets were now high and dry. The change was noted with pleasure by the thousands of prosperous farmers and small-town merchants, lawyers, doctors, and bankers who now looked to Chicago to break the monotony of life in Dubuque, Racine, and Muncie. Typical of them was a tall, thin young attorney from Springfield. Whenever Abraham Lincoln got up to Chicago on business, usually a case for the Illinois Central—he almost always found time for a show.

Undoubtedly, the grandest theater in Chicago at this time was McVicker's. A handsome $85,000 brick structure on Madison Street, just west of State, McVicker's exterior boasted twin cupolas, while its interior was brightened by a drop curtain depicting the railroad bridge connecting Rock Island, Illinois, and Davenport, Iowa. The house featured a stock company headed by James H. McVicker himself, and was soon attracting stars of the magnitude of E. A. Sothern and Lotta Crabtree; in 1858, Edwin Booth headed the bill in *Brutus* and *Richelieu*. Ultimately, he would play Romeo to McVicker's daughter Mary's Juliet, and, as though to prove that life follows art, would marry her.

If Chicago was the entertainment capital of the heartland, it was, almost from the beginning, also the shopping center. As early as 1840, ladies wishing something smart to wear could find at Gray & Company cambrics, merinos, and satinets, not to mention Vauxhall cloaks and palm leaf hats. If their palates also craved luxuries, Lefort's "Parisian Establishment" offered a wide selection of chocolates, sultanas, and nougats, as well as a confection called a "pyramid." In the midst of the 1847 building boom, the infant city had, along with $88,000 worth of iron and nails, brought in $68,000 worth of hats, capes, and furs and $51,000 worth of jewelry.

Yet, as the old Sauganash gave way to the Briggs House and the city's first primitive theaters were eclipsed by the splendor of McVicker's, so the little shops of the '40s were about to be overshadowed by the behemoth of the department store. One man, Potter Palmer, was chiefly responsible for the transition. Born of Quaker parents in New York State, Palmer learned his trade from the highly successful New York City merchant A. T. Stewart, and when he came to Chicago in 1852 with $5000, he was prepared to revolutionize the selling of dry goods. Palmer was Chicago's first shopkeeper to appeal primarily to women. His store on Lake Street was the first to have tastefully decorated show windows, to sell goods on credit, and to guarantee that if a customer was dissatisfied with merchandise it could be exchanged or her money refunded.

As time passed, Palmer's interest shifted more and more to real estate development, centering on his dream of making State Street Chicago's supreme shopping avenue. To help him run his department store, he brought in two young men as partners, Marshall Field and Levi Leiter. Before long Potter Palmer had retired altogether from the retail business, and in 1863 he built for Field and Leiter—on State Street naturally—an

elegant white marble palace which he rented to them for the then unheard-of sum of $50,000 a year. Here was the beginning of Marshall Field & Company.

This booming, bustling town was strongly Democratic, having been born during the heady days of Andrew Jackson's administration and agreeing with him wholeheartedly in his dislike and distrust of the so-called eastern aristocracy. The city found its spokesman in Stephen A. Douglas, the five-foot-tall senator from Illinois. It was Douglas who, as the powerful chairman of the Committee of Territories, pushed through statehood for territory after territory to place Chicago in the center of an "ocean-bound republic"; it was Douglas who fought for the city as the eastern terminus of the great transcontinental rail lines, fought for it against Memphis, New Orleans, and St. Louis. Yet it would be a single issue, the supreme issue, that would destroy him—slavery.

The growing controversy over slavery could not fail to erode the once almost unanimous support the Democrats had enjoyed in Chicago. The institution was profoundly hated in the city: by the Germans because many were liberals who had escaped from Prussian oppression, by the growing number of Scandinavians—Norwegians, Danes, Swedes—who had come to Chicago carrying a deep loathing of their native aristocracy, by the Yankees who were often dedicated abolitionists. In 1856, while Illinois was backing the Democrat James Buchanan for President, Chicago turned to the Free Soil advocate, John C. Frémont. That summer Abraham Lincoln had been in Chicago. He had come to speak at a banquet for Frémont—to speak against slavery:

> The human heart is with us; God is with us. We shall again be able not
> to declare that "all states as states are equal," nor yet that "all citizens as
> citizens are equal," but to renew the broader, better declaration . . . that
> "all men are created equal."

If the diminutive Stephen Douglas was, as his admirers called him, the "Little Giant," then perhaps the new Republican party had found a giant killer.

The first great confrontation came in the senatorial election of 1858. In April of that

Abraham Lincoln's funeral cortege at Park Row, May 1, 1865, with the train which carried the assassinated President's body from Washington in the background. The wooden arch erected for the occasion was embellished with Gothic Revival, Masonic, and patriotic motifs. "[H]ere the mourning began to take on a character distinctly different from what had marked it in the East. The people who now met the coffin, who followed it to the court-house, ... dated their trust in him many years earlier than 1861. Man after man of them had come to pay their tribute, not to the late President of the United States, but to the genial lawyer, the resourceful, witty political debater who had educated Illinois to believe that a country could not endure half slave and half free. . . ." —Ida Tarbell, Life of Lincoln.

year, the Democrats nominated Douglas for another term, and in June the Republicans named Lincoln. A month later, Douglas returned to Chicago from Washington and was given a hero's welcome by a throng from Little Egypt, as downstate Illinois was called because of its metropolis, Cairo. Up Lake Street the crowd moved with its idol to Wabash, Washington, down Dearborn to the Tremont House. Stepping out onto a balcony, Douglas eloquently defended his concept of "popular sovereignty," arguing that each state, individually, should decide whether it wanted to be slave or free.

Standing silently in the crowd, listening, was Lincoln. The next night he stepped out onto the same balcony. His words were very different from those of the "Little Giant": he spoke of the Union, of one law for all; he warned that "a house divided against itself cannot stand." Thus the great Lincoln-Douglas debates began. Chicago once more voted Republican, but Illinois went Democratic and Douglas was returned to the United States Senate. But it was only a battle that was lost, not a war.

Lincoln and Douglas would face each other again in 1860 as the presidential standard bearers of their two parties. It was as though Chicago, which a mere thirty years before had been a blowing field of wild onions, now bestrode the nation. The Democrats met in Baltimore, but it was Chicago for the Republicans, the first national political convention held in the city that would become America's number one convention town, the site of the selection of Grant, Garfield, Cleveland, Benjamin Harrison, Theodore Roosevelt, Taft, Harding, Franklin Delano Roosevelt, and Eisenhower, as well as those vice presidents who moved up to the highest office in the land, Chester Arthur, Coolidge, and Truman.

Chicago sought the convention because it was a Republican city, but also because it wanted to show off. With its population quadrupled to more than 100,000, with its fifteen railroads bringing in the wealth of Kansas, Missouri, Iowa, Minnesota, Wisconsin, and Nebraska, with its wholesale houses sending their own drummers into St. Louis and Cincinnati, underbidding local manufacturers and bringing back orders that kept 500 factories booming day and night, Chicago was in no mood to be different. The island had done all right. It was proud when men such as William Howard Russell of the august London *Times* came out for a visit in 1860 and took seriously the title it had bestowed upon itself:

> The scene now began to change gradually as we approached Chicago, the prairie subsided into swampy land, and thick belts of trees fringed the horizon; on our right glimpses of the sea could be caught through openings in the wood—the inland sea on which stands the Queen of the Lakes.

The "Queen of the Lakes" wanted to take her visitors to the Sherman House to mingle with Cyrus McCormick, William Ogden, and Nelson Morris—men who could match dollars with anyone from Boston or New York. Besides, the dining room featured fresh lobster, chilled champagne, and pheasant under glass. She wanted the visitors to see Elijah Peacock's dazzling jewelry store on Randolph Street with its trays of Brazilian diamonds and pigeon-blood rubies. She wanted to suggest an evening at McVicker's, where one night Adah Isaacs Menken, half naked and tied to the back of a running horse, was performing in *Mazeppa's Ride* and, on the next, the extraordinary New Orleans pianist Louis Moreau Gottschalk was charming the city with his syncopated compositions. The more serious-minded might drive down to Cottage Grove Avenue and Thirty-fourth Street to see the astonishing Gothic castle William Boyington had just built for the new University of Chicago.

The city had every right to be pleased with itself that May day in 1860 when the Republican National Convention convened in the Wigwam, a plain pine structure which the local Republican Club had built on the site of Mark Beaubien's Sauganash Hotel. The ladies of Chicago had attempted to disguise the hall's utilitarian lines by covering as much of it as possible with garlands, wreaths, flags, marble busts, and portraits of American notables. And just to add a touch of history, the official gavel was fashioned from a timber of the *Niagara,* Commodore Perry's flagship in the Battle of Lake Erie.

It is unlikely that any of the 10,000 Republicans who crowded into the Wigwam were very much concerned with aesthetics. For days the city had been a maelstrom of political parades, processions for New York's favorite son, William H. Seward; for the popular Ohio governor, Salmon P. Chase; for John C. Frémont; for Illinois's own Abraham Lincoln. And there was no dearth of marchers. More than 2000 people came out from New York alone. Every one of Chicago's railroads offered special excursion rates for those who wanted to see the convention and the city. The trains from New England stretched for miles around the south end of the lake into Indiana. This was, in a sense, Chicago's first great fair. The new city, as well as the new party, had attracted the whole country. Chicago, as a single man, wanted Lincoln, the Illinois candidate, the rail-splitter. It took three ballots, but on the third he won. In a moment of wild enthusiasm, a man climbed up through a skylight in the Wigwam's roof and passed the triumphant word to the crowd packed in the streets below. When he was told, Lincoln took it calmly. "Just think," he said, "of such a sucker as me as President."

In the election, Chicago gave Lincoln ten thousand votes to two thousand for its old hero Douglas. And when Fort Sumter was fired on, Joseph Medill's *Tribune,* which had been one of the first newspapers to support Lincoln, set the tone:

> Let expressed rebuke and contempt rest on every man weak enough to
> be anywhere else in this crisis than on the side of the country against
> treason. . . . We say to the tories and the lickspittles in this community,
> a patient and reluctant, but at last an outraged and maddened people
> will no longer endure your hissing. You must keep your venom sealed,
> or go down! *The gates of Janus are open, the storm is on us. Let the cry be:*
> THE SWORD OF THE LORD AND OF GIDEON!

The gates of Janus were indeed opened, and the sword of the Lord—his fiery, swift sword—was quickly unsheathed. When Lincoln called for volunteers, Governor Richard Yates found that Chicago alone was ready to supply the entire six regiments he had requested. Sumter surrendered on the thirteenth of April and a week later the first Chicagoans, numbering some six hundred, boarded an Illinois Central train and headed south. Eventually, Chicago sent some twenty-two thousand troops to fight for Lincoln, to fight at Fort Donelson and Chickamauga, at Shiloh and Vicksburg, at Pea Ridge and Malvern Hill. More than three thousand did not return.

Yet the Civil War was, without doubt, a great economic boon for the city; the bloody conflict between the nation's two halves was the event which finally raised Chicago to dominance in the heartland. While its rivals—Louisville, Cincinnati, and St. Louis—were all border cities whose river trade was disrupted by the war, Chicago, far to the north, with its untrammeled railroads, flourished. The city became the chief supplier of the Union army, and eastern investors, spotting a good thing, poured money into its plants and warehouses.

Throughout the bloodshed, Chicago never stopped building. The huge Union Stock Yards at Halsted and Thirty-ninth streets was constructed. There were new additions to the university, an immense hall for the 1864 Democratic convention, Uranus Crosby's magnificent $600,000 opera house, the refurbishing of hotels such as the Tremont, and the erection of splendid mansions like the one Leander, Cyrus McCormick's brother, built on Rush Street. Factories, warehouses, and grain elevators grew ever thicker along the river.

As victory seemed nearer and nearer, as Atlanta and then Richmond fell, Chicago waited expectantly. When news of Appomattox came, the crowds in the streets sang first the Doxology and then "The Battle-Cry of Freedom," composed in the dark summer of 1862 by the city's own George F. Root in his office at Root and Cady, music publishers, on Clark Street:

> Yes, we'll rally 'round the flag boys,
> We'll rally once again,
> Shouting the Battle-Cry of Freedom!

OPPOSITE: *Flags and bunting were always popular ways of marking a patriotic occasion in Chicago. The Fair Store on the northwest corner of State and Adams streets is here in full panoply for a visit to the city of President William McKinley, October 7, 1899. The Fair, founded in 1875 by Ernest J. Lehmann, lived up to its motto of "Everything for Everybody" by stocking goods affordable by a broad spectrum of Chicagoans. It was the Fair which attracted the heroine of Theodore Dreiser's Sister Carrie: "Without much thinking, she reached Dearborn Street. Here was the Great Fair store with its multitude of delivery wagons about, its long window display, its crowd of shoppers." The building, constructed between 1890 and 1891, was the work of William Le Baron Jenney. In 1965 it was extensively remodeled and became Montgomery Ward's Loop flagship. The historic structure was demolished in the 1970s.*

Then at the moment of triumph, when it seemed true indeed that the Union dead had not died in vain, one last life was added to their awesome number.

Chicago got word of Lincoln's assassination early in the morning of April 16. Like a whirling carousel whose works have jammed, all motion ceased. The saloons, the theaters, shops, the Board of Trade, the courts, all closed. The city waited as the funeral train slowly wound its way westward—Baltimore, Harrisburg, Philadelphia, New York, Albany, Buffalo, Cleveland, Columbus, Indianapolis—and then, on the morning of May 1, over the tracks of his own Illinois Central, the black-palled cars reached Chicago and stopped at Park Row, just off Michigan Avenue. The afternoon before he was shot, Lincoln had gone for a drive with his wife Mary and told her: "with God's blessing we may hope for four years of peace and happiness, then we will go back to Illinois, and pass the rest of our lives in quiet." Now he was back, for that spring, for that summer, for the ages.

Witnesses reported that the city was eerily quiet, a quiet like that stillness which descended at Appomattox when, at last, the guns fell silent. It had been raining, the heavy spring rain of Illinois which is guaranteed to make the corn "knee high by the Fourth of July," and the streets once again were muddy. Yet few rode that day. The citizens of Chicago walked like kings come to bury a fellow monarch. There were young women in white dresses before the black-plumed hearse; there were soldiers just returned from battle; there were distinguished pallbearers, his old friends such as Mayor John Wentworth and Francis Sherman, at whose hotel he had often dined, and John B. Rice, who presented the plays he so enjoyed. In all, forty thousand walked with him to Van Osdel's Court House, and there a quarter of a million moved silently past the ebony and silver coffin to glimpse his chalk-white face. Yet there was one sound, a sound that all who heard it never forgot; it was, in the words of the famous prima donna, Clara Louise Kellogg, "the sound of those shuffling feet, shuffle, shuffle,—in the Court House grounds in Chicago: a sound like a great sea or forest in a wind as the people of the nation went in to look at their President whom they loved and who was dead."

There was also music, the German choirs of the city singing Bach and Handel, and a new song by George F. Root:

> Farewell Father, Friend and guardian,
> Thou has joined the martyrs' band;
> But thy glorious work remaineth,
> Our redeemed, beloved land.

"He was received with a solemn magnificence of pageantry and funeral pomp unexcelled anywhere," a local paper announced proudly. But the next day the city had one final tribute for its hero. To carry Lincoln's body and his grieving widow home to Springfield, Chicago brought forth George Pullman's resplendent Palace Car.

—‖ THE LIVING CITY ‖—

ONE OF THE CHIEF functions of a city is to give to the lives of its citizens and to visitors a sense of celebration. Its streets should be avenues for the manifestation of moments of great national solemnity and rejoicing. They must also be stages for the small passing delights of shopping, strolling, and observing one's fellow creatures. The city must also contain places of worship and parks in which to refresh the body and the spirit.

In one of her short stories, "Madame de Treymes," the novelist Edith Wharton, an astute critic of architecture and design, has a character observe: "he was always struck anew by the vast and consumately ordered spectacle of Paris: by its look of having been boldly and deliberately planned as a background for the enjoyment of life." The secret of the urban success of Paris is that while the parade grounds and boulevards—the Champ-de-Mars and Champs-Élysées—

created by the Bourbon kings and Napoleon III are promenades of glory, always, nearby is a network of small, vital byways lined with those establishments which give cities life: bookshops and bars, pharmacies and food stalls, periodical kiosks and pensions. A great city is a complex city. It must have both majesty and mud, the divine monument and the dive. Of course, public safety, reasonable order, and a certain degree of salubriousness are necessary, but when these become a city's planning obsessions they can kill. Streets are not kitchen floors to be eaten off of; the city is not the suburb, not the gated estate, and for a metropolis to attempt to emulate them is to invite the dullness which destroys. Chicago has done well with its great boulevards, but the streets which once lit up the night and proffered food and drink and song have too often been bulldozed into silent oblivion.

: BUNTING AND ARCHES :

ABOVE: *Temporary triumphal arch on Michigan Avenue honoring the encampment of the Grand Army of the Republic, August 31, 1900. The arch, inspired by that of Constantine in Rome, and its sculpture by Lorado Taft, was constructed of plaster over wooden lathing.*

RIGHT: *The surprisingly modernistic World War I Victory Arch was erected parallel to Michigan Avenue at the entrance to Grant Park in 1918. It was decorated, not with militaristic sculpture, but with the names of battles in which Chicago doughboys took part. Its demolition shortly after the victory celebrations marked the demise of Chicago's tradition of heroic street decoration.*

: PLACES OF WORSHIP :

ABOVE, LEFT: *The first University of Chicago contained a large chapel, which is not surprising since one of the school's prime purposes was the training of Baptist ministers. The University, whose cornerstone was laid on July 4, 1857, stood at the corner of 34th Street and Cottage Grove Avenue on a ten-acre campus which had been donated by Senator Stephen A. Douglas. Designed by William W. Boyington, the cream-colored stone building—seen here during*

a Baptist ministers' convention—was described in a guidebook as being in the "Norman or Romanesque style." It bore a marked resemblance to James Renwick's Smithsonian Institution in Washington. The edifice was severely damaged by a fire in the 1880s and afterward demolished.

ABOVE, RIGHT: *Trinity Episcopal Church, on the south side of Jackson Boulevard between Wabash and Michigan avenues, was an important downtown parish before*

the Great Fire. Constructed between 1860 and 1861 from plans by Theodore Vigo Wadskier, a Dane born in St. Croix, who came to Chicago about 1857, Trinity combined Romanesque-style segmental arched windows with Gothic pinnacles. Its façade and towers were of "Athens marble" from Joliet. The church's impressive frescoed interior, with furniture supplied by Potter Palmer, held 1400 worshipers. It was consumed in 1871.

COPELIN & MELANDER, PHOTOGRAPHERS, 131 LAKE STREET, CHICAGO.

STEREOSCOPIC VIEWS OF CHICAGO AND VICINITY.

154—Interior Grace Church Wabash Ave.

ABOVE: *Grace Episcopal Church, on South Wabash Avenue at 14th Street, designed by Sanford E. Loring and William Le Baron Jenney, was consecrated on Easter Sunday 1869. The Gothic Revival edifice had a Victorian polychromatic interior with a blue ceiling, walls of soft violet gray relieved by purple and gold, and trusses edged with vermilion. The parish, which served the affluent Prarie Avenue neighborhood, led the way in caring for the ill among the thousands of Confederate soldiers imprisoned during the Civil War at Camp Douglas on 31st Street. In 1915 Grace Church and its new chapel designed by Bertram G. Goodhue were gutted by a fire.*

RIGHT: *This photograph, taken February 1, 1921, just before the structure was razed, clearly reveals that Jenney used iron framing for this project begun the year after his arrival in Chicago in 1867. While Jenney was studying in Paris in the 1850s, the influential architect and theorist Eugène Emmanuel Viollet-le-Duc was advocating this very use of iron in Gothic Revival structures.*

LEFT: *Originally built by Edward Burling and Dankmar Adler in 1875 and remodeled by Adler and Sullivan in 1892, Sinai Temple, at the southeast corner of Indiana Avenue and 21st Street, was a center of the German-Jewish Reform movement. It counted among its members Julius Rosenwald of Sears, Roebuck and Philip Dee Block of Inland Steel. The temple was demolished in the 1920s after the congregation had moved to South Shore.*

ABOVE: *The Chicago Avenue Church, popularly known as the Moody Tabernacle, founded by the renowned evangelist Dwight L. Moody, whose hymns, such as "In the Sweet By and By," were among the most popular anthems of Victorian Protestantism, stood at the corner of La Salle Street and Chicago Avenue. Built between 1873 and 1876, the Venetian Gothic sanctuary was demolished in 1939. It was important in the history of Chicago design because its architects, Johnston and Edelmann, assigned the interiors to a young draftsman in their office, Louis Sullivan. This was Sullivan's first appearance as a designer.*

In the nineteenth and early twentieth centuries park structures permitted builders to give untrammeled
play to their imaginations. This
1906 photograph shows a fanciful

lost pavilion on the beach at 78th
Street which allowed Edwardian
Chicagoans to savor Lake Michigan
without fear of getting their feet wet

RIGHT: *"Drouet had taken three
rooms, furnished, in Ogden Place,
facing Union Park, on the West Side.
That was a little, green-carpeted
breathing spot, than which, today,
there is nothing more beautiful in
Chicago. It afforded a vista pleasant
to contemplate. The best room looked
out upon the lawn of the park . . .
where a little lake lay sheltered."*
—Theodore Dreiser, Sister Carrie.

*Dreiser lived in a room overlooking
Union Park and this, with the spires
of the Congregational Church in the
background, is the view he described.
Today, the park and its little lake are
buried beneath a blanket of concrete.*

Water—in the form of pools, formal basins, and Lake Michigan coves—provided one of the perpetual delights of Chicago's parks. These Lincoln Park photographs show a swan boat in 1899 and the park's graceful iron bridge. Both the bridge and the swan boat have departed.

STREETS FOR PEOPLE

ABOVE: *Open-air markets, the delight of Americans abroad, flourished in our own cities in the nineteenth and early twentieth centuries. Shown is Maxwell Street's Jewish secondhand clothing mart around 1905, only one aspect of the varied ethnic mix of Chicago's West Side, described by Jane Addams, whose pioneering settlement was nearby, in* Twenty Years at Hull-House: *"Between Halsted Street and the river live about ten thousand Italians. . . . To the south of Twelfth Street are many Germans, and side streets are given over almost entirely to Polish and Russian Jews. Still farther south, these Jewish colonies merge into a huge Bohemian colony, so vast that Chicago ranks as the*

third Bohemian city in the world." The beginning of the end for many of the West Side neighborhoods came in 1957 with the Dan Ryan Expressway. The new Chicago Circle Campus of the University of Illinois did its best to finish the job in the mid-1960s, demolishing, among other things, most of Hull House. The planned expansion of the University of Illinois at Chicago would overwhelm the 58 acres encompassed by the Maxwell Street neighborhood. In a peculiarly bizarre bow to the history it will destroy, the University has proposed saving some façades from Halsted Street and restructuring them on the school's new parking garage.

OPPOSITE: *". . . [Y]ou take your life in your hand when you attempt the crossing of State Street, with its endless stream of rattling wagons and clanging trolley-cars," warned William Archer, the English author of* The Green Goddess. *By the time this photograph was taken, in 1907, State Street had fulfilled Potter Palmer's dream of making it one of the world's leading retail centers. No other city had so many famed department stores standing in such close proximity: Carson, Pirie, Scott; Mandel's; Rothschild's; The Fair; the Boston Store; Lytton's; Marshall Field. Now many of its superb emporiums live only in memory.*

ABOVE: *South Water Street, paralleling the south bank of the Chicago River, was the city's first commercial street, already well established by 1834. The South Water Street Market, seen here about 1910, was, like Paris's now-vanished Les Halles, the city's belly. The market was famed for its fish, especially Lake Michigan white fish and pickerel, poultry, and dairy products; vegetables were sold in the Haymarket on Randolph Street. In the nineteenth century, when Chicago was the world's greatest purveyor of game, the market was most renowned for its wild ducks, geese, prairie chickens, snipe, and venison. The supporters of the Chicago Plan of 1909 found the lively market "an economic waste." It closed in August 1925, and its site was obliterated by a double-decked 110-foot-wide highway. Even its*

historic name disappeared, for South Water Street has been supplanted by Wacker Drive, named for Charles H. Wacker, one of those instrumental in implementing the Chicago Plan.

OPPOSITE, TOP: *In her ground-breaking study* The Death and Life of Great American Cities *Jane Jacobs makes this profound statement: "Intricate minglings of different uses in cities are not a form of chaos. On the contrary, they represent a complex and highly developed form of order." The north side of Washington Street, between State and Dearborn, seen here in the 1950s, offered a beguiling diversity of establishments which served well both the workers in the surrounding offices and visitors. Because it was a block of older buildings, the rents were low enough to attract the types*

of businesses necessary to the health of an urban center: inexpensive restaurants, auction houses, bookshops, dance studios, food stores. Not only was the north side of Washington a wonderful example of urban vitality, it was composed of structures of great architectural significance. At the far end of the block was the McCarthy Building by John Van Osdel, built in 1872, the year after the Great Fire; next to it the Stop & Shop was a 1928 work in polychromed terra-cotta of the distinguished firm of Schmidt, Garden & Erickson; while the Western Methodist Book Corner, the narrow building with bay windows, an 1898 design by Harry B. Wheelock, echoes the contemporary work of Louis Sullivan. At the beginning of the 1990s all of these buildings were demolished.

LEFT: *"Another phase of Chicago night life is jazz music,"* Windy City columnist Irv Kupcinet wrote in the October 1951 issue of Holiday Magazine. *One of the prime spots to hear jazz and blues was the Blue Note, seen in this 1958 view of the corner of Madison and Clark streets. Opened by impresario Frank Holzfiend in a basement at 56 West Madison in 1947, the club moved to a large L-shaped room on the second floor at 3 North Clark in 1954. In addition to Ellington, in residence when this photograph was made, the Blue Note presented, among others, George Shearing, Louis Armstrong, Ella Fitzgerald, Billie Holiday, Benny Goodman; and Sarah Vaughan, who got her start there. The block, with its spirited signage advertising a Chinese restaurant, a Turkish bath, a movie theater, a bar, and a coffee shop, exemplifies what a thriving big city downtown should be. The Blue Note closed in 1960, killed, in part, by the advent of television. Most of its neighbors disappeared with the massive redevelopment of the North Loop which began with the construction of the Civic Center in 1962.*

ABOVE: *After the completion of the Michigan Avenue Bridge in 1920, Chicago developed a natural and exciting division in its central retail life. State Street remained the site for the grand retail establishments, such as Marshall Field & Company and Carson Pirie Scott & Company. Upper Michigan became an avenue of small, upscale speciality shops, selling fine linens, one-of-a kind hats, designer dresses, and luxurious furs. State was the equivalent of New York's Fifth Avenue; North Michigan echoed Paris's Faubourg St. Honoré.*

"Get out of your train and drive up Michigan Avenue," the Chicago novelist Mary Borden exclaimed. "I defy you not to respond to the excitement in the air. . . not to throw your hat to the sky and shout. Beautiful! How beautiful it is as you whirl northward past the Tribune Tower. . . ." In this view from Chicago Avenue in the 1920s, the new Gothic Tribune Tower by Howells & Hood on the left, and the Renaissance Wrigley Building by Graham, Anderson, Probst & White on the right, appear in the distance like shimmering mirages. All the buildings in the foreground, except the Allerton Hotel on the left, vanished in the mammoth redevelopment of North Michigan Avenue following World War II.*

OPPOSITE: *Randolph Street was Chicago's "Great White Way." In this 1960 photograph looking west from State Street, remnants of the vitality of this thoroughfare are still evident. All of the structures on the near right were demolished in 1999 to provide the site for a dormitory for the School of the Art Institute. The picturesque façade of Robert and Max Eitel's Old Heidelberg — a 1934 project of Graham,* Anderson, Probst & White—was saved, but its spacious interior, which would have made a superb student lounge or dining hall, was destroyed. The Old Heidelberg, which specialized in Czech and German dishes, was beloved by generations of Chicagoans.*

"Wass willst du haven?" he said. "You remember that?" "Yes, indeed, Louie and the Hungry Five, the comic German brass band from Old Heidelberg on Randolph Street, near the Oriental," said Corde.—Saul Bellow, *The Dean's December.*

The Oriental, now the Ford Center for the Performing Arts, still stands, though it has been stripped of its furnishings. The Woods, designed in 1917 by Marshall and Fox, with a striking Venetian Gothic inspired exterior, was not so lucky. It was felled by the wreckers in 1989.

The Great Fire

THE LATE SIXTIES continued the boom begun in the war years. With its population of 300,000 far outdistancing its old rivals St. Louis and Cincinnati, with only the long-established cities of the East selling more goods, with its exports exceeding $178 million a year, with its industrial development spreading south and west of the river, Chicago looked confidently to the future. Impressive mansions lined the well-paved streets of the North Side and, on the South Side, Prairie Avenue now began that progress toward opulence which would, in time, make it a rival of Philadelphia's Rittenhouse Square and New York's Fifth Avenue. The palatial Field & Leiter emporium on State Street was joined by an equally grandiose one under the aegis of Samuel Carson, John Pirie, and Robert Scott, while Peacock's had fresh competition in the sale of diamonds and rubies from S. Hoard & Company, which would one day become the elegant Spaulding's. Chicagoans liked to boast of the quality of education at the Rush Medical College, whose Dr. Daniel Brainard had been elected to the French Academy of Sciences, and to point out that the swing bridge designed by Newton Chapin and Daniel L. Wells had become a model throughout Europe. To top it all, the new Palmer House was, without doubt, to be counted among the finest hotels in the United States. One of its selling points was a telegraphic fire alarm in each room, a fire hose on each floor, and huge tanks of water on the roof.

The summer and autumn of 1871 had been exceptionally dry. Scarcely an inch of rain had fallen between July and October. All fall Chicago had been plagued by fires; a particularly serious one had occurred on October 7 at the Lull and Holmes planing mill on South Canal Street. Four blocks of modest frame dwellings had been destroyed before the blaze was finally brought under control. The ordeal had exhausted the city's fire department. The next day, a Sunday, a strong southwest wind had sprung up, parching the earth and drying the city even more. That night about nine o'clock, at the stable in the rear of the Patrick O'Leary house on De Koven Street on the far Southwest Side, a historic accident took place.

The usual form of the tale is that while Mrs. O'Leary was milking, her cow kicked over the kerosene lamp, thus setting fire to the hay in the barn. Though there can be little doubt that the O'Leary barn was where the fire started, the circumstances surrounding its beginning are difficult to ascertain. And certain questions must be asked. It seems a bit odd that a woman who milked her own cow every night would have placed a lantern in a position where the animal could easily kick it over. It also seems odd that most versions of the story say that the lantern was behind the cow when it was kicked over. Cows do not kick backward. There is one universally overlooked clue in all of the

OPPOSITE: *The ruins of the Honoré Block at Adams and Dearborn streets, the property of Mrs. Potter Palmer's father. The block's façade was of cast iron, which accounts for its dramatically surviving presence. Many of Chicago's pre-fire commercial buildings had cast-iron first-floor storefronts ordered through local dealers from the preeminent New York firm of Daniel Badger.*

testimony surrounding this incident; that is Mrs. O'Leary's statement that there was an "explosion" when the lantern ignited the hay. A burning kerosene lamp does not explode. But that word may provide a solution to the mystery. At this time, long before the internal combustion engine, gasoline had almost no value, for it was merely that portion of raw petroleum which distilled off at a lower temperature than kerosene. It was usually thrown away. In the years before and after the Chicago fire, company after company was accused of adding gasoline to its kerosene, and one state after another passed legislation forbidding the practice. An "explosion"? Did Mrs. O'Leary's kerosene contain gasoline?

The blaze spread rapidly; the fire department was not notified for half an hour, and given that start and the high wind, the flames were already out of control before any apparatus arrived on the scene. At the Sherman House, Alexander Frear, a visiting politician from New York, was waiting for friends from Milwaukee. "There was a large crowd of strangers and businessmen of the city in the hotel," he remembered later. "The corridor and parlors were full of idlers, much as usual. While looking over the register some one said, 'There go the fire-bells again. . . . They'll burn the city down if they keep on.'"

The strong wind drove the fire north, and within an hour the mills and furniture shops west of the river were ablaze and the flames began eating at the huge grain elevators along the bank. The homes of thousands of poor workers jammed in among the mills and shops were also consumed, and their terrified inhabitants fled north and east like refugees before a conquering army. Though by now the conflagration had attracted the attention of most of the city, in the more prosperous districts people still felt safe. The burned blocks of the previous night stood in the fire's path, creating what seemed like an impassable barrier, and beyond that was yet another wall, the vaunted fireproof stone edifices of the city's business district, the five- and six-story office buildings of Van Buren and Adams streets.

At the gleaming new Palmer House, Mr. and Mrs. Alfred Hebard and their daughter were preparing for bed. They had stopped over in Chicago for a bit of shopping and sightseeing before proceeding home to Iowa after a visit back east. The Hebards heard that there was a big fire in the city, but there didn't seem to be any reason for concern. Didn't the Palmer House have those telegraphic fire alarms and those hoses and those tanks of water on the roof? But, as Mrs. Hebard remembered, they did want to have a look:

> We immediately took the elevator to the upper story of the Palmer,
> saw the fire, but, deciding that it would not cross the river, descended
> to our rooms in the second story to prepare for sleep. Husband and
> daughter soon retired; I remained up to prepare for the morrow's journey,
> and thus gain a little time for shopping before the departure of the train
> at 11 a.m. Feeling somewhat uneasy, I frequently opened the blinds,
> and each time found the light in the streets increase until every spire and
> dome seemed illuminated.

The fire had leaped the wasteland left from the previous night and had been carried into the heart of the city by wind-blown pieces of burning wood which hurtled through the air like deadly missiles. Now graveled roofs and stone or cast-iron walls and alert watchmen counted for nothing. Aided by the blazing bridges and the fiercely flaming ships packed on the river for the annual fall sailings before the lake froze, the fire easily slipped within the gates at a hundred points. In a hot shower of light the tar works exploded, then the gas works, then the armory and the central police station. Like two arms of an invading host, the fire split, half heading east across Fifth Avenue and up La Salle, destroying the leading banks, the Board of Trade, and the most prestigious office buildings, while the other half moved north to devour the mansions on Monroe, Madison, and Washington streets. Above the shouts and screams of the panicked citizens and the roar of the inferno could be heard the Court House bell, a dirge for a dying city.

Joseph Chamberlin, a twenty-six-year-old reporter for the *Evening Post*, tried to find out what his paper was doing about the fire:

> When I crossed the river, I made a desperate attempt to reach my office
> on Madison Street beyond Clark. I pressed through the crowd on
> Randolph Street as far as La Salle, and stood in front of the burning
> Courthouse. The cupola was in full blaze, and presented a scene of the
> sublimest as well as most melancholy beauty.

Sweeping up La Salle, the flames destroyed the luxurious Grand Pacific Hotel and then turned on the Michigan Southern terminal. By now it was a firestorm, nearly white-hot with very little smoke, lapping up oxygen like a dog lapping up water, an ancestor of those firestorms set off by World War II incendiary bombs in Hamburg and Dresden. In

OPPOSITE: *No single building's destruction in the Great Fire marked the passing of Old Chicago more dramatically than that of the Tremont House. This engraving, published within weeks of the conflagration, gives a highly accurate picture of the hostelry, which stood on the southeast corner of Lake and Dearborn streets. The Tremont had roots going back to 1832, but the structure shown here is the 250-room building designed in 1850 by John Van Osdel. On July 9, 1858, Senator Stephen A. Douglas opened his reelection campaign on the Tremont's side balcony; the next day, his opponent, Abraham Lincoln, spoke from the same balcony. And it was at the Tremont, during his first visit to Chicago after the 1860 Republican convention, that Lincoln met his vice-presidential running mate, Hannibal Hamlin.*

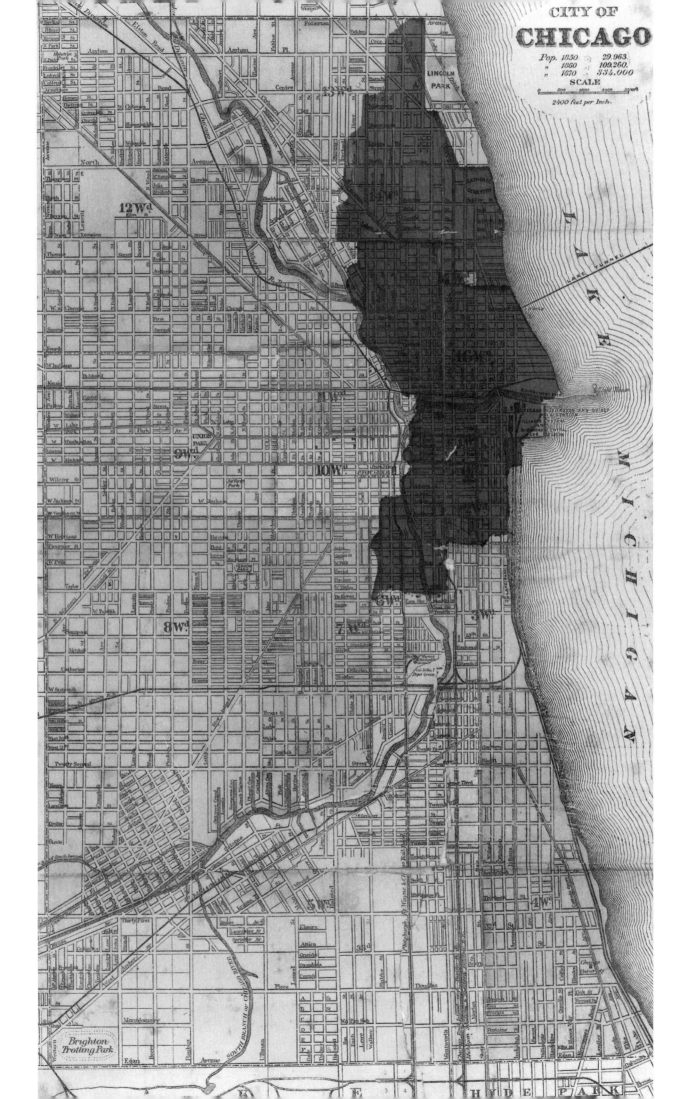

CITY OF
CHICAGO

Pop. 1850   29.963.
"   1860   109.260.
"   1870   334.000
SCALE

2400 feet per Inch.

a desperate attempt to halt its progress, gunpowder was used to blow up buildings in its path, but to no avail. A grim gallows humor infected the dazed populace. "Chicago does nothing by halves," it was said, "not even its fires."

Northward the conflagration pressed, up Market Street and Wells and Franklin, burning the cheap buildings at the river end of Jackson, Quincy, and Adams. As it approached the Nevada Hotel, a popular rendezvous of visiting journalists and touring theatrical troupes, the manager had difficulty convincing some of the actresses, many of whom had just gone to bed, that the place was in danger. The burning wall next moved along South Water Street, consuming the lumber exchange and the densely clustered warehouses filled with millions of dollars' worth of French wine, Chinese tea, and Java coffee. At the lake end of the street, the Richmond House, where the Prince of Wales had stayed, and the Tremont both quickly vanished. They were soon followed into oblivion by the Briggs and the Metropolitan. Nearby, dazzlingly new, was the half-million-dollar Bigelow House, its scheduled opening coinciding with the fire itself. Only the flames drank the contents of the already filled punchbowls standing on damask-covered tables in its dining room. And then it was the Sherman's turn. Alexander Frear reports that the fire suddenly was no longer a joking matter:

> The corridor was a scene of intense excitement. The guests in the house were running about wildly, some of them dragging their trunks to the stairway. Everything was in confusion. . . .

Soon the splendidly refurbished Crosby's Opera House went, and Hooley's, and the Field & Leiter store, and the newspapers: the *Evening Post,* the *Evening Mail,* the *Staats-Zeitung,* the *Tribune.* Eventually even the supposedly impregnable Palmer House was threatened. Mrs. Hebard had at last convinced her sleepy husband that he must do something:

> Evidently the Palmer House was in great danger, and it was better to leave it now than to wait; but how to remove our baggage was the next question. Once we thought we had secured a cart or a wagon, but no sooner was the trunk thrown on than it was pulled off again by someone claiming a prior right. . . .

The city was indeed in chaos. People staggered in the streets, drunk from the wares of the untended saloons; looting was rampant; children were lost; the main avenues were choked with treasures—paintings, pianos, mirrors, furniture—all carried a little way and then abandoned by their fleeing owners.

On Monday morning there was a rumor that the fire had been checked, but the story proved false. The flames leaped the river to the North Side and thirstily set to work first on the great breweries and then on the grand houses of Ohio and Rush and Cass and State streets before turning on the churches: the New England and the Unity, Holy Name Cathedral and fashionable St. James'. Exhausted, despairing, Chicagoans stood by the thousands in the waters of Lake Michigan or huddled in the empty graves of the old cemetery north of the city, which was being cleared to create Lincoln Park. Finally, about midnight on Monday, it began to rain. The flames died down; the embers ceased to glow. The Great Chicago Fire was history. The toll: three and a quarter square miles burned, 18,000 buildings destroyed, 100,000 persons homeless, 300 dead, more than $200 million in property lost. Certain irreplaceable things had been swept away: the Academy of Design, filled with paintings for an upcoming exhibition, the Chicago Historical Society, with Lincoln's own copy of the Emancipation Proclamation.

OPPOSITE: *This map shows the area destroyed by the great fire of 1871 set against the city's later expansion. The burned district comprised the heart of Chicago, a densely built-up urban area four miles long and two thirds of a mile wide.*

The prairie giant was, for a moment, as still as death. Bret Harte wrote a eulogy:

> Blackened and bleeding, helpless, panting, prone
> On the charred fragments of her shattered throne
> Lies she who stood but yesterday alone.
> Queen of the West! by some enchanter taught
> To lift the glory of Aladdin's court,
> Then lose the spell that all that wonder wrought.
> Like her own prairies by some chance seed sown,
> Like her own prairies in one brief day grown,
> Like her own prairies in one fierce night mown.

Certain disasters continue to linger in men's memories, held there either because of their drama or their magnitude. The names come quickly to mind: the San Francisco earthquake, the sinking of the *Titanic,* the *Hindenburg*'s destruction. The holocaust that swept over Chicago on October 9, 1871, is without doubt to be included among them. To those caught in its path, its power seemed almost satanic. In his *History of the Great Fires in Chicago and the West,* the Reverend Edgar J. Goodspeed of the Second Baptist Church wrote: "McVicker's Theatre and the *Tribune* building formed the northern boundary of the [fire] . . . it was here that the few workers now left with courage enough to contest with miserable fortune made their final stand. The *Tribune* building was believed to be fire-proof, if any structure devised by man could be proof against such a combination of the elements as was now raging. McVicker's yielded first, and was instantly a heap of brick and ashes, and the *Tribune* structure was not long in following."

⫴ A CITY IN RUINS ⫴

The burned-out Court House seen from the corner of Clark and Washington streets. The nearest portion is one of the new wings Van Osdel added just before the fire.

ABOVE: *A drawing of the palatial new Grand Pacific Hotel, by W. W. Boyington, occupying the entire block bounded by Clark, Jackson, La Salle, and Quincy streets. It was just preparing to open its doors when the fire struck.*

RIGHT: *The shell of the* Tribune *building, at the corner of Dearborn and Madison streets, thought by its owners to be fireproof. By Tuesday morning, October 10th, the Great Fire had burned itself out. A rainstorm extinguished its last glowing embers. The next day, using a job-printing office on Canal Street purchased by publisher Joseph Medill, the* Tribune *put out a one-page newspaper. The Thursday paper had two columns of heart-breaking personal notices from people looking for family members. Among them: "Peter Grace lost wife and children, Church, Carpenter and Washington Streets; Mrs. Tinney lost little girl six years old, Katie, Harrison House. A little girl, cannot speak her name, at Desplaines Hotel."*

ABOVE: *The gutted Grand Pacific Hotel after the flames had done their work. Its backers had at least one consolation: the hotel's ruins were considered the most impressive in the city. Quickly rebuilt, using Boyington's plans, the Grand Pacific was one of Chicago's preeminent railway hotels providing luxurious accommodations for those wishing to break their journey with a stop in Chicago. It was managed by the noted hotelier John B. Drake, who made its game dinners nationally famous. The opulent caravansary was pulled down in the 1890s to be replaced by the Illinois Trust and Savings Bank.*

LEFT: *The entrance to the Insurance Exchange on La Salle Street.*

ABOVE: *This view, near Randolph Street, shows how quickly after the fire Chicago began rebuilding. Alfred T. Andreas, in his* History of Chicago, *reports that the city rang with "the noise of countless saws and hammers and chisels and axes and planes. . . ." Indeed, by December more than 200 substantial brick and stone buildings were under construction in the downtown district.*

LEFT: *"I know that as I turned wildly back once toward Dearborn Street, I saw the beautiful Episcopal Church of St. James in flames. But they came on all sides, licking the marble buttresses one by one, and leaving charred or blackened masses where there had been white marble before. But the most wonderful sight of all was the white, shining church tower, from which, as I looked, burst tongues of fire. . . ."*
— *"A Woman's Story of the Fire" reported in* History of the Great Fires in Chicago and the West *by the Rev. E. J. Goodspeed.*

St. James, at the southeast corner of Wabash Avenue and Huron Street,

was constructed in 1857 from designs by Edward J. Burling. In 1875 the church, now the cathedral of the Episcopal diocese of Chicago, was rebuilt by Burling and Adler. The stones of the church tower still show the effects of the Great Fire's searing heat.

ABOVE: "I remember driving downtown with my father through streets ragged and broken. . . . And everywhere around us, and northward as far as the eye could reach, nothing but charred ruins, with only the castellated water tower rising intact high above the ghostly devastation," wrote Harriet Monroe in A Poet's Life. The water tower, on Pine Street, now North Michigan Avenue, one of the rare surviving structures in the city's burned district, became a symbol of Chicago's will to survive, a striking example of the importance of historic landmarks in the lives of people.

CHICAGO WILL RISE AGAIN.

A Phoenix Rising

THE MORNING AFTER THE FIRE, Joseph Chamberlin witnessed an astonishing sight: "As I passed up West Madison Street, I met scores of working girls on their way 'down town' as usual, bearing their lunch-baskets, as if nothing had happened. They saw the fire and smoke before them, but could not believe the city, with their means of livelihood, had been swept away during the night."

It took days for Chicagoans to comprehend the full extent of the holocaust. Government officials, for instance, assumed that the currency stored in the Post Office and Custom House vaults had survived, protected by their three inches of boiler plate and a wall of brick. When, after four days, the smoking mass had cooled, it was discovered that the fire's 3000-degree heat had incinerated more than a million dollars. The story was the same at the city's banks.

John Greenleaf Whittier expressed the consensus of an appalled nation:

> On three score spires has sunset shone,
> Where ghastly sunrise looked on none;
> Men clasped each other's hands and said:
> The City of the West is dead.

The obituary was premature. The keystone of Chicago's being, its island location, the prime reality which had allowed it to rise from a haunt of wolves to near greatness, was still there. Its rich hinterland had not burned, nor its lake, nor, above all, the bright rails reaching out to the Atlantic, the Pacific, and the Gulf. Many of its industries too had survived: the Union Stock Yards, 75 percent of its grain elevators, 80 percent of its lumberyards. Out on the West Side stood more than 600 untouched factories. There was something else, too, something which in a later pretentiously unsentimental age, it is easy to discount: the city's spirit. In that first post-fire edition, the *Tribune* had extorted the citizens to "Cheer Up!"

> In the midst of a calamity without parallel in the world's history, looking upon the ashes of thirty years accumulations, the people of this once beautiful city have resolved that CHICAGO SHALL RISE AGAIN!

Before the last coals had cooled, the marks of new life had appeared. Just days after the fire, the first commercial structure, a 12-by-16-foot shanty on Washington Street

"Chicago may be taken as a fair type of American material energy. We are proud to claim her as a representative city, so far as vigor, boldness, self-poise, industry, and far-reaching enterprise are the characteristics of the American Republic . . . As Chicago was a representative city in the nation, so it shares in all the recuperative qualities of the Republic."
—New York Tribune *editorial shortly after the fire.*

Chicago did indeed show amazing recuperative powers. Within days of the blaze, the Chamber of Commerce began clearing away the ruins of its old building and started construction of an even larger edifice, which was officially dedicated by Mayor Joseph Medill on the first anniversary of the fire. In this picture, taken in 1872 looking northeast from La Salle and Madison streets, workmen can be seen finishing the new Chamber's roof. The site is now occupied by the American National Bank Building.

between Dearborn and Clark, was put up by W. D. Kerfoot, a leading real estate agent. The sign on the shanty was significant: "W. D. Kerfoot. Everything gone but Wife, Children and Energy." Field & Leiter soon opened for business in a carbarn. Chicagoans even found a constructive use for the ruins themselves. When they had ceased to smoke, the debris was pushed out into Lake Michigan to extend the city's shoreline. Today, under Grant Park's green lawns, a lost world lies buried.

The city's morale was helped immeasurably by an outpouring of sympathy and aid from the nation and the world. Louisville and Pittsburgh sent food. The city of Brooklyn and the New York Stock Exchange each pledged $100,000; A. T. Stewart, the dry-goods magnate, contributed $50,000 to be used exclusively for needy women. Money came from St. Louis and Cincinnati; from the hackmen of Washington, D.C.; from financiers such as Morgan and the Rothschilds, from Canada, Germany, and France. The British donated 8000 books for a public library. Edwin Booth, Mrs. John Drew, and Charlotte Cushman all gave benefit performances. The Philadelphia Athletics played a benefit baseball game.

The help was desperately needed. Winter, the long, gray, brutal midwestern winter, was coming on, and in the city 100,000 were homeless and more than 35,000 faced starvation. The $1.98 worth of food distributed weekly to each needy family meant, in many cases, the difference between life and death. There was another matter, almost as urgent, that deeply concerned the thousands of unemployed: would the city's devastated industries rebuild? No industry was more basic to the city's economic welfare than the McCormick Company, whose $2 million plant lay in ruins.

Cyrus McCormick, already in his sixties, was known to be considering not rebuilding in Chicago and letting his other plants scattered across the country carry on his business. But when McCormick and his wife Nettie visited the rubble of his once-proud works, a moving, and perhaps decisive, demonstration took place. Cyrus McCormick had always been a popular employer, and now, as he walked amidst the twisted metal and piles of brick, the men cheered. Within three months a new McCormick Reaper Works had risen on Western Avenue.

Potter Palmer was in far more serious straits than was Cyrus McCormick. In a single night he had lost his magnificent new hotel, as well as the marble emporium he had constructed for Field and Leiter, and a mile of buildings on State Street. At the ripe age of forty-five he had just married the much-younger Berthe Honoré, the town's undisputed belle, and had looked forward to spending the rest of his life enjoying the good things of this world. Palmer was a man with a taste for the best: dining off vermeil, drinking champagne from crystal goblets, dashing about town in a four-horse barouche. Now, for the moment, all of that had to be put aside. Borrowing nearly $2 million from an insurance company—the largest loan ever made to an individual at that time— Palmer scoured the country buying materials to rebuild his beloved State Street. Day and night, by sunlight and arc-light, the frantic work went on as his mercantile mile grew ever more splendorous. Its centerpiece was his new hotel. Using Van Osdel's plans for the lost building, Palmer had them greatly expanded to create one of the most sumptuous edifices in the United States.

That the post-fire Palmer House was the pre-fire Palmer House writ large brings up an important point. Within six weeks after the fire, 318 permanent structures with a total frontage of three and one half miles had been begun. The sudden demand was so great that it was impossible for Chicago's architects to draw up new plans for every building, and many, following Palmer's lead, resurrected whatever blueprints they had salvaged and used them to reconstruct the city. It should not be surprising, therefore, that it is often difficult to distinguish buildings constructed just after the fire from those put up just before it.

The hodgepodge of architectural styles—Gothic Revival, Tuscan, Moorish—that had marked the Chicago of the '60s was not to survive for long. In its place rose one supreme aesthetic ideal: the Paris of the Second Empire of Louis Napoleon and his empress, Eugénie. There had been elements of this taste in the Civil War city, but now, in the seventies, it swept aside most competitors. Louis Napoleon's political empire had already ceased to exist, destroyed in the debacle of the Franco-Prussian War of 1870, but his aesthetic empire had just begun its reign, surviving intact in the Paris created for him by the superb city planner Baron Haussmann. It was this, the Paris of grand boulevards, of glittering new palaces, of rich hotels and eye-catching department stores, that Chicago and all America now sought to emulate.

The hallmarks of the style, referred to in France as "Le Style Napoléon III," were excessively tall plate glass windows, a prodigal use of attached and semiattached Corinthian columns, and high mansard roofs topped by lacy cast-iron crestings. These elements were inspired, in particular, by Charles Garnier's opulent new Paris Opera house and by the recent additions to the Louvre carried out for the Emperor by Visconti and Lefuel. The latter is of profound significance to American architecture, for, when he was a student at the École des Beaux-Arts in the 1840s, Richard Morris Hunt's patron was Hector Martin Lefuel. Hunt would also enter Lefuel's *atelier*, the studio where École students received guidance in their work from notable practicing architects. After the young American left the École, Lefuel would employ him as "inspector of works," the man in charge of the Louvre's new Pavilion de la Bibliothèque on the rue de Rivoli. When Richard Morris Hunt returned to his native land in 1855, he longed to build in the grand style based on ancient classical and Renaissance precedents which the École espoused. In time, with the palaces of the Vanderbilts in New York and Newport and, above all, with Chicago's White City, the moment for that would come. But at first, the architect had to work in the Second Empire mode. One of his supreme achievements in that style was the mansion he designed on Prairie Avenue in 1876 for the "Merchant Prince," Marshall Field. Its very Parisian Le Style Napoléon III exterior and its glittering ivory and gold drawing room were highly appropriate for the man whose great emporium gloried in selling annually gallons of Guerlain scent and thousands of yards of silk from the looms of Lyon.

Of all the city's architectural firms, none understood the Second Empire ideal better than Cudell & Blumenthal. Its senior partner, Adolph Cudell, a native of Germany, was responsible for Aldine Square on the South Side, an impressive post-fire achievement which, with its separate houses screened behind a handsome uniform façade, suggested a Parisian residential quarter. Cudell and Blumenthal's most spectacular commission was the mansion they designed in 1875 for Cyrus McCormick on Rush Street. An exuberant confection of columns, garlands, rusticated stonework, and crestings inspired by the recently completed Richelieu wing of the Louvre, it was truly a palace for a Reaper King.

It was not a residence, though, which would present the Beaux Arts style in all its panoply, but, rather, the new City and County Building. It would be easy to trace the whole history of taste in Chicago through its court houses, as they rose one after another, ever larger, ever grander, from the little temple of the first years, through Van Osdel's fine Greek Revival structure and his French wings, to the bedizened edifice that now became the seat of government for Chicago and Cook County. Three days after the fire, the City Council authorized the erection of a new court house. A competition for the project attracted some fifty designs, designs with names such as "Semper Resurgens" and "Legibus et Populis" and "In Hoc Signo Vinces." After this prodigal use of Latin, the council, in the best aldermanic tradition, announced that it had no qualified adviser to judge the entries and that, anyway, there had been no guarantee that the winner would get the job. It then promptly gave the commission to its personal favorite, James J. Egan, the county architect.

"There is over a square mile of space in the yards, and more than half of it is occupied by cattle pens; north and south as far as the eye can reach there stretches a sea of pens."
— Upton Sinclair, The Jungle.

ABOVE: *The Union Stock Yards, covering a square mile between 39th and 47th streets and Ashland Avenue and Halsted Street were, according to the Chicago Tribune, "the eighth wonder of the world." Inaugurated on Christmas Day 1865, the new facility unified the operations of various stockyards that had been scattered across the South Side. By the time this photograph was taken in 1905, the Yards employed 75,000 workers, supported another 250,000 people in their immediate neighborhood, received some 17 million cattle, sheep, and hogs a year, and processed $500 million worth of meat products annually.*

The animals became not only steaks and hams, but glue, gelatin, fertilizer, soap, and buttons.

OPPOSITE, TOP: *The Yards were a city unto themselves, with streets with names like "Packers Avenue," their own water and electric systems, a bank, and a daily newspaper,* The Drovers' Journal. *The Yards even had their own hotel, the Transit House, built in 1869. Here, in the lush days of the late nineteenth century, cowboys, cattlemen, and commission merchants mingled with the purchasing agents of the armies and navies of the German, French,*

and British empires and with the Princes of Packingtown, Nelson Morris, Philip D. Armour, and Gustavus Swift. The Transit House burned in 1912 and was replaced by the Stock Yards Inn. With the shift of meatpacking to stockyards which were nearer the sources of supply, such as those in Omaha, the Union Stock Yards became obsolete. They ceased operation in 1971. Now the only remnant of the vast complex which made Chicago the "Porkopolis" of America is the ochre stone gate which Burnham and Root designed for it in the 1870s.

LEFT: *A visit to the Stock Yards was de rigueur for any celebrity coming to Chicago, whether it was Rudyard Kipling, Sarah Bernhardt, or Queen Marie of Rumania. In October 1924, the Prince of Wales—seen here with Louis Swift—made the obligatory stop. He recalled the experience in* A King's Story: *"I paid a quick visit to my ranch in Alberta, stopping off on the way back at Chicago and Detroit. These stops gave me my first glimpses of the American Middle West and the prodigies of American industry. In Detroit the late Mr. Henry Ford took me along his assembly line at River Rouge, where I saw an automobile assembled in sixteen minutes; and while in Chicago another leading captain of industry, Mr. Louis F. Swift, showed me how a steer could be dismembered in about the same period."*

The vast building's walls and cost rose with equally astonishing extravagance. Standing on a tall two-story, cut-stone base, 35-foot Corinthian columns of polished granite reached up to an elaborate entablature. Above that was an attic story embellished with allegorical groups representing Agriculture, Commerce, Peace, the Mechanic Arts, Science, and, for good measure, Plenty. Over it all was to loom a gigantic dome, but this final flourish was never attempted. The publicly announced cost of the structure was more than $4 million, and the council members did not occupy their palatial new chambers until 1885.

Long before that, in 1873 to be exact, Chicago felt itself sufficiently recovered to stage an Inter-State Industrial Exposition in the huge iron-and-glass hall William Boyington had constructed on Michigan Avenue. The exposition attracted thousands who wanted to see for themselves if "The City of the West" had been truly resuscitated. The signs of life were indisputable. From the genuine silver dollars paving the floor of the Palmer House's barber shop to the Grand Pacific's game dinners offering comestibles such as buffalo, antelope, bear, quail in plumage, and partridge in nest, the city's new hotels far surpassed those that had existed before Mrs. O'Leary's accident. The theaters, too, partook of the new magnificence. McVicker's had reopened on its old site with a spectacular pinnacled building, and it now had stiff competition from Hooley's, which had been inaugurated in October 1872 with a bill that featured a pantomime, a Mardi Gras divertissement, and the Mademoiselles Elise and Marie Gratz giving "their Tyrolean eccentricities in song."

But for the discerning, the best show in town was not to be found at McVicker's or Hooley's or at any of the other dozen new theaters built in the post-fire years, but on the floor of the Chicago Board of Trade on La Salle Street. For now the dream of cornering the market took hold of men's minds, a dream tellingly dissected in Frank Norris' powerful novel of the Chicago Grain Exchange, *The Pit*. No one was more adept at getting a corner than Benjamin P. Hutchinson, "Old Hutch" as he was called on La Salle Street, who had arrived in Chicago as a bankrupt shoe manufacturer from Lynn, Massachusetts, and went on to found the Corn Exchange Bank. In 1888, Hutchinson cornered September wheat and made more than a million dollars in the process.

If the visitor was in town to shop, there was no place in the country quite like Field & Leiter's new store on State Street, which, with the withdrawal of Leiter in 1882, became officially Marshall Field's. Building on Potter Palmer's merchandising acumen, Field made his store the Midwest's supreme emporium. A trip to Chicago became synonymous with a visit to Field's. It was the dream of schoolgirls, the goal of brides, the happy memory of elderly ladies in all the little towns of the heartland. At Field's one could find gowns inspired by Charles Frederick Worth, French kid gloves, and Oriental rugs made by special order in Persia to fit the size and shape of a modern house. In 1872 sales totaled $3 million; ten years later the firm was doing an annual business in excess of $24 million.

There was one place that was always at the top of any Chicago visitor's sightseeing list: the Union Stock Yards. In the years since the Civil War, Morris & Company had been joined by Swift, Armour, and Cudahy, and together they made up the Big Four which shared among themselves most of Chicago's meat packing. There was a good deal to share. Incoming hogs alone increased from 3 million in 1872, to 5 million in 1882, to 7 million in 1892, and the number of cattle and sheep soared proportionately. More than any other industry, the Yards exported the name Chicago around the world. By the late '70s, the packers had perfected the canning of meat—corned beef, roast beef, ox tongue, potted ham—and in the golden age of empire building, this Chicago invention became a necessity for European countries with armies in tropical climes.

During the 1883 Sudan expedition against the Mahdi, the British government ordered no less than 740,000 pounds of Chicago beef, an order expanded the next year to 2 1/2 million pounds. The event was noted by an anonymous rhymster:

> The roast beef of Old England
> Is famed in song and story,
> Without it where was English brawn
> That won old England glory?
> But in these days of England's gloom,
> When war's dread notes alarm her,
> What does she send to save Khartoum?
> Corned beef canned by Phil Armour.

Around the great packing houses, an almost self-sufficient town grew up—"Back-of-the-Yards," as it was called. Here, in row upon row of dilapidated wooden houses the workers lived: first Germans, then Irish, then Poles, Czechs, and finally, Lithuanians. At the turn of the century, Upton Sinclair's vivid portrait of their stunted lives in *The Jungle* would arouse an entire nation.

There was another company town in Chicago. The use of *The Pioneer* to carry Lincoln's body back to Springfield had sparked a rage for sleeping cars, and George Pullman rapidly expanded his hold on the market, not only by the excellence of his product and services, but by buying out his competitors. By 1890 the Pullman Company was carrying nearly 5 million passengers a year, offering such luxurious innovations as steam heat, electric lights, and separate toilets for men and women. It even had a company song:

> Hurrah for a ride without jostle or jar!
> Hurrah for a life on the iron bar!
> Hurrah for a ride in a Pullman car!
> *Vive la compagnie!*

As a monument to his success, the sleeping car magnate built in 1882, on the South Side near 111th Street, America's most spectacular privately owned town. Designed by Solon S. Beman, one of Chicago's most inventive architects, Pullman was modeled on the Krupp complex near Essen, Germany. Here, in a perfectly planned community, George Pullman offered his employees a shopping arcade, a theater, a library, a hotel, and decent housing, all in an attractive park-like setting. The idea was good, the execution brilliant, but the continuing company ownership of the workers' houses bore the seeds of a terrible conflict.

It was indeed an impressive Chicago which rose in the dozen years after the fire. The city, all agreed, was the fastest-growing metropolis in the world; with its population already more than 500,000, there were those who predicted that in another decade it would reach a million. Lady Duffus Hardy, who had made a splash with a string of best-selling novels including *Beryl Fortescue* and *Paul Wynter's Sacrifice,* had expected, when she paid a visit in the '80s, to find the Chicagoans still living among ruins. The reality surprised her:

> Knowing of the fiery scourge which a few years ago had marred and
> scarred the beauty of that fair city, we expected to find traces of ugliness
> and deformity everywhere. . . . But, Phoenixlike, the city has risen up out
> of its own ashes, grander and statelier than ever.

George M. Pullman's favorite architect, Solon S. Beman, was born in Brooklyn in 1853. After working for the noted Gothic Revival designer Richard Upjohn in New York, Beman came to Chicago in 1879 at the request of Pullman to remodel the interiors of his Prairie Avenue mansion. The young architect was soon hired to design the model town of Pullman. In the following years, Beman would design the Pullman building, add a wing to Pullman's residence, and create the sleeping car magnate's impressive classical monument in Graceland Cemetery. The architect had a highly successful practice until his death in 1914.

ABOVE: *The beginnings of the Chicago hotel lay in small establishments such as the Green Tree Inn, built by James Kinzie at the corner of Canal and Lake streets in 1833. The Green Tree was later moved to Milwaukee Avenue, where it stood when George Ade visited it in the 1890s. Ade was touched by the old building, which he said was the only one in the city that an officer from Fort Dearborn would recognize. "He would find the same old roof, the same square-paned little windows and the clapboarded walls growing rusty in spite of repeated paintings."*

When this photograph was taken in 1901, the group shown was trying to save the structure. Their efforts were in vain. The next year Chicago's oldest landmark was razed.

OPPOSITE, TOP: *Typical of the large pre-fire hotels was the Briggs House, designed by John Van Osdel and constructed in 1856 at the northeast corner of Wells and Randolph streets. Its lobby windows were handsome examples of the arched Victorian style which replaced the more severe square-topped windows of the Greek Revival. The hotel was a victim of the Great Fire.*

OPPOSITE, BOTTOM: *Starting in 1849, the City Coucil passed ordinances requiring that the street grade be raised anywhere from 4 to 14 feet, depending on the location, because the Chicago water table was by that time almost at street level. Large structures, like the Briggs House, were lifted by dozens of men turning jacks in synchronization. Afterward a new foundation would be constructed beneath the building.*

CHICAGO'S HOTELS had both a national and an international reputation for size and luxury, but they held a very special place in the hearts of Midwesterners. It was most likely a Chicago hotel that figured in a honeymoon, in that all-important business trip, in the memorable excursion to the Columbian Exposition of 1893 or the Century of Progress of 1933. Due to the city's role as America's favorite political convention site, its hotels also had a place in history. It was the Blackstone which supplied the "smoke-filled room," where, in 1920, Warren Gamaliel Harding was chosen as the Presidential standard-bearer of the Grand Old Party. It was also at the Blackstone where, in 1952, Dwight D. Eisenhower set up his command post in the titanic struggle which gave him the victory over the hero of the heartland Republicans, Senator Robert A. Taft.

THIS PAGE: *The Sherman House, named for its owner, Francis C. Sherman, the city's Civil War mayor, had one of the longest runs of any Chicago hotel. The first was built in 1845; the second (*TOP*), constructed on the original site at the northwest corner of Clark and Randolph streets, was designed by* William W. Boyington in 1861. *When it was destroyed in the fire, Boyington was called back to design its successor (*BOTTOM*), which survived until 1910.*

OPPOSITE: *The fourth Sherman House, which opened its doors in 1911, was the work of the distin-* guished firm of Holabird & Roche. *Its owner, Ernie Byfield, made its College Inn a gathering place for show people and the headquarters of Chicago's favorite bandleader, Isham Jones. In the expansion of the hotel in the 1920s, the Sherman was shorn of its distinctive green terra-cotta mansard roof.*

FIRST ANNUAL BALL SHOW MAN'S LEAGUE OF AMERICA
COL. W.F. CODY (BUFFALO BILL) PRESIDENT.
HOTEL SHERMAN MAR.-4-1914 CHICAGO.

ABOVE: *The ballroom of the Sherman with the First Annual Ball of the Showman's League of America in progress, March 4, 1914. The League's president, the goateed Colonel William F. Cody, a.k.a. Buffalo Bill, is eighth from left, in the front row.*

RIGHT: *A view of the Celtic Room the last day the Sherman was open, February 2, 1973. People waited two hours to be seated in the handsome oak-paneled grill. The Sherman House was finally demolished in 1980.*

110

Supreme among the post-fire hotels was the $2 1/2 million Palmer House at State and Monroe streets. The design of the hotel was based on plans by John Van Osdel which were expanded by C. M. Palmer, an architect who did much work in Chicago in the 1870s. The Palmer House gloried in thirty-four varieties of marble, a 25-foot-high rotunda, an Egyptian parlor, and furniture imported from France and Italy. It also claimed to be the world's first fireproof hotel—a strong selling point in Chicago—and 600 tons of Belgian iron was used in its construction. This Palmer House was demolished in 1925 to make way for the current hotel of that name.

ABOVE: *The Palmer House's Grand Dining Room, 64 feet wide and 76 feet long, was enriched with gilded Corinthian columns, a marble floor, and frescoes painted by Italian artists. The damask table linen was made especially for the hotel in Belfast. The room was the scene of a spectacular banquet for Ulysses S. Grant in 1879, featuring Mark Twain as speaker and a game dinner of saddle of venison, roast prairie chicken, buffalo steak, breast of duck, and filet of wild turkey. The Grand Dining Room was the place where guests on the American Plan, that is,*

with one bill covering both room and board, ate. The Palmer House also had a restaurant to serve both guests who had chosen the European Plan, which did not include meals in the price of a room, and diners who were not staying at the hotel.

RIGHT: *The Ladies' Entrance of the Palmer House on Monroe Street. The hotel opened in sections as they were completed. This section, as the date on the elaborate marquee makes clear, opened in 1872, though the entire hotel was not ready for occupancy until the following year.*

LEFT: *The Morrison, one of the Loop's preeminent commercial hostelries, was the creation of Harry Moir, who arrived in Chicago in 1899. Its 3400 rooms made it one of the world's largest hotels, while its forty-five stories made it the world's tallest. The Morrison was constructed in four stages between 1913 and 1932. The first section, at the southeast corner of Clark and Madison streets, was designed by Marshall & Fox and opened in 1914. A second section opened in 1915. The hotel's third section, on Madison between Clark and Dearborn, and the fourth section were the work of Holabird & Roche.*

In this 1930 view, the hotel soars above the old Arcade which connected Clark and La Salle streets. The Morrison was razed in 1965 and replaced by the new headquarters of The First National Bank.

ABOVE: *In 1935 after the repeal of Prohibition, the Morrison's Terrace Room, which became one of Chicago's most popular downtown nightspots, was created.*

OPPOSITE: *Located at 190 East Pearson Street, near the Water Tower, the Pearson Hotel, which opened in 1923, was a refined red brick and limestone interpretation of the Georgian style. Its architect, Robert S. DeGolyer, was much influenced by the recently completed Ritz-Carlton Hotel by Warren & Wetmore in New York. Curiously, the Pearson was demolished in 1972 to clear the way for construction of Chicago's Ritz-Carlton.*

ABOVE: *The 105-room Victoria Hotel, designed in 1892 to house those attending the 1893 Columbian Exposition, was the heart of downtown Chicago Heights. The hotel was an important element in the oeuvre of Adler & Sullivan and of the firm's young assistant, Frank Lloyd Wright, who participated in the design. With its bold clock tower rising above the lobby entrance, its rhythmical Richardsonian arches framing the ground-floor shop windows, and the exaggerated overhang of its eaves,*

the Victoria looked back to Adler and Sullivan's Pueblo, Colorado, Opera House of 1889 and their Charnley House of 1891 and forward to Wright's Winslow House of 1894. In the halcyon days of thoroughbred racing in Chicago in the 1930s, '40s, and '50s, the Victoria would be filled in the summer with horsemen participating in the meetings at Lincoln Fields and Washington Park. This unique caravansary closed its doors in 1958 and was knocked down in 1961.

EDGEWATER BEACH HOTEL
CHICAGO

In 1916 Benjamin H. Marshall of the firm of Marshall & Fox brought a delicious note of fantasy to the shore of Lake Michigan with his yellow stucco Edgewater Beach Hotel. Located at 5349 North Sheridan Road, the 500-room hotel, with its tennis courts, miniature golf course, and sandy beach, would not have been out of place in Florida. In this view the hotel still has immediate access to the lake. But when, in the 1950s, the city extended Lincoln Park north of Foster Avenue and built a new highway along the lake by filling in the shoreline, the Edgewater Beach was no longer on the water's edge. The hotel closed in 1967 and was razed in 1970.

European visitors were immediately struck by the perpetual bustle in the lobbies of Chicago hostelries. Typically, Harold Spender, an English author and lecturer, reported in November 1920: "The lounge of the LaSalle was like the lobby of the House of Commons on a day of political crisis." Holabird and Roche, the architects of the 22-story LaSalle, which opened in 1909, at the northwest corner of La Salle and Madison streets, would have been delighted by Spender's comparison. They had intended that the lobby (TOP), with its rich paneling of Circassian walnut, should have a club-like English ambiance as befitted a hotel in the heart of Chicago's financial district. Opening off the lobby was both a formal Louis XIV–style dining room and the airy pearl gray Palm Room (LEFT). This room was one of the supreme examples of the use of Rookwood tile and terra-cotta, from the internationally-renowned pottery in Cincinnati. On June 6, 1946, a fire in the LaSalle killed sixty-one people. The hotel was renovated by Rapp & Rapp, but was razed in 1977.

An Architecture for a Democracy

LOUIS SULLIVAN concludes his essay "The Tall Office Building Artistically Considered" with these words:

> . . . when we know and feel that Nature is our friend, not our implacable enemy . . . then it may be proclaimed that we are on the high-road to a natural and satisfying art, an architecture that will soon become a fine art in the true, the best sense of the word, an art that will live because it will be of the people, for the people, and by the people.

That the words of the supreme architect of the heartland should echo the words of its supreme statesman is no coincidence. The same forces that shaped the man who saved the Republic and who proclaimed, "As I would not be a slave, so I would not be a master," made Chicago the natural site of America's first school of democratic architecture. They were the forces that would make the heartland the seedbed of America's realistic literature and transform our speech from the tight circumscribed tongue of England into the broad expression of a vast continent. In *The American Language,* H. L. Mencken saw it all beginning with Chicago's first hero, Andrew Jackson:

> [I]t was his fate to give a new and unshakable confidence . . . at the Battle of New Orleans. Thereafter all doubts began to die out; the new Republic was turning out a success. . . . The hordes of pioneers rolled down the Western valleys and on to the great plains. America began to stand for something quite new in the world—in government, in law, in public and private morals, in customs and habits of mind, in the minutiae of social intercourse.

Chicago, the most American of cities, was at the center of this new creation. It was not surprising, therefore, that here were felt the first stirrings of a native architecture which was not provincial, not colonial, which proudly asserted the United States' aesthetic independence by at last breaking with European precedents. As Pullman and McCormick had changed America, as Lincoln had, now came men who would transform its very appearance: William Le Baron Jenney, Dankmar Adler, Louis Sullivan, John Wellborn Root.

Indeed, in the 1880s and 1890s Chicago gave its name to a new school of architecture, now known as the First Chicago School (as distinguished from the Second Chicago

Burnham & Root's Masonic Temple of 1890–1892 was among the handsomest Chicago School skyscrapers and also one of the most famous. "There was also the Masonic Temple of twenty-one stories, at the time the tallest building in the world, from the top of which . . . one could see Council Bluffs, Iowa, 230 miles distant," Edgar Lee Masters wrote in his memoirs. "I had to try that out, and Uncle Henry took me to the Masonic Temple." The structure, at the northeast corner of State and Randolph streets, was one of the keystones of the Loop's urban fabric. Its roof garden and Temple Theatre tied it into the Randolph Street rialto, while its shops purveying furs and other luxury goods linked it to Marshall Field's, just across Randolph, and to the other State Street emporiums. The demolition of the Masonic Temple in 1939 was a devastating loss for downtown Chicago. Next to the Masonic Temple, on East Randolph, may be glimpsed Adler & Sullivan's vanished six-story Martin A. Ryerson Building of 1884.

School of Mies Van der Rohe and his followers, and Frank Lloyd Wright), whose work was to have a profound effect not only in the United States but throughout the world. The early buildings of the Chicago School relied for their inspiration on the work of Louisiana-born architect Henry Hobson Richardson, whose ideal was the rugged Romanesque of the south of France. Ironically, although Richardson unequivocally rejected the concept of the metal-framed building, championing instead lithic structures with load-bearing walls, it was to be the metal skeleton frame that allowed the architects of the School to perfect their signature edifice, the skyscraper, and it was the aesthetic realities of the materials themselves—iron and steel—that gave them their distinctive style.

The architectural historian James Marston Fitch, in his *American Building,* describes the environment in which the Chicago School developed as:

> . . . the electric environment of a vigorous and progressive capital,
> intellectual center of the Midwest. In the older cities of the eastern
> seaboard, the Wall Street capitalists had already consolidated their power
> and settled down for a long period of intensifying conservatism. Chicago,
> on the other hand, was the pivot of industrial and agrarian forces
> which resisted, for the time at least, the long arm of eastern monopoly.
> It faced huge new problems and had no choice but to try new solutions.

The problems or, better, the challenges were indeed huge. Travelers noted an actual hum as they approached Chicago. "Conceive a city all [of] whose principal streets correspond to Victoria Street in London, or the most central parts of Glasgow and Manchester," an Englishman, Sir John Leng, wrote in the mid-'70s, "and you will understand the style of the Chicago of to-day." Seventy-five passenger trains now served it daily, while its port annually cleared more than 10,000 vessels. In the two decades after the Great Fire of October 1871 had swept away much of the city's business center, the value of construction amounted to more than $300 million and by 1890 land in the Loop (so named because of the loop made first by cable cars and later by the elevated around the city's business section) was selling for $900,000 a quarter-acre.

The first buildings erected in the wake of the fire were little more than copies by architects such as John Van Osdel and William Boyington of pre-fire structures. Their style, generally a Second Empire pastiche, was criticized even as the structures were completed. But, curiously, it would be their height—five or six stories—which would eventually seal their fate.

Hard-pressed to keep up with the demand, Chicago's builders invented one revolutionary method of construction after another. Salt was added to mortar so that bricks could be laid in winter; lights were placed under temporary roofing to permit excavation at any time and in any weather; straw was packed around concrete so that it could be poured even in a blizzard. As early as 1873, Frederick Baumann had published his pioneering study, *The Art of Preparing Foundations for All Kinds of Buildings, with Particular Illustration of the Method of Isolated Piers as Followed in Chicago.* Baumann proposed that each vertical element of a building should have a separate foundation ending in a broad pad which would distribute its weight over the marshy ground. It was this type of foundation which Burnham and Root used for their Montauk Block on West Monroe Street of 1882. But as the architects discovered, Baumann's foundation had a serious disadvantage. It took up so much room that it occupied almost all of the valuable basement space. In addition, the upper limit of a building standing on this type of foundation was ten stories.

A decade later, Adler and Sullivan developed a far better solution than Baumann's to the problem of Chicago's spongy soil—and at the same time to the problem of producing more space in Chicago's crowded commercial center. Their most significant innovation came with the Chicago Stock Exchange on La Salle Street of 1894. In order not to disturb the surrounding structures with pile driving, Adler and Sullivan dug shafts into the bedrock 50 feet below the surface and then filled them with concrete. This type of caisson construction quickly became routine for tall buildings across the United States.

It was William Le Baron Jenney, an engineer who had graduated from the École Centrale des Arts et Manufactures in Paris and who had built bridges for the Union army, who came up with the most momentous innovation of all. In 1884, at the corner of Dearborn and Washington streets, Jenney constructed for the Home Insurance Company the world's first iron-and-steel-framed building. After that it was possible to reach up to almost any height, to do away with thick stone or brick supporting walls and to replace them with thin curtain walls which could be cut away to permit larger and larger windows. Though it would take time for the full implication of the Home Insurance Building to be understood, Jenney had prefigured the skyscraper and the all-glass tower.

Major Jenney's office was an atelier for the architects of the Chicago School. Through it passed Martin Roche, William Holabird, Irving K. Pond, James Gamble Rogers, Alfred Granger, and Howard Van Doren Shaw, and to it, in 1873, came Louis Henri Sullivan. After training at the Massachusetts Institute of Technology in his native state and a stint in a Philadelphia architect's office, Sullivan was searching for a larger field of action, and when he saw Chicago he knew that he had found it. In his *The Autobiography of an Idea,* a book which ranks with *The Education of Henry Adams* as one of the most intriguing self-revelatory works in American literature, Sullivan recorded his first emotions toward the city of his destiny:

> Louis thought it all magnificent and wild: A crude extravaganza:
> An intoxicating rawness: A sense of big things to be done.

The Jenney atelier was a congenial place for a bright, energetic young man. Not only was the Major a fine teacher, but he was also a delightful human being. Sullivan was to remember him as "a *bon vivant,* a gourmet" who "knew his vintages, every one." Because he felt it important for an architect to experience the good things of life, Jenney encouraged his staff to go to the theater, to restaurants, to concerts, and, above all, to the beer gardens the Germans had introduced into the city. Scattered across town, from Henry Schoelkopf's Relic House on the North Side to Baum's Pavillion on the South, they offered wine and beer, Wiener schnitzel and sauerbraten, good orchestras, and, often on Sunday afternoons, operetta, and gave the city a surprisingly continental air.

Sullivan's guide to this new world was Jenney's foreman, John Edelmann, an enthusiastic, well-read young man of twenty-four. Edelmann introduced Sullivan to the progressive political theories that were swirling about the Middle West—the single tax, and the need for an exclusively greenback currency—and to German metaphysics and books such as Charles Darwin's *On the Origin of Species.* On Sundays Edelmann and Sullivan went to Turner Hall on the North Side to hear Hans Balatka's orchestra perform Wagner, then the musical rage. A passion for serious music seems to have been common to almost all of the architects of the Chicago School. It was a passion easily satisfied in a city boasting a symphony under the brilliant baton of the German-born conductor Theodore Thomas, as well as the Bush Temple of Music with its fine conservatory and the Chicago Musical College, presided over by the popular Dr. Florenz Ziegfeld, whose son would one day employ melody to glorify the American girl.

Carved decoration from the north façade of Adler & Sullivan's Walker Warehouse of 1888.

This *joie de vivre* shared by Jenney, Edelmann, Sullivan, and the other members of the Chicago School is an important factor in understanding their architecture. It was a natural element in a metropolis without a strong Puritan tradition, which from its beginnings delighted in plays, music, and dancing. It is significant that the consummate expressions of the School were to be office buildings, hotels, concert halls, cafes, beer gardens, and theaters. It was to be a supremely public architecture, an enhancement of places where the people gathered.

It was because of this awareness of the people as equal citizens of a republic—an awareness as intense as that felt by Lincoln himself—that the Chicago architects wanted buildings which would reflect the political and economic realities of the United States. The Chicagoans were not satisfied merely to build structurally innovative edifices; they wanted them to be stylistically revolutionary as well. They sought reality, not fantasy, and the reality of America as seen from the heartland did not include the pavilions of princes or the castles of kings. Sullivan's colleagues agreed with him when he called pseudo-Gothic churches and ersatz Palladian office buildings mere "architectural theology." They found their inspiration not in the Venice of the doges, or in the Rome of the Caesars, or in the Paris of the Bonapartes, but in Joseph Paxton's Crystal Palace in London, John Roebling's Brooklyn Bridge, and the new fireproof Chicago warehouses of George H. Johnson and Frederick Baumann. Here were no Philadelphia waterworks disguised as Greek temples, no Hartford, Connecticut, firearms factory pretending to be an Oriental seraglio. Sullivan, the chief theorist of the Chicago School, would call for buildings where "form followed function," just as it had in the sanctuaries of ancient Greece and in the twelfth-century Gothic cathedrals. He would call for a decoration based not upon the copybooks in the university libraries but on natural forms, the living reality of the American land. And always, at the very heart, was the belief that architecture must celebrate its own time and that this time was one of technology, industry, and, above all, democracy. The Roman temple had no place in our cities. To use it as the form of a bank, he would write later in his *Kindergarten Chats,* was as ridiculous as requiring a banker to "wear a toga." Elsewhere in the *Chats,* in a passage suggesting Gertrude Stein's "A rose is a rose is a rose is a rose," Sullivan reiterated why our architecture must be American:

> Furthermore, if the pseudo-Roman temple were good for any one thing in America, it must, *ipso facto*, be good for anything and everything American, because American means American, and expresses the genius of the people. But Roman does not mean American, never did mean American. Roman was Roman; America is, and is to be, American.

This was the authentic voice of the heartland.

Sullivan was not the only Chicago architect deeply concerned with perfecting an American stylistic theory. John Wellborn Root was another. Born in Georgia and educated in England and in New York as a civil engineer, Root had worked in the office of James Renwick, the architect of the Smithsonian Institution in Washington. After arriving in Chicago in 1871, he linked up with Daniel Burnham, who had come to architecture by way of selling plate glass and mining and who had one consuming ambition: to be a millionaire. Their first important commission, in 1874, was for a house on Prairie Avenue for John B. Sherman, "the father of the Yards." Of pressed brick and sandstone, its strong, simple lines stood out in sharp contrast to the extravagant palaces surrounding it. In 1882 Burnham and Root carried the aesthetic ideals of the Sherman residence into the commercial world with their Montauk Block, where, within the very shadow of the Parisian grandeur of the Palmer House, the young architects put up an unadorned

Louis Sullivan about 1885.

nine-story brick structure which proclaimed proudly that it was nothing more and nothing less than an office building. Burnham and Root's Reliance Building on State Street of 1895, completed after Root's death by Charles B. Atwood, brilliantly exemplified yet another innovation with far-reaching implications for American architecture: the deliberate celebration of the rigid nature of metal. There is about the Reliance a marvelous sense of the sharp, almost dangerous edges of the steel frame lying just beneath its thin, white terra-cotta walls. This sensation is enhanced by the fact that two-thirds of the walls are of glass, producing a structure of rare brittle beauty.

The startlingly straightforward elevations of the Montauk Block and the angular beauty of the Reliance Building were no accident. In the '80s, Root had begun writing a series of pioneering essays for Chicago's progressive building journal the *Inland Architect,* which expressed concepts given form in the Sherman residence, the Montauk Block, and the Reliance Building:

> We must especially beware of the servile imitation of those greatest
> and completest styles that mark the end of long periods of architectural
> development.

And:

> As far as material conditions permit it to be possible, a building designated
> for a particular purpose should express that purpose in every part.

Because Root was to die at forty, it would be Louis Sullivan who would give final form to these ideals.

By the time Sullivan met the man who would be his partner in accomplishing this task, he had spent a frustrating term at the École des Beaux-Arts which had deepened his conviction that the architectural solutions for America did not lie in Europe. The introduction came through his old friend John Edelmann. "Further away stood Adler at a draftsman's table," Sullivan was to write. "He was . . . heavy-set, well-bearded, with a magnificent domed forehead which stopped suddenly at a solid mass of black hair." Dankmar Adler was the son of a German Jewish rabbi and cantor who for more than thirty years was the spiritual leader of Chicago's prestigious Anshe Mayriv congregation. After serving, like Jenney, as an engineer in the Union army, he had formed a partnership with Edward Burling, and, in the years after the fire, Burling and Adler were responsible for more than a hundred buildings in Chicago, including the *Tribune* offices, Delmonico's restaurant, and the Methodist Church Block.

Adler was both popular and successful and, in 1879, encouraged by the commission to design the important Central Music Hall at the corner of State and Randolph streets, he decided to go into business for himself. Needing a draftsman, he hired Louis Sullivan, whose first task was to design the new hall's organ grilles. The Central Music Hall was the prototype of the kind of theater that would make Adler and Sullivan famous, an effective combination of shops, offices, and an auditorium with perfect acoustics. Indeed, Adler was the greatest acoustical engineer of his time, with a knowledge of sound unique in the nineteenth century. He was responsible for the splendid acoustics of the Chicago theaters he and Sullivan built, such as the Schiller, as well as those of New York's Carnegie Hall.

It was Adler and Sullivan's skill in designing theaters that brought them their greatest commission. After hosting the 1880 and 1884 Republican conventions, the barnlike Inter-State Exposition building on the lakefront had stood empty for months. Ferdinand Peck, heir to a large Chicago real estate fortune and a serious patron of music, conceived the idea of using the building for a summer festival featuring Theodore Thomas' orchestra. Adler was asked to convert the cavernous interior into a concert hall, and the ingenious plan he devised not only provided seats for 6000 but also enabled all to hear each instrument distinctly. The success of the festival led Peck to begin thinking of a permanent concert hall on a grand scale, and who could better design it than Adler and Sullivan?

In 1886, when the Auditorium commission came to them, Adler was forty-two and Sullivan thirty. They were at the height of their powers and they would need all of their strength and skill for the monumental job ahead of them. Fortunately they had a staff of unusual talent. There was George Grant Elmslie, who would design some of the most glorious small buildings of the twentieth century; Paul Mueller, a brilliant construction engineer who would share the honors for Tokyo's Imperial Hotel; and a young man still in his teens, Frank Lloyd Wright.

Sullivan's first designs show a picturesque structure complete with oriel windows, a high gable roof, dormers, and pinnacles. But nearby was rising Henry Hobson Richardson's Marshall Field Wholesale Store, and it was an unmistakable lesson in how a modern building should look. Richardson was the one eastern architect unreservedly admired by the men of the Chicago School. His Trinity Church in Boston, his Ames Memorial Library in North Easton, Massachusetts, his Allegheny County buildings in Pittsburgh were all impressive examples of a virile, modified Romanesque style. The final and most complete statement of that style was his building for Marshall Field. A solid block of masonry-supporting walls, it was stripped of almost all decoration, achieving its breathtaking beauty by means of fine workmanship and the powerful rhythms of its fenestration: uniform for the first two floors, doubled for the upper two, quadrupled in the attic. Years later, in his *Kindergarten Chats,* Sullivan was to call the Field building "this oasis in our desert"; now he was to learn from it. Leveling gables and pinnacles and dormers, Sullivan sketched a simplified lithic structure with but a single, massive tower.

From the moment in 1887 when President Grover Cleveland laid the cornerstone of the Auditorium, Chicago sensed that it was a very special building. In the first place, the effort required for its construction reminded observers of the pyramids. At its acre-and-a-half site on Michigan Avenue at Congress Street, 200 men and 30 teams of horses labored day and night digging a stupendous pit for its foundations. These consisted of an ingenious floating network of huge timbers, steel rails, and iron I-beams strong enough to support the 4000 pounds per square foot pressed down upon them by the massive load-bearing walls of Indiana limestone and Minnesota granite. To insure that the seventeen-story tower, which alone weighed 15,000 tons, would settle at the same rate as the rest of the building and thus not crack the walls, Adler devised a brilliant mathematical formula which allowed him to load the lower floors artificially and then gradually empty them as they rose above the main body of the structure. The Auditorium Tower immediately became the city's leading tourist attraction—Chicago's equivalent of the dome of St. Paul's in London—the place where all went to view this astonishing prairieland capital. Paul Bourget (1852–1935), a French novelist who visited the United States in 1893 and two years later published *Outre-Mer: Impressions of America,* found it like nothing else in the world: "It is two hundred and seventy feet high, and it crowns and dominates a cyclopean structure which connects a colossal hotel with a colossal theatre."

"Colossal" was indeed the word heard time and again when, on December 9, 1889, President Benjamin Harrison dedicated the Auditorium. (The packed house—many of whom had paid $2000 for a box seat—not only got to see the President, but also heard the soprano Adelina Patti sing "Home, Sweet Home.") And colossal was an accurate description, for the Auditorium Theatre, seating 4000 with room for another

3000 on special occasions, was the largest opera house in the world. Its enormous orchestra pit could hold 110 musicians, and the stage could be extended out over the parquet to form the nation's biggest ballroom. Yet Adler had made its acoustics so perfect that every word of a conversation on its mammoth stage could be heard with ease in the top gallery, some six stories up and half a block away. The structure was rich in innovations. It was the first new building in the world to be electrically lit, and enormous fans, drawing air down shafts from the roof and forcing it through sprays of water and over blocks of ice, made it the first to be air-conditioned.

There was another word which was often heard that December night: beautiful. In the decoration of the interior, Sullivan proved beyond doubt that architects need not look to Greece or Rome or medieval Europe in order to create beauty. The forms based on nature, which he so strongly advocated, were more than sufficient. The theater ceiling was a series of sweeping gold-leaf-covered arches set with diamond-like, carbon-filament lights. The effect was to crown every citizen of the republic at every performance with an equally brilliant tiara. Sullivan's genius was evident in all aspects of the building's decoration: in the subtle variations of the ivory and gold stenciling on the walls, in the carpets and ironwork, in the designs of the fifty million tesserae which made up the mosaic floors. But in the Auditorium's long bar, Sullivan surpassed himself, and in so doing he made artistic history. Here he gave his theories of decoration untrammeled play and enriched the room's ceiling and columns with a wondrous foliate flowering, an early expression of the aesthetic principles that characterized Art Nouveau, the style that was to dominate European and American architectural circles during the last decade of the nineteenth century and the first decade of the twentieth. In *The Roots of Modern Design,* the English architectural historian Sir Nikolaus Pevsner gives Sullivan his due:

> The two creators of Art Nouveau were Louis Sullivan in Chicago and
> Victor Horta in Brussels. Sullivan was probably essentially original. . . .
> By the time Sullivan designed the interiors of the Auditorium Building
> in Chicago, this is by 1888, his ornamental style was complete.

The Auditorium was an unqualified success from the moment it opened. Adler and Sullivan moved their offices into the tower, the hotel at once joined the august company of the Palmer House, the Sherman, and the Grand Pacific, its restaurants and banqueting rooms became the gathering places of the city's fashionable; but it was the theater which was its glory. To it came Enrico Caruso, Amelita Galli-Curci, John McCormack, Luisa Tetrazzini, and Dame Nellie Melba, who said, "I wish I could fold it up and take it with me everywhere." Richard Strauss, Sergei Prokofiev, and Nikolai Rimsky-Korsakov all conducted there. On its stage Booker T. Washington and President McKinley made their

The caption to this turn-of-the-century collectible trading card read "Waiting for the arrival of Montgomery Ward & Co's catalogue." Not only did Ward's catalogues change the way rural and small town America shopped, they were also used as teaching tools in innumerable one-room schoolhouses with few textbooks. Teachers used the catalogues' text for reading lessons and their postal zone maps to teach geography.

Among the many examples of Sullivan's matchless details were the ivory and gold leaf stencils behind the boxes of the Auditorium Theatre. In the 1890s these were judged to lessen the effect of the gowns of the ladies seated in the boxes whose color scheme was often just that: ivory and gold. The color was changed to red.

joint appeal for racial tolerance, Theodore Roosevelt launched his Bull Moose campaign, and Will Rogers first found fame with his heartland humor. Near the end of his life, Frank Lloyd Wright reminisced about working there for the two geniuses whose monument it will always be, and called it "the greatest room for music and opera in the world."

The Auditorium was indeed an extraordinary building, perhaps the most extraordinary ever constructed in America, but suddenly Chicago was full of remarkable buildings, all reaching up as high as their load-bearing walls would carry them. This desperate race for height was the result of a combination of a continuing boom and the extreme restriction of the city's central business district. Bound on the north and west by the Chicago River, on the south by an impassable network of railroads, and on the east by Lake Michigan, its total area was barely three quarters of a square mile. The only direction to go was up. The architects who first accomplished this feat with a high degree of perfection were undoubtedly Burnham and Root. Their Rookery of 1885, at the southeast corner of La Salle and Adams streets in the heart of the financial district, set a standard for office size, width of corridors, and placement of elevators which was to be followed in commercial buildings for fifty years; while the three-story entrance court of glass and iron was one of the Chicago School's finest interiors. Burnham and Root matched this triumph with their awesomely sophisticated sixteen-story Monadnock Building on West Jackson Boulevard. In subtle tribute to the city which gave it life, the Monadnock's severe, Egyptian-inspired walls flared out at base and parapet to form the silhouette of a growing papyrus or of its relative, the wild onion.

The Monadnock was at once the supreme load-bearing-wall skyscraper and the last. By the time it opened in 1892, the Chicago architects had mastered all the lessons of Major Jenney's Home Insurance Building. William Holabird and Martin Roche not only used an iron-and-steel frame for their handsome Tacoma, but also introduced the idea of riveting it into place, thus greatly reducing the time it took to construct a building. Soon, Holabird and Roche were dotting the Loop with their distinctive structures: the Caxton, the Pontiac, the Old Colony, the splendid Marquette. Chicago now became a forest of true skyscrapers, their iron-and-steel trunks growing upward toward the dizzying height of twenty stories. There was the Chamber of Commerce by Baumann and Huehl; the Manhattan by the still-active Le Baron Jenney; and Adler and Sullivan's exquisitely decorated Stock Exchange. Standing on top of the Auditorium Tower, Paul Bourget was awed:

> It needs but a few minutes for the eyes to become accustomed to the strange scene. Then you discern differences of height among these levels. Those of only six or seven stories seem to be the merest cottages, those of two stories are not to be distinguished from the pavement, while the "buildings" of fourteen, fifteen, twenty stories, uprise like the islands of the Cyclades as seen from the mountains of Negroponte.

Again it was a Burnham and Root building that focused the attention of America and Europe on the Chicago skyscraper. Everything about their Masonic Temple of 1892 on the northeast corner of State and Randolph streets was worthy of a superlative. At twenty-two stories it was by far the tallest building in the world. Its basement restaurant seated 2000, its interior shopping galleries were huge, its elevators numbered fourteen, its roof garden rested literally in the clouds. During the 1893 Columbian Exposition, knowledgeable European visitors turned their backs on the fair's Beaux Arts architecture and asked to see the Masonic Temple. Along with Adler & Sullivan's Wainwright Building, constructed in St. Louis at the same time, the Temple—with its distinct base, its soaring shaft uninterrupted by horizontal divisions, and its fine functional cape—gave the basic form to the powerful skyscrapers of the '90s.

With such buildings the Chicagoans frankly and joyously celebrated the life of the new industrial age about them. Thomas Tallmadge, in his *Architecture in Old Chicago,* gives the true meaning of the city's glorious new creations:

> [T]hey present a distinct bracket in architectural design in which the
> men of the eighties in presenting the steel skeleton to the world clothed
> it in a dress they thought appropriate and which came near to being
> indigenous. . . . It must be remembered that all of these giants were built
> in a period of élan, almost all by young men, fired with a conviction
> that Chicago was the wonder-city of the world and bolstered up in the
> idea by the amazement of Europe and by the grudging admiration of
> New York.

It is not surprising that it was a Chicago writer, Henry B. Fuller, who became the first American novelist to take for his subject the life of the great industrial city. The opening of his appropriately named *The Cliff-Dwellers* is an evocation of the world of the skyscraper:

> Between the former site of old Fort Dearborn and the present site of
> our newest Board of Trade there lies a restricted yet tumultuous territory
> through which, during the course of the last fifty years, the rushing
> streams of commerce have worn many a deep and rugged chasm. . . .
> Each of these cañons is closed in by a long frontage of towering cliffs,
> and these soaring walls of brick and limestone and granite rise higher
> and higher with each succeeding year, according as the work of erosion
> at their bases goes onward. . . . Ten years ago the most rushing and
> irrepressible of the torrents which devastate Chicago had not worn its
> bed to a greater depth than that indicated by seven . . . "stories."
> This depth has since increased to eight—to ten—to fourteen—to
> sixteen, until some of the leading avenues of activity promise soon to
> become little more than mere obscure trails half lost between the bases
> of perpendicular precipices.

A new architecture had been born, an architecture without fluted columns or the white statues of long-dead gods, an architecture voicing Lincoln's dream of a nation without master or slave. Louis Sullivan summed up its creed in his *Kindergarten Chats:*

> Bank upon democracy, for your country is as surely and will remain
> surely a democracy, as it is sure that the sun will rise and set.
> Do not give yourself a moment's worriment about this. And arrange
> your architecture for Democracy, not for Imperialism. . . .

In its flowering, the Chicago School did indeed arrange its architecture for democracy.

—‖ AMERICAN METROPOLIS ‖—

IN THE LAST QUARTER of the nineteenth century, Chicago felt that it was destined to give expression to a new, a wholly American, civilization. There was undoubtedly an element of boosterism in this conviction, stemming from the metropolis's phenomenal growth to more than 1 million in the two decades following the Great Fire. A Scots visitor, Emily Faithful, encapsulated this "go-aheadism" when, in *Three Visits to America*, she quoted a Chicago friend:

> When a true-spirited citizen from Chicago first visits New York, he exclaims, "This isn't much of a city after all," when he drinks New York whiskey he complains it isn't half as good as he gets at home, for it only burns 'half-way down!' The Sunday newspapers can't compare with his;

and as for the feet to be seen on Fifth Avenue, he contemptuosly remarks, "Call that a foot!—our girls have them twice the size!"

But there were also incontestable foundations for the belief in Chicago's destiny. In Abraham Lincoln the city had already given the Republic a new political being; its writers, such as Theodore Dreiser, were fashioning a revolutionary, realistic approach to literature; and its architects were ready to turn away from the thralls of the past to fashion buildings fit for the New World. Studying the structures they had already produced by the early 1890s, the French novelist Paul Bourget quickly grasped their meaning: "It is the first draught of a new sort of art—an art of democracy. . . ."

MONUMENTS OF COMMERCE

OPPOSITE: *If any one building may be said to have begun the new art, it was Burnham & Root's Montauk, built in 1882 on West Monroe Street and first rented to the Hartford Insurance Company. The architectural historian Thomas Tallmadge asserted that "what Chartres was to the Gothic Cathedral the Montauk Block was to the high commercial building." Casting aside classical columns and Victorian furbelows, its young designers raised a straightforward structure of brick, relieved only by bands of terra-cotta. The Montauk was destroyed in 1902 and replaced by the First National Bank Building.*

ABOVE: *What the Montauk was to the history of commercial design, William Le Baron Jenney's Home Insurance Building, begun in 1884, was to the history of construction. While it is true that iron-framed structures, including a shot tower designed by James Bogardus in 1855 in New York and a warehouse by Hippolyte Fontaine in Paris of 1864, had made their appearance, Jenney's building was a great leap forward. Carl W. Condit, in his* The Chicago School of Architecture, *succinctly sums up what Jenney achieved: "The decisive step for the tall office building, however, remained to be taken. This was the*

reduction of the exterior wall to a mere curtain or envelope that is supported throughout by the interior framing and nowhere supports itself or any part of the building load." The Home Insurance, which stood at the northeast corner of La Salle and Adams streets, was the world's first iron-and-steel-framed building. Originally ten stories high, two more were added to it in 1890. This key to a history of the evolution of the American skyscraper was demolished in 1931.

One of Chicago's earliest examples of the Romanesque Revival style, a style which would have a profound effect upon the city's architecture, was Solon S. Beman's brick and granite Pullman Building of 1883. Its arched entrance was particularly admired. The structure, at the southwest corner of Michigan Avenue and Adams Street, had a highly sophisticated mixed use plan of offices, luxurious apartments whose residents included Chicagoan Florenz Ziegfeld, Jr., and one of the city's first restaurants with a view, the Tip Top Inn, favored by Anna Held and George M. Cohan. The Pullman Building was destroyed in 1956.

BASEMENT LEVEL FLOOR PLAN, THE PULLMAN BUILDING

79

"Four-square and brown, it stands, in physical fact, a monument to trade, to the organized commercial spirit, to the power and progress of the age, to the strength and resources of individuality and force of character. . . ."

— *Louis Sullivan*, Kindergarten Chats.

ABOVE: *Henry Hobson Richardson's Marshall Field Wholesale Store, commissioned in 1885, a year before Richardson's death, was an icon for Louis Sullivan, who had long admired the Boston architect's lithic Romanesque Revival buildings. The massive structure, built of rock-faced red Missouri granite, filled the entire block bounded by Adams, Quincy, Wells, and Franklin streets. The structure housed Field's wholesale division, which, when it was built, far outstripped the profits from Field's State Street retail emporium. The merchant from Indiana or Wisconsin, coming to* Chicago to restock his store, would find in the Field Wholesale Store 500,000 square feet of beautifully organized merchandise. And the choice was astounding, everything from fine French veiling to Victrolas. After two days—the usual stay— the merchant would complete his order and return home. By the 1920s, Field's wholesale business became unprofitable. In 1930 Richardson's Romanesque masterpiece—one of the structures by which he hoped posterity would judge him—was cavalierly obliterated.

THE AUDITORIUM

Adler & Sullivan's seventeen-story Auditorium Building, the tallest building in America at the time, brilliantly incorporated three separate entities within a single structure. The 400-room Auditorium Hotel occupied the Michigan Avenue and most of the Congress Street sides of the edifice, while the 136 offices in the office building portion were located on the Wabash Avenue side and in the tower. Symbolically, at the center of the building was the Auditorium Theatre, the nation's largest theater.

OPPOSITE, BELOW: *The influence of Richardson's Marshall Field Store is readily observable in Adler & Sullivan's Walker Warehouse of 1888, originally built for Martin Ryerson, Jr. The building's visual excitement results from the rhythmic play of its arches and the carved decoration of a type which would become a Sullivan trademark, at the ground-floor level. (A carved detail from the north façade is shown on page 121.) The Walker Warehouse,* which stood at 210-14 South Market Street, was demolished in 1953 for the extension of Wacker Drive.

ABOVE: *A view north on Michigan Avenue in 1889, with the Auditorium Building under construction on the left. On the right is the Exposition Building, designed in 1873 by William Boyington and built to proclaim Chicago's recovery from the fire. In the Exposition Building, James* Garfield was nominated for President in 1880, and Grover Cleveland in 1884. Afterward it was the setting for the Chicago Symphony Orchestra concerts conducted by its founder, Theodore Thomas, which revealed such a vast audience for serious music in Chicago that their chief backer, Ferdinand Peck, commissioned the Auditorium. The Exposition Building was razed in 1891 to make way for the present Art Institute.

ABOVE: *The entrance to the Auditorium Hotel, on Michigan Avenue.*

RIGHT: *Visitors on the observation tower atop the Auditorium Building in the 1890s when it was the place to view the wonders of the prairie metropolis.*

The open loggia above the entrance formed part of the Auditorium Hotel's second-floor reception room. By the 1930s the aging hotel could not compete with new hostelries like the nearby Stevens. It became the Chicago Servicemen's Center during the Second World War. After the war the Auditorium Building was acquired by Roosevelt College, now Roosevelt University, and the hotel's rooms

were converted into classrooms. The open loggia has been enclosed, the second-floor reception room is now a student lounge, and the observation tower has vanished.

OPPOSITE: *Sullivan's sinuous designs in wood and plaster in the long bar on the hotel's ground floor gave him the right to be called one of the creators of Art Nouveau. When the hotel was a servicemen's center, the fabled oak bar was removed to supply space for a cafeteria steam table. Then, in an act of staggering vandalism, when Congress Street was widened in 1952, the seminal room was obliterated to make way for a pedestrian arcade through the south end of the Auditorium Building.*

The Auditorium's 175-foot-long main dining room (ABOVE) and its 4200-seat opera house (OPPOSITE) were superb examples of Sullivan's love affair with the arch, expressed in his Kindergarten Chats: *"It is a form so much against Fate, that Fate, as we say, ever most relentlessly seeks its destruction. Yet does it rise in power* so graciously, floating through the air from abutment to abutment, that it seems ever, to me, a symbol and epitome of our own ephemeral span.* To emphasize his beloved arches, Sullivan, in this, the world's first fully wired new building, made brilliant use of electric lighting. The dining room on the hotel's tenth floor offered spectacular views over Lake Michigan. Its ceiling was originally stenciled in a luxuriant white and gold pattern. This has now been painted over.

When the Auditorium project began in 1886, the Board of Directors was so concerned about the structure's expense that it insisted on

a cost-conscious austerity for the exterior. But as the project took shape the Board's enthusiasm increased and it let Adler and Sullivan expend money much more lavishly. (The structure would eventually cost more than $3 million.) One result was the sensational decoration Sullivan gave to the theater. The Auditorium Theatre was the center of opera in Chicago from 1889 until 1929, the house where Puccini supervised the production of his new La Fanciulla del West, where Prokofiev conducted the world premier of The Love for Three Oranges, and where Chicago's own Mary Garden's sensual portrayal of the lead in Richard Strauss's Salome so shocked the Law and Order League that the production was shut down. But in the autumn of 1929, Chicago Opera moved to Samuel Insull's new Art Deco Civic Opera House. Since then the matchless hall's role in the cultural life of Chicago has never been satisfactorily defined.

Another Adler & Sullivan monument was the Chicago Stock Exchange at 30 North La Salle, completed in 1894. In the Stock Exchange, Adler & Sullivan made abundant use of the large Chicago window, a startlingly modern design consisting of a broad stationary central pane flanked by smaller panels which open. The building's oriels not only brought light and air into the interior, but helped lessen the impact of wind on the structure's elevations. Though the Stock Exchange was listed by the Landmarks Commission as one of the most significant structures in Chicago, it was destroyed in 1972. This view of its La Salle Street façade was taken by the Chicago photographer and preservationist, Richard Nickel, shortly before the Exchange was razed. Nickel, visiting the site alone on a weekend after demolition had begun, was killed when a section of the building collapsed. Nickel is buried in Graceland Cemetary, near his hero, Louis Sullivan.

OPPOSITE: *The distinctive arched entrance of the Stock Exchange, seen on the right in this 1930s photograph, looking north on La Salle Street, was judged by the architecture critic Hugh Morrison to be "one of the most beautiful single features in all of Sullivan's work." The building was notable for its second-floor 64-by 181-foot trading room, whose brilliant steel framing by Adler made it obstruction-free and with equal ease carried the eleven floors of offices above it.*

The Stock Exchange also possessed important decorative metalwork. The iron elevator grills were ornamented with small spheres representing seed pods, a design resulting from Sullivan's love of natural forms. The elevators' Art Nouveau cast bronze T-plates possessed a sumptuousness that carried them into the realm of jewelry.

One of the realities of iron was that it lent itself to the sinuous curve, leading the Chicago architects who employed it, as it did their European contemporaries, to Art Nouveau. This stairway is reminiscent of the design elements used by Hector Guimard, the dominant Art Nouveau designer in France, for the railings of his Paris Mètro stations.

"*Most of the panes that enclosed this central space were of great height and breadth . . . others, smaller, gave light and some ventilation.*" —Henry B. Fuller, The Cliff-Dwellers.

The novelist Fuller coined the now-famous appelation "cliff-dwellers" to describe the office workers in the preeminent early Chicago skyscraper, the Rookery. Its great lobby, shown here shortly after completion in 1888, was one of the Chicago School's most dynamic interiors. The building, at 209 South La Salle Street, is one of three survivors out of a total of twenty-seven by Burnham & Root which once graced the Loop. The lobby, though, was considerably altered during a 1905–07 renovation by Frank Lloyd Wright. At that time its delightful Art Nouveau lighting fixtures were replaced by massive planters and Wrightian vertical elements fastened to the top of the stairway. These diminished the essential element of the stairway which the architect Henry Van Brunt, writing in 1871, found irresistible: "*One may admire the audacity of the double iron staircase which, supported by ingenious cantilevers, ramps with double curvature out into open space, meeting at a landing in the sky.*"

3913 – Chicago. Womans Temple

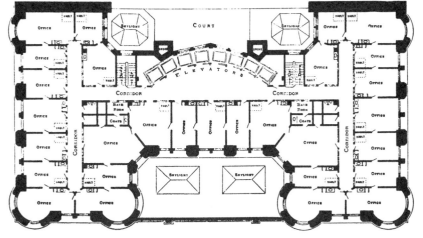

FIRST FLOOR PLAN OF THE WOMEN'S TEMPLE

OPPOSITE: *Among John Wellborn Root's last designs was the splendid headquarters for Frances Willard's Woman's Christian Temperance Union. For this building, popularly known as the Woman's Temple, which opened in the spring of 1892 on the southeast corner of La Salle and Monroe streets, Root turned away from the more virile Romanesque style and found his inspiration in the chateaux of France's Loire Valley. All of the structure's $987,628 cost was raised by the women of the W.C.T.U. Ironically, the Woman's Temple was demolished in 1926, when the organization it housed was at the height of its power.*

LEFT: *"These great Olympian buildings strike me as having beauty of a very high order," the British painter John Lavery told Harriet Monroe in 1911, after looking at Chicago's skyscrapers. "There has been nothing on earth like it since Egypt built the pyramids." One of the earliest of the Olympians was the Tacoma, on the northeast corner of La Salle and Madison streets, completed in 1889. Its architects, Holabird and Roche, were, along with Adler and Sullivan and Burnham and Root, key to the development of the First Chicago School of Architecture. William Holabird, born in New York State in 1854, attended West Point and came to Chicago in 1875. His partner, Martin Roche, grew up in Chicago and while still in his teens entered the office of William Le Baron Jenney, where he met Holabird. The Tacoma was the first building constructed by using rivets, the first whose design openly revealed the steel structure beneath, the first to inch toward the concept of the all-glass wall. This Olympian was toppled in 1929.*

Not all of the city's skyscrapers followed the aesthetic precepts of the Chicago School. One of the more notable mavericks was the Columbus Memorial Building at the southeast corner of State and Washington streets, an 1893 creation of the still-vigorous William Boyington. The flamboyant building got its name from Moses Ezekiel's bronze statue of Christopher Columbus, which had originally graced the Italian Pavilion at the 1893 Fair and which now stood in a niche above the State Street entrance. In the statue, elevator grilles (ABOVE), and other fittings the Columbus Memorial possessed some of the city's finest bronze work.

Another memorable departure from the Chicago School was located just to the east of the Columbus Memorial, at 15 East Washington

Street: the Venetian Building, completed in 1892 (seen here just to the left of the Columbus Memorial). This project from Holabird & Roche had a distinctive façade of buff-colored Roman brick which culmi-

nated in a broad band of Venetian-inspired terra-cotta ornament topped by a pitched red tile roof. Both the Columbus Memorial and the Venetian Building were demolished in 1959 to make way for a parking garage.

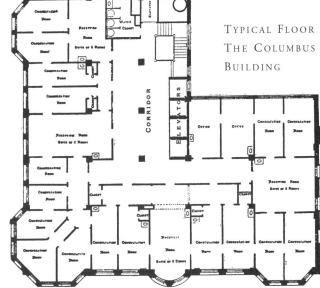

TYPICAL FLOOR PLAN,
THE COLUMBUS MEMORIAL
BUILDING

There was a time when few Americans would not have recognized this building as "The Busy Beehive" headquarters of Montgomery Ward & Co. Another architectural maverick, the distinctive Italian Renaissance-inspired skyscraper at 6 North Michigan Avenue was an 1899 design by Richard E. Schmidt, one of Chicago's most prolific twentieth-century architects, with important input by Hugh M. G. Garden, an architect and renderer who also worked with Louis Sullivan and Frank Lloyd Wright. Pictured with its outer walls removed to show the frenetic activity inside, it was regularly used by the firm to advertise the mail-order business founded by A. Montgomery Ward in 1872. The 390-foot-high edifice was crowned by a beloved Windy City work of art, "Progress Lighting the Way for Commerce," an 18-foot-high weathervane by J. Massey Rhind, whose many projects included the sculpture for Grant's Tomb in New York. (The form of the statue was undoubtedly influenced by Augustus Saint-Gaudens's Diana atop Stanford White's Madison Square Garden.) Montgomery Ward sold the building in 1908. After being judged unsafe, the impressive tower portion of the structure was removed in 1947. In the process, "Progress" was destroyed.

ABOVE, LEFT: *With its crisp lines, light piers, and large Chicago windows, Holabird & Roche's Republic Building on the southeast corner of State and Adams streets marked the last stage in the development of the tall commercial building of the Chicago School. Originally 12 stories high when it opened in 1905, in 1909 it was raised to 19. Still structurally sound and financially viable, this architecturally significant State Street office building was demolished in 1961.*

ABOVE, RIGHT: *Among Chicago's finest Art Deco office towers was the McGraw-Hill Building at 520 North Michigan Avenue, of 1928, by Thielbar & Fugard. The designing partner on the project, John Reed Fugard, was born in Iowa in 1886 and attended the University of Illinois, and by 1912 was designing apartment houses in Chicago. In his unpublished thesis on Fugard, Zurich Esposito discusses the outstanding luxury apartment buildings that Fugard was responsible for in the 1920s when he was in partnership*

with George Knapp. Among them are 229 East Lake Shore Drive, 232 East Walton Place, and 20 East Cedar Street. The McGraw-Hill Building, commissioned by the publishing company, was a sleek limestone structure whose geometric massing reflects French Art Moderne precedents. Integrated into the façade were stylized Art Deco panels by Eugene and Gwen Lux depicting mythological subjects. Though an official Chicago landmark, this beacon of 1920s sophistication, on the near left in this 1957 photograph, was leveled in 1999.

VIII

Dreams of Empire

AS THE FOUR-HUNDREDTH ANNIVERSARY of Columbus' discovery of the New World approached, the federal government announced that there would be a national exposition to commemorate the event. America's cities entered the competition like thoroughbreds at the Derby. New York, Washington, St. Louis, as well as Chicago, were all strong contenders. But Chicago worked hardest and it had impressive credentials. Since the fire, it had passed both Philadelphia and Brooklyn to become the nation's second largest city and its citizens were convinced that in ten years it would take first place. Mayor Carter Henry Harrison saw the Fair as the crowning achievement of his colorful five-term reign, and he soon had a committee of three hundred working to bring the Columbian Exposition to the shores of Lake Michigan. To show just how determined it was, by 1890 Chicago had issued stock worth $5 million to begin construction. These efforts were only spurred on by the snide comments of the eastern press, which predicted that if Chicago got the Exposition it would be a cattle show. When Charles A. Dana, editor of the New York *Sun,* pontificated: "Don't pay any attention to the nonsensical claims of that Windy City," Chicagoans seized the appellation and made it their own. All the hard work paid off when, on April 21, 1890, Congress designated the Windy City as the Fair's official site. One of the reasons for the selection of Chicago was the fame of its architects. The Fair, it was assumed, would provide a spectacular showplace for this exciting native American school. The assumption was proven correct when Daniel Burnham and John Root were appointed its architectural directors, for all America knew them as the men who had built the Rookery and the Monadnock.

Before a single structure could be raised, there was the all-important matter of location. Within the city an intense rivalry broke out between the North, West, and South sides; and Chicago turned for guidance to the greatest landscape architect of the day, Frederick Law Olmsted, the creator of New York's Central Park. Olmsted was no stranger to Chicago. In 1868 he had, to the west of the city, laid out the town of Riverside, whose well-planned greenswards and winding tree-lined streets became a model for garden suburbs across the country. Afterward, the South Park Commissioners had retained Olmsted and his partner, Calvert Vaux, to furnish plans for the improvement of Chicago's recreational facilities. The result was the most complete and elaborate scheme adopted by an American city until that time. Olmsted called for a ring of parks around Chicago, a kind of green belt, connected by broad, tree-screened boulevards. In time, these parks—Washington, Garfield, Jackson—would become the pride of the city and an undeniably civilizing influence. Here it was possible for urban workers to have an occasional green thought in a green shade.

LEFT: *The essence of the Beaux Arts architecture of the 1893 Columbian Exposition is exemplified by the triumphal arch in the center of the Colonnade designed by Peabody & Stearns which led to the amphitheater where, among other events, horse shows were held. Here are many of the hallmarks of the style: paired Corinthian columns, an arch whose underside is decorated with rosettes and whose façade carried bas-relief classical figures; an entablature embellished with swags and wreaths and topped by a balustrade; and, finally, colossal sculptural groups which relate to the function of the structure, in this case, appropriately, animals.*

Olmsted and his young assistant, Henry Sargent Codman, eventually settled on Jackson Park on the South Side. It was undeveloped—a mixture of swamp, sand, and scrubby trees—but it had two significant advantages: it was easily accessible to the heart of the city and it lay along the lake. The latter was extremely important, for Olmsted and Codman felt that an international exposition honoring Christopher Columbus must have water as its central element. Now, at the very beginning, they made possible that shimmering assemblage of formal pools, canals, and lagoons which, more than any other single factor, was to make the Columbian Exposition memorable.

Meanwhile, Root had found a worthy architectural model for Chicago. The nation's last fair, the Philadelphia Centennial Exposition of 1876, had become a byword for tasteless vulgarity. But in 1889 France had astonished the world with its *Exposition Universelle.* Root went to Paris to study the Exposition in detail and returned filled with admiration for the daring 360-foot span of Ferdinand Dutert's iron-and-glass Galerie des Machines and for its centerpiece, Gustave Eiffel's elegant, soaring 1000-foot tower. Chicago's fair, too, would display modern technology with style and panache. As Root's sister-in-law, the poet Harriet Monroe, wrote in her biography of him:

> . . . it should be a great, joyous, luxuriant midsummer efflorescence,
> born to bloom for an hour and perish—a splendid buoyant thing,
> flaunting its gay colors between the shifting blues of sky and lake
> exultantly, prodigally.

It would, in essence, be a reflection of the Chicago School and of the vibrant city that had nurtured it.

Though Root felt that the fair should be, above all, an expression of the heartland, he believed just as strongly that architects from other sections of the country should participate. In line with this he sent out invitations to Richard M. Hunt, to McKim, Mead, and White, and to George B. Post, all of New York; to Peabody and Stearns of Boston; as well as to Van Brunt and Howe of Kansas City. Following guidelines set down by Root, these architects would be allowed to design a circle of buildings around the Court of Honor. All the fair's other structures would be allocated to Chicagoans.

Ever since he had begun his task, John Root had driven himself at a terrible pace. Not only had he been traveling almost constantly, drawing and redrawing plans, speaking to business and civic groups, and personally guiding important visitors over the fair's bleak, windswept site, but he had been attempting to carry on the work of his own busy office. He was, in fact, exhausted. Just as all of his efforts were beginning to bear fruit, on the very day the architects of the fair were to meet, John Root became ill. That night his ailment was diagnosed as pneumonia, and four days later, on January 15, 1891, he was dead. Root had been the ideal spokesman for the inland architects; more than any other man, he possessed a true vision of what a fair held in Chicago should be. Harriet Monroe expressed his hopes:

> He wished to offer to the older nations a proof of new forces, new ideals,
> not yet developed and completed, but full of power and prophetic
> charm. He wished to express our militant democracy as he felt it, pausing
> after victory for a song of triumph before taking up its onward march.

Now there would be no proof of new forces, no vivid expression of democracy. After Root's death, Daniel Burnham assumed command, and Burnham was a man with little feeling for such ideals. As he told Louis Sullivan, this was a time "to work up a big business, to handle big things, deal with big businessmen." Sullivan had been shocked by these words, but Burnham, like a hound sniffing the air, had caught the correct scent. The egalitarian age of Lincoln had been succeeded by the era of the trusts, whose monopolies in sugar, oil, steel, coal, beef, and even ice created two nations within the Republic, one of capitalists and one of workers. Burnham was aware that Chicago itself had ceased to resist the long arm of eastern monopoly. A Philadelphian, Charles Tyson Yerkes, with the backing of the traction magnate Peter A. B. Widener, had taken over the city's streetcar system. In 1889 the important grain elevator company of Munger, Wheeler had been bought by an English syndicate. More and more New Yorkers and New Englanders sat on the boards of Chicago's banks and owned its choice real estate; the latter development was vividly illustrated in 1890 when Hetty Green, "the witch of Wall Street," opened an office in the city. But nothing so starkly revealed the change as the sale of that quintessential Chicago institution, the grand old Union Stock Yards, to a New Jersey corporation. The Yards' new president was no Morris or Armour or Swift, but Mr. Nathaniel Thayer of Boston, Massachusetts.

John Wellborn Root, near the end of his life.

Now the Fair would express this new reality. With a score of brilliant Chicago architects to choose from, Burnham passed over them all, and selected as Root's replacement Charles B. Atwood, a draftsman in the fashionable New York firm of Herter Brothers and a close friend of Richard Morris Hunt. If one had to choose a moment when the seed was planted which grew into Chicago's Second City complex, this is that moment. The Fair, which was to proclaim to the world in blazing colors the ideals of the heartland metropolis, was transformed by that act into a gleaming white advertisement of eastern taste. Atwood himself built the Palace of Fine Arts; Hunt the Central Administration Building; McKim, Mead, and White the Agricultural Pavilion; Peabody and Stearns the Machinery Hall; Van Brunt and Howe the Electricity Building; George B. Post the 30-acre Manufactures and Liberal Arts Building.

The central figure in the decision to make the official architecture of the Fair Beaux Arts and eschew the more rugged style developed in Chicago out of Henry Hobson Richardson's Romanesque Revival was Richard Morris Hunt. Hunt had, in 1845, become the first American to enter the architecture section of Paris's prestigious École des Beaux-Arts. There he had absorbed the École's dictum that the classical was the ultimate expression of the beautiful in architecture, as well as the school's enthusiastic acceptance of modern construction methods and materials such as iron and steel. By the time that Hunt was chosen chairman of the Fair's board of architects his prestige was enormous. He had designed, among other things, the base of the Statue of Liberty, been president of the American Institute of Architects, and was, in the words of Dankmar Adler, "The leader of the profession of architecture in America." But there was an additional and practical reason behind the choice of the Beaux Arts style. The Fair's architects began meeting only in February of 1891, giving them but two years to complete their gigantic task. It was Hunt who argued that the Fair could rise most quickly by giving its buildings skeletons of iron and steel and covering them with staff—a mixture of inexpensive plaster of Paris and hemp fibers—which could then be molded into any form. The classical Beaux Arts style, Hunt added, with its ready repertory of columns, pilasters, and cornices, would lend itself to the process better than any other style. Painted white, he noted, it would resemble marble, Beaux Arts architects' favorite material.

Indeed the Fair can be viewed as a paradigm of the teaching of the École des Beaux-Arts that while Athens' Parthenon and Rome's Pantheon and the Renaissance buildings of Bramante exemplified the ultimate expression of beauty, architects must also embrace the modern world of the elevator and the rivet. So many craftsmen were needed to give everything just the right pseudo-classical cast that the sculptor Augustus Saint-Gaudens seized

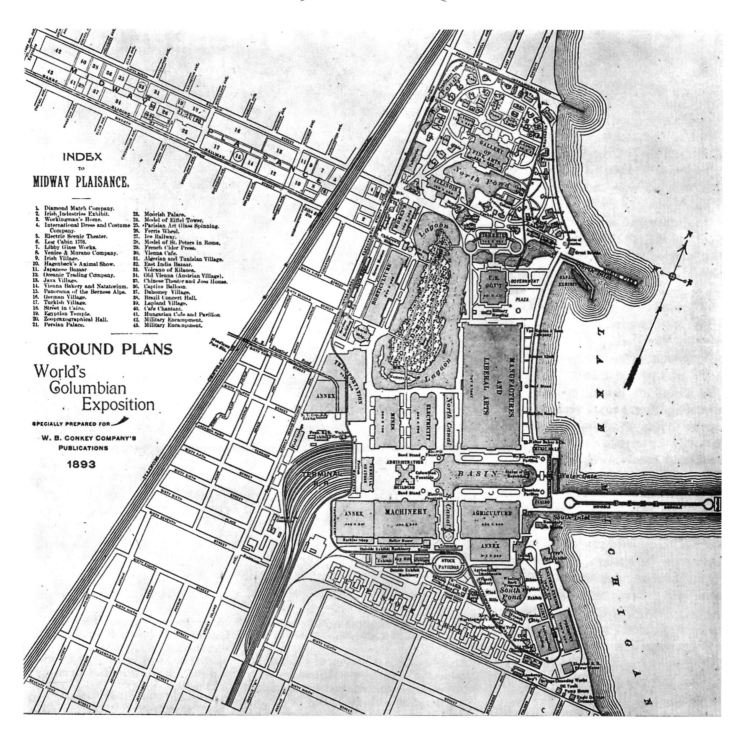

INDEX

TO

MIDWAY PLAISANCE.

1. Diamond Match Company.
2. Irish Industries Exhibit.
3. Workingman's Home.
4. International Dress and Costume Company.
5. Electric Scenic Theater.
6. Log Cabin 1776.
7. Libby Glass Works.
8. Venice & Murano Company.
9. Irish Village.
10. Hagenbeck's Animal Show.
11. Japanese Bazaar.
12. Oceanic Trading Company.
13. Java Village.
14. Vienna Bakery and Natatorium.
15. Panorama of the Bernese Alps.
16. German Village.
17. Turkish Village.
18. Street in Cairo.
19. Egyptian Temple.
20. Zooprazographical Hall.
21. Persian Palace.

22. Moorish Palace.
23. Model of Eiffel Tower.
24. Parisian Art Glass Spinning.
25. Ferris Wheel.
26. Ice Railway.
27. Model of St. Peters in Rome.
28. French Cider Press.
29. Vienna Cafe.
30. Algerian and Tunisian Village.
31. East India Bazaar.
32. Volcano of Kilauea.
33. Old Vienna (Austrian Village).
34. Chinese Theater and Joss House.
35. Captive Balloon.
36. Dahomey Village.
37. Brazil Concert Hall.
38. Lapland Village.
39. Cafe Chantant.
40. Hungarian Cafe and Pavilion.
41. Military Encampment.
42. Military Encampment.

GROUND PLANS
World's
Columbian
Exposition

SPECIALLY PREPARED FOR

W. B. CONKEY COMPANY'S
PUBLICATIONS

1893

Daniel Burnham and cried, "Look here, old fellow, do you realize that this is the greatest meeting of artists since the fifteenth century?" A close look at Frederick MacMonnies' fountain, which one wag said resembled nothing so much as eight parlormaids attempting desperately to sweep the water out of the lagoon while their mistress sat imperiously above them on a precariously placed chair, might make one question Saint-Gaudens' enthusiasm, but he undoubtedly sounded convincing to Burnham.

Two structures broke the Fair's Beaux Arts pattern. Henry Ives Cobb, who had built a castle for Potter Palmer on Lake Shore Drive, designed an imaginative assemblage of circular pavilions containing aquariums and angling displays for the fisheries exhibit. And Adler and Sullivan made the centerpiece of their exotic Transportation Building a bright, welcoming door of carved arabesques sheathed in silver and gold. It alone was true to Root's dream, the one "joyous, luxuriant midsummer efflorescence" in the White City.

Nevertheless, the Columbian Exposition was a titanic achievement for a municipality which had been pronounced dead scarcely twenty years before. Chicago had every reason to be proud when, on May 1, 1893, Grover Cleveland—in the presence of Mayor Harrison; the Infanta Eulalia representing the successors of Ferdinand and Isabella; the Duke of Veragua, who claimed descent from the Discoverer himself; and an assembled throng of about one million—officially opened the fair. As the President touched a golden telegraph key, ten thousand electric lights flashed on, the sprays of a dozen fountains shot into the air, a hundred flags unfurled, Theodore Thomas's orchestra struck up the "Columbian March," and over on the Midway the giant Ferris Wheel, the first in America, and Little Egypt simultaneously began their gyrations. In a country where few had ever seen a finished town and almost none had beheld outdoor electric illumination, the White City seemed a miracle, a paradise complete.

Foreign visitors also were impressed. William Stead, the English editor of the influential *Review of Reviews,* whose book, *If Christ Came to Chicago!,* is one of the most interesting studies of the city of the '90s, began his four-month stay by going to the fair. His praise was unqualified:

> Never before have I realized the effect which could be produced by architecture. The Court of Honour, with its palaces surrounding the great fountain, the slender columns of the peristyle . . . and the golden dome of the Administration Building, formed a picture the like of which the world has not seen before.

The Fair brought people to Chicago from the far corners of the world. An Indian, Mulji Devji Vedant, writing in the *Asiatic Review,* was no less enthusiastic than Stead:

> To me the World's Fair presented a spectacle that exceeded all my expectations of grandeur. The majestic *White City* where poverty has no place to live, exercises over the mind such a charm, that its defects, like the dark spots of the sun, are invisible to the naked eye, owing to the great halo of lustre that pervades throughout.

There was one man who saw the dark spots. Louis Sullivan, already an incipient alcoholic and more and more exhibiting those personality disturbances which, two years later, would lead to the disastrous dissolution of his partnership with Adler, saw the Columbian Exposition as the death knell of the democratic architecture he hoped for. In his *The Autobiography of an Idea,* he recalled:

> These crowds were astonished. They beheld what was for them an amazing revelation of the architectural art, of which previously they in comparison had known nothing. To them it was a veritable Apocalypse, a message inspired from on high. Upon it their imagination shaped new ideals. They went away, spreading again over the land, returning to their homes, each one of them carrying in the soul the shadow of the white cloud. . . . They departed joyously, carriers of contagion, unaware that what they had beheld and believed to be truth was to prove, in historic fact, an appalling calamity.

The millions who came to the Fair would indeed carry the example of the White City across the land. It would be imitated in a thousand museums and libraries and

The main exhibition grounds of the 1893 World's Fair covered the area from Lake Michigan to Cottage Grove Avenue and from 56th Street to 67th Street. The design of the grounds was the last major work of Frederick Law Olmsted, the landscape architect responsible for New York's Central Park. After the Fair closed, the site became Jackson Park. The Midway Plaisance, which stretched a mile to Cottage Grove Avenue, was the exhibition's entertainment section, reserved for such attractions as a reproduction of Ireland's Blarney Castle, the streets of Cairo, replete with a live camel, and the Ferris Wheel. Many visitors to the Midway took time to inspect the new, refounded University of Chicago which was rising alongside it. Because of its stone Gothic buildings, the University was deemed the "Gray City" as opposed to the Fair's "White City."

courthouses whose monumental stairways, gargantuan columns, and echoing halls would be a sincere flattery to the shimmering mirage on the shores of Lake Michigan. For Sullivan, the compliment brought no joy. "The damage wrought by the World's Fair," he said prophetically, "will last for half a century."

Though Sullivan would excoriate the Fair as a kind of plague spreading across the nation, there were inescapably practical reasons for the triumph of the Beaux Arts style. One of them is embedded in Daniel Burnham's famous words: "Make No Little Plans!" Burnham would, after the Fair, make large plans for Washington, D. C., Cleveland, San Francisco, and most notably, for Chicago. He understood that the burgeoning American metropolises, if they were to provide attractive settings for their citizens, needed some careful urban planning. The First Chicago School, in its splendid proclamation of American individuality, built structures which were essentially unrelated one to another. Their skyscrapers were like those tall keeps which noble Italian families in towns such as San Gimignano built in the Middle Ages for their protection. The École, on the other hand, could summon up the great example of Baron Haussmann's planning for nineteenth-century Paris, where broad, straight thoroughfares led to perfectly sited structures such as the Opera. Thus the Beaux Arts and its satellite, the City Beautiful movement, could easily provide American cities with boulevards and parks and public squares.

In addition, while the Beaux Arts style could call upon the rich panoply of classical statues and columns and porticos and domes with which to make it inescapably evident that a structure was a museum or a library or a city hall, the First Chicago School never developed a readily readable vocabulary for civic structures. Typically, Burnham & Root's 1885 Art Institute might have been a clubhouse or a school. Thus when a new Art Institute was built in 1893, Chicago turned to the Boston firm of Shepley, Rutan & Coolidge to produce an edifice which, in its Italian Renaissance form, inescapably proclaimed its purpose.

The make-believe world of the Columbian Exposition ended even before the gates shut, for in the Fair's final hours Mayor Harrison was assassinated by a demented job-seeker. The act heralded bad times to follow. The closing of the Fair found the United States in the worst business depression of the nineteenth century, and Chicago, flooded with men who had flocked to the Columbian boomtown, was particularly hard hit. Hundreds slept in the corridors of the County Building; thousands were saved from starvation by the saloons' free lunches.

The city's workers were not prepared to accept the situation without protest. Chicago was the center of labor union organizing in the United States; a Chicago poem had become the anthem of the all-important Eight-Hour Day movement:

> We mean to make things over, we are tired of toil for naught,
> With but bare enough to live upon, and ne'er an hour for thought;
> We want to feel the sunshine, and we want to smell the flowers,
> We are sure that God has willed it, and we mean to have eight hours.

The first great confrontation had come in 1886 in Haymarket Square. An orderly meeting of workers, listening to speeches by anarchists and others protesting the shooting of six strikers who had demanded an eight-hour day from the McCormick Reaper Works, was charged by a phalanx of 200 policemen. Someone—never identified—threw a bomb into the midst of the police. Instantly there was a barrage of pistol shots from both sides, killing outright one policeman and one civilian. Eventually, seven more officers died from their wounds. During the hysteria that followed, eight anarchist leaders were brought to trial and four were hanged on the tenuous charge of inciting to violence. Illinois's new

Democratic governor, John Peter Altgeld, had just pardoned those anarchists still in prison in 1893 when he had to deal with a far greater conflict.

The worsening economic situation was being felt with appalling sharpness in George Pullman's model town. With the demand for railroad cars declining, Pullman had reduced his workforce, shortened hours, and cut wages by 25 percent while refusing to lower rents in his company-owned houses. In 1894, his desperate employees joined Eugene Debs's American Railway Union and there soon followed a nationwide boycott in which railway workers refused to handle Pullman cars. Pullman demanded that the Governor ask for federal troops to break the strike, but Altgeld replied that since there had been no violence he had no legal grounds for such a request. Pullman then appealed directly to President Grover Cleveland, and on July 2, 1894, Cleveland, swayed by arguments that the strike was affecting the United States Post Office and the federal courts, ordered the troops to Chicago. The Railway Union was temporarily smashed, Debs was arrested for conspiracy, and a young lawyer who stepped forward to defend him, Clarence Darrow, began his magnificent career on behalf of the poor, the oppressed, and the unpopular.

These sounds of distant battle rarely intruded into the drawing rooms of Chicago's millionaires, who now began living on such a scale that, for the next half century, "Chicago packing fortune" and "Chicago dry-goods fortune" became, in American and English fiction, literary shorthand for limitless wealth. Along Prairie Avenue on the South Side the very rich dwelt in a proximity the likes of which could be found only in the upper reaches of New York's Fifth Avenue. There, side by side, stood the mansions of George Pullman, Philip D. Armour, John J. Glessner of International Harvester, William B. Kimball of pianos, and Marshall Field, whose dwelling by Richard Morris Hunt was the first in the city to be electrically lit. Field's former partner, Levi Z. Leiter, gave society something to talk about in 1895 when his daughter, Mary Victoria, married George Nathaniel Curzon, Marquess of Kedleston and future viceroy of India. The bride's father sweetened the deal by presenting the happy couple with $700,000 in cash and a guaranteed annual income of $30,000. Field too could be magnificent on occasion, as when he threw a $75,000 costume ball for his son, Marshall Field, Jr., and his daughter Ethel. Gilbert and Sullivan's *Mikado* was very much the rage just then, and so everyone was asked to come *à la Orientale*. As a final fillip, Field had James McNeill Whistler design the party favors.

All the magnificence was not on the South Side. North of the Loop, near the old

Water Tower, the real estate tycoons John V. and Charles B. Farwell lived in brotherly harmony next door to one another. Charles's mansion, by the firm of Treat and Foltz, was in the popular Queen Anne style and appropriately baronial as befitted a United States senator at whose table Generals Grant and Sheridan had dined. Charles's special passion was rare sixteenth-century books, and his library contained one of the world's half dozen best collections. But when it came to books, Charles Farwell was no match for the Bordens, farther north at the corner of Lake Shore Drive and Bellevue Place. The Bordens not only read books, they wrote them. William Borden, a lawyer and mining engineer who had made a fortune in the Leadville, Colorado, strike, had proclaimed his good luck by having Hunt run up for him an impressive limestone French chateau. His daughter Mary became a well-known novelist—*Woman with White Eyes, Sarah Defiant, Flamingo;* his son John wrote about his Arctic Circle explorations; his second wife Courtney penned *Adventures in a Man's World;* while a granddaughter became a leading patron of *Poetry* magazine and the wife of America's most literate twentieth-century politician, Adlai Stevenson.

But if Chicago had a Buckingham Palace in these years it was without doubt the crenelated "Norman" castle Henry Ives Cobb and Charles Sumner Frost built at 1350 Lake Shore Drive. For here dwelt Chicago's queen, Bertha Honoré Palmer, intelligent, handsome, awesomely energetic. Arrayed in her famous pearls and wearing a diamond tiara, she seemed more regal than royalty, especially, Chicagoans noted, when, during the Fair, she returned the haughty snubs of the Spanish Infanta with charm and good manners. Mrs. Palmer could, with equal ease, handle real estate investments, give dinner parties that delighted everyone from President McKinley to struggling artists, and persuade Mary Cassatt to paint the murals for the Columbian Exposition's Woman's Building. One of the reasons Mrs. Palmer chose Cassatt to paint a tympanum was to popularize the artist's work in America, for though Cassatt had been born in the United States, she had spent most of her adult life in France and was not well known in her native land. The central panel of the mural, which had been executed outside of Paris on canvas and was intended to illustrate the theme of women plucking the fruits of Knowledge and Science, depicted two young women gathering apples in an orchard. It was flanked by smaller panels symbolizing young girls pursuing Fame. Cassatt's work was considered daring because the figures were not shown in classical garb, but wearing contemporary dress. The mural disappeared after the Fair.

Artists were often invited to 1350, for art was Bertha Palmer's passion. The gallery of her castle glowed with more Impressionist paintings than any room in any other private house in the world. When she discovered that among the 600 works sent by the French government for display at the Palace of Art there was not a single Impressionist canvas, she corrected the oversight by loans from her own collection, so that the crowds at the Fair might see pictures by Renoir, Monet, Pissarro, Sisley, and Degas.

Mrs. Palmer's avant-garde taste in painting is indicative of the atmosphere of the city of the '90s. For the next two decades there would be scarcely a movement in architecture, literature, education, or social theory which did not have either its roots or some of its best expression in Chicago. Nowhere was this more evident than at the University of Chicago, which under the leadership of William Rainey Harper had been newly refounded on the Fair's old Midway. There in the '90s John Dewey was conducting classroom experiments and writing his epoch-making *The School and Society,* which would transform American education. There too, Thorstein Veblen was studying Chicago's rich and using his observations for *The Theory of the Leisure Class.*

The university, though, had no monopoly on the city's educational efforts. On Halsted Street on the West Side, Jane Addams had established her "Cathedral of Humanity," Hull-House, the nation's pioneer settlement house. Here she and her fellow

Sculptured decoration over the doorway of the 1908 Mary Crane Nursery of Jane Addams' Hull-House. This photograph was taken March 31, 1963, the day before the property at Halstead and Polk streets was turned over to the city for razing.

workers not only fed and clothed and counseled men, women, and children, but created a dynamic cultural center which they hoped would transform the lives of the inhabitants of the slums around them. Hull-House's theater reached such heights that William Butler Yeats went there to see his verse drama performed; its lecture series became the one platform in America where a Russian anarchist or a union leader or a suffragette could always get a hearing. It was at Hull-House, too, that the concept of the university extension course was born, with law taught by Clarence Darrow, economics by Henry George, and architectural theory by Frank Lloyd Wright, who delivered there his seminal "The Art and Craft of the Machine."

The city's cultural ferment was also reflected in its twenty-five daily newspapers, whose staffs were the envy of editors across the country. None could match the glamour of the *Record,* with George Ade, whose witty "Stories of the Streets and of the Town," illustrated by the deft hand of John T. McCutcheon, proved him one of America's finest humorists, and Eugene Field who alternated between his "Sharps and Flats," one of the first newspaper columns, and his delightful children's poems: "Wynken, Blynken, and Nod" and "Little Boy Blue." The *Record*'s chief competitor for literary laurels was the *Chicago Evening Post.* The *Post* had the incomparable Finley Peter Dunne, "Mr. Dooley," who expressed the uncomplicated but profound wisdom of the Irish living "Back-of-the-Yards."

If the Windy City had a supreme voice in this decade, though, it belonged to a young man named Theodore Dreiser, who arrived from Indiana just as the '90s began. His recollection of the excitement he felt, expressed in *A Book about Myself,* strongly echoes Louis Sullivan:

> It is given to some cities, as to some lands, to suggest romance, and to
> me Chicago did that hourly. It sang, I thought . . . and I was singing
> with it.

Dreiser also worked on a Chicago paper, the *Daily Globe.* His coverage of all aspects of urban life would surface again in the rich details of *Sister Carrie,* for that novel is, in fact, a kind of Baedeker of the metropolis of the '90s. On the train bringing Carrie Meeber to the capital of the Midwest, Drouet, the man who will initiate her into a new world, remarks, "Chicago is getting to be a great town. . . . It's a wonder. You'll find lots to see here." For Dreiser, this was a rare case of understatement.

IT IS NOT SURPRISING that the two most architecturally significant of America's fairs should have been held in Chicago, for, beyond all other American cities, Chicago has expressed its creative drive in building. The World's Columbian Exposition of 1893, organized to celebrate the four-hundredth anniversary of the discovery of the New World, marked the triumph in the United States of the Beaux Arts style. The Century of Progress, held in 1933 on the centennial of Chicago's incorporation as a town, just as clearly signaled the demise of that fashion and the advent of the modern, International style. Both fairs were a tribute to the vigor of the city in which they took place: the first, a wonderland created only two decades after the nation had questioned whether Chicago would rise again from the ashes of the Great Fire; the second, a brave show in the face of the Great Depression.

: THE COLUMBIAN EXPOSITION—1893 :

The Palace of Mechanic Arts, by the distinguished Boston firm of Peabody & Stearns, was said to be inspired by the architecture of Renaissance Spain. This view looking south shows the side of the structure which faced a canal branching from the Fair's Grand Basin. The obelisk, a copy of the Egyptian one in New York's Central Park, was the Columbian monument. The moose is by Edward Kemeys, the sculptor of the familiar bronze lions flanking the entrance to the Art Institute.

ABOVE: *Princess Eulalia, the Infanta of Spain, representing Ferdinand and Isabella and the nation which financed Christopher Columbus's voyage, on the Midway with her escort. The twin pagodas mark the entrance to the Chinese theater, where daily a troop of singers and actors, brought from Peking, presented performances of authentic Chinese opera.*

The heart of the Columbian Exposition was the Court of Honor. Daniel Chester French's statue of the Republic gazes across Frederick Law Olmsted's 1100-foot-long Grand Basin toward Richard Morris Hunt's Administration Building, whose dome, 275 feet in the air, was 57 feet higher than that of the Capitol in Washington. On the left is McKim, Mead & White's Agricultural Building; on the right, George B. Post's Manufactures and Liberal Arts Building. With their uniform cornice line and luminous white color, the majestic structures presented an awesome image to the more than 25 million people who visited the exhibition.

The novelist Theodore Dreiser wrote that no one who saw the Court of Honor would ever forget "its monumental stateliness and simple grandeur. . . ."

OPPOSITE, TOP: *The Exposition's official Beaux Arts style was deemed appropriate for any sort of display. Behind its fanciful façade, William Le Baron Jenney's Horticultural Hall was an expression of the Major's continuing interest in the creative use of iron and steel. The crystal dome of its central pavilion, which housed full-grown palms, tree ferns, and giant cacti, was 187 feet in diameter.*

OPPOSITE, BOTTOM: *One of the Fair's most interesting pavilions, because of what it represented, was the Woman's Building, the large structure in the rear. The inspiration of Mrs. Potter Palmer, President of the Fair's Board of Lady Managers, the 400-foot-long structure was the work of Sophia Hayden, a twenty-one-year-old Bostonian. Not only was the building designed by a female, its interiors were decorated exclusively*

with murals by women artists, including the noted Impressionist Mary Cassatt. One of the features of the Woman's Building was an exhibition of labor-saving devices which would make women's lives easier, including the first gas kitchen range.

BELOW: *A revolutionary feature of the pavilion was the nursery and playroom where mothers visiting the Fair could leave their children.*

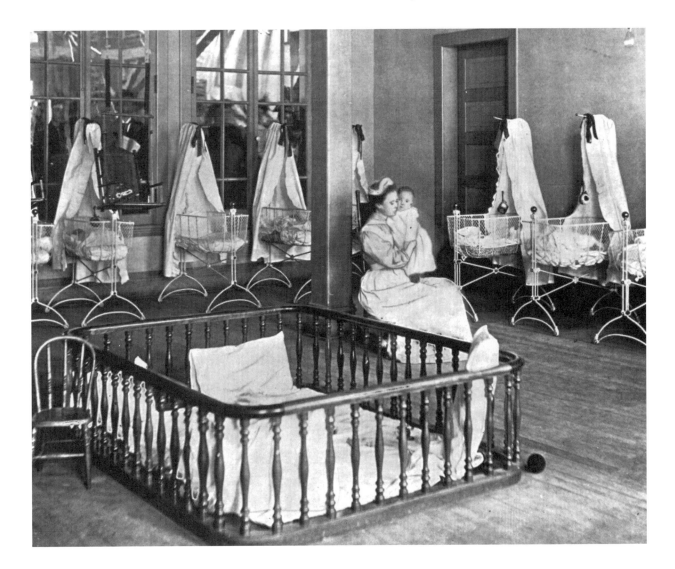

ABOVE: *The Columbian Exposition was a breathtaking mix of staggering engineering and exquisite painting and sculpture. George B. Post's mammoth Manufactures and Liberal Arts Building dominated the Fair's romantic lagoon. The domed structure is the United States government building, while the* circular pavilion in front of it is part of Henry Ives Cobb's Spanish Romanesque Fisheries Building, which strikingly dissented from the Exposition's classical canon.

OPPOSITE, BOTTOM: *The skeleton of the Manufactures and Liberal Arts Building under* construction. Covering 31 acres, it boasted steel arches with an unsupported span of more than 250 yards, which, at their highest point, were more than 212 feet above the ground. The building was reputed to be able to accommodate 300,000 people at one time.

ABOVE, RIGHT: *Among the many sensational exhibits in the Manufactures and Liberal Arts Building was the Yerkes telescope, made by the American company Warner & Swasey, whose 40-inch-diameter lens was the world's largest. After the Fair closed, the telescope was presented to the University of Chicago by Charles T. Yerkes.*

ABOVE: *The entertainment sensation of the Columbian Exposition was the Ferris Wheel, the world's first, designed by George Washington Ferris. The impetus behind the wheel was Daniel Burnham's challenge for Chicago to have something as "daring and unique" as the Eiffel Tower, which had been the sensation at the International Exposition held in Paris in 1889. The inventor of the wheel was a thirty-three-year-old Nebraska native who had been educated at the Rensselaer Polytechnic Institute in Troy, New York. The scale of Ferris's wheel was gargantuan. It was 264 feet (26 stories) high, supported by twin 140-foot steel towers, and powered by a 1000-horsepower steam engine. Its 36 passenger compartments, when fully loaded, held a total of 2160 persons. One was reserved for a band which played, time and again, the Exposition's hit song, "After the Ball Is Over." After the Fair, the wheel eventually reappeared in 1904 in St. Louis to delight visitors to the Louisiana Purchase Exposition. In 1906, following that event, Ferris's captivating wheel was brought to earth by 100 pounds of dynamite.*

OPPOSITE, TOP: *MacMonnies's Columbian Fountain, which stood in the Grand Basin opposite French's statue of the Republic, exemplified the devotion of the artists of the Fair to the human form and to allegory.*

OPPOSITE, BOTTOM: *Adler & Sullivan's Transportation Building, along with Cobb's Fisheries Building, was a striking dissent from the Fair's classical orthodoxy. The structure, covering five and a half acres in addition to four great train sheds holding an astonishing collection of locomotives, was one of the Exposition's largest. It was an eye-catching composition of Sullivan's adored arches and his voluptuous molded decoration along with elements of exotic Moorish design. The Transportation Building's long flanking walls were painted red, orange, yellow, green, and blue, while its main entranceway, "The Golden Door," blazed with gold and silver.*

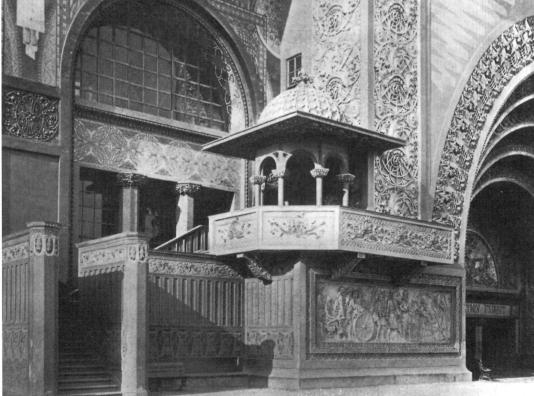

To celebrate the achievement of creating the Columbian Exposition, the city honored itself with "Chicago Day" on October 9, the anniversary of the Great Fire, shortly before the Fair closed. Some 751,000 paid admissions were recorded, a one-day record, and the throng packed the 633-acre Fairgrounds to witness the mammoth parade of military units, floats, and civic organizations. In this photograph, taken on Chicago Day, the Agricultural Building, topped by Augustus Saint-Gaudens' 19-foot statue of Diana, is in the background. The man standing in the electric launch is Harlow Davison Higinbotham, son of Harlow Niles Higinbotham, President of the Fair. After the close of the Exposition, there was a move to preserve the Court of Honor, but after a devastating fire on the night of January 8, 1894, the effort was abandoned.

: A CENTURY OF PROGRESS — 1933 :

IN 1933 CHICAGO DECIDED to hold a fair, the Century of Progress, both to commemorate its centennial as a city and, with unemployment rampant, to give the metropolis an economic and psychological boost. In contrast to the architecture of the 1893 Columbia Exposition, which echoed the glory of Greece and Rome, this Fair was to be an optimistic expression of the present. If the Century of Progress had to be categorized, it was, in its cubist volumes, its bright colors, and its affinity for artificial lighting, Art Deco. (The term "Art Deco" derives from the Éxposition des Arts Decoratifs et Industriels Modernes, held in Paris in 1925.) A number of decorative precedents of the Paris fair were evident in structures at the Century of Progress. One of the most striking was the sunburst motif above the entrance of the pavilion designed by Hiriart, Tribout & Beau for the famed department store, Galeries Lafayette. It boldly reappeared on the Travel and Transportation Building. Economically, the Century of Progress was a success, repaying its costs and ending up with cash in the bank. By the time it closed in October of 1934, more than 35 million people had passed through its turnstiles.

OPPOSITE: *The northern entrance to the Century of Progress at Twelfth Street, now Roosevelt Road, led to the Avenue of Flags, which terminated at the Hall of Science. In the midst of the national self-doubt engendered by the Great Depression one of the buoyant themes of the Fair was the patriotic belief that, for the United States, progress was inevitable.*

ABOVE: *The Sky Ride, which carried passengers from the mainland near Soldier Field to Northerly Island, now the site of Meigs Field, was the Century of Progress's answer to the Columbian Exposition's Ferris Wheel. (The 1909 Plan of Chicago had envisioned a number of man-made islands in Lake Michigan, but Northerly was the only one created.) The semicircular structure on the near right is a portion of the Hall of*

Science, designed by Paul Cret, the Philadelphia architect responsible for Washington's Folger Library. Within the Hall the Exhibition's central theme, applied science, was illustrated with imaginative exhibits, including a ground-breaking one on atomic energy. The striking twin towers on the far left belong to the Federal Building (see page 173).

OPPOSITE: *This night view looking south from the West Tower of the Sky Ride captures one of the notable aspects of the Fair, its dramatic lighting. This was the work of the eminent Austrian-born architect and set designer, Joseph Urban, who was in charge of the Century of Progress's overall design, its color scheme, and its lighting. The beams in the distance emanate from Urban's great Fountain of Light. In the dark mood of the 1930s, the Fair's concentration on light was more than aesthetic. As* The Literary Digest *noted when it discussed the Fair's pavilions: "Bathed in extraordinary effects of light, they signal Chicago's invincible optimism."*

The chronological and conceptual distance between Chicago's 1893 and 1933 fairs was dramatically illustrated by the types of transportation featured at the two events. Adler & Sullivan's Transportation Building at the earlier exposition displayed colossal new steam locomotives; some of the most dramatic exhibitions at the Century of Progress pertained to the automobile.

ABOVE, LEFT: *Among the Fair's finest structures was the white metal and wood pavilion designed by Holabird & Root for the Chrysler Corporation, a dynamic composition consisting of four 125-foot-high pylons centered on an open court. Encircling the pavilion was an elegant two-story glass promenade and exhibition deck. Here seen at night bathed in silver and gold light,* programmed by Joseph Urban and mirrored in its reflecting pool, the structure shows how good modern architecture could be. Architectural Forum *chose the Chrysler Building as the Fair's best, and the distinguished architectural critic Royal Cortissoz, writing in the* New York Herald-Tribune, *said that it "gave you something of that sensation which is evoked by architecture in its real sense." The one building from the 1933 Exposition that should have been saved, it, like the others, was swept away after the Fair closed.*

ABOVE, RIGHT: *The open Walter P. Chrysler Hall at the center of the building.*

ABOVE: *Buckminster Fuller in his Dymaxion car at the Fair. Its three wheels and rear engine, its inventor hoped, would revolutionize automobile design.*

LEFT: *The Century of Progress was a much-needed showcase for American industry in the depths of the Great Depression. In its pavilion the Ford Motor Company dramatically made the point that its automobiles were indeed well built.*

OPPOSITE: *"The individual who goes to Century of Progress hoping to walk in the midst of what he might look upon as classic splendor," Franklin Booth wrote in a brochure on the architecture of the Fair, "will not find the thing that he hopes for." Among the numerous notable pavilions was the Federal Building, whose architects, Arthur Brown of Los Angeles and Edward Bennett of Chicago, surrounded a traditional dome with three soaring concave towers.*

ABOVE: *Ironically, one of the most structurally innovative of the Century of Progress buildings was that for Travel and Transportation, a joint effort of the Exposition's architectural commissioners, including Hubert and Daniel Burnham, Jr., sons of the man who invited Richard Morris Hunt to take charge of the architecture for the 1893 Fair. In order to keep expenses to a minimum, the structure's sheet metal walls were bolted together and its roof hung from a series of cables in the manner of a suspension bridge. The cost was about 14 cents a cubic foot of space.*

RIGHT: *The Communications section of Raymond Hood's Electrical Pavilion, the prototype of the windowless building.*

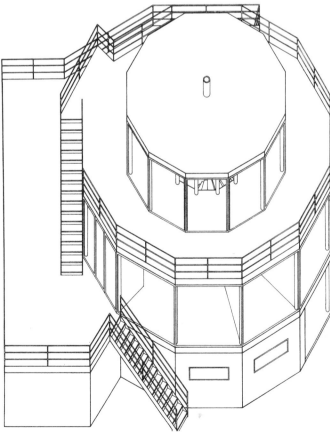

One of the most innovative and influential designs at the Fair was George Fred Keck's House of Tomorrow. The house's glass walls and its sparely furnished rooms, by Chicago interior decorator Mabel Schamberg, did truly lead the way to tomorrow in residential design.

IX

Where Is Athens Now?

AT THE BEGINNING of the new century, Hamlin Garland, who would lovingly celebrate the heartland in *A Son of the Middle Border*, journeyed from Chicago, where he was living, to New York. There he saw powerful forces at work:

> On my return to New York City in January, 1900, I found it in the midst of rebuilding, and I soon discovered that changes in the literary and artistic world were keeping pace with the swift transformations of the business world. New publishing houses were being established and new magazines. . . . The esthetic life of all America was centralizing, with appalling rapidity, on this small island. . . . The inland writer, like the inland publisher, was persuaded that in order to gain a national reputation he must speak from Manhattan.

Chicago's industry was being quickly linked to the East with golden chains, and its architecture now, more often than not, was in the classical manner embraced by the Columbian Exposition. Indeed, by the end of the '90s Chicago's architects had mastered all the nuances of the Beaux Arts style, and their buildings, both in beauty and quality of construction, equaled those of East Coast firms such as McKim, Mead & White and Hunt & Hunt.

Louis Sullivan had good reason to wonder why the bankers did not wear togas. On the site of the old Grand Pacific Hotel, D. H. Burnham & Company, as Burnham & Root was now called, constructed for the Illinois Trust & Savings Bank one of the world's most spectacular money-changing halls. Behind its 100-foot-long façade adorned with 36-foot monolithic Corinthian granite columns, the Illinois's vast banking room reveled in Siena violet, Alps green, and Numidian red marbles, as well as gold leaf, stained glass, and bronze. In 1905, Burnham sought to surpass this *tour de force* with his First National Bank Building. The First National consumed not only tons of sumptuous varicolored stone from Europe and Africa, but 150 railroad cars of pure white Vermont marble as well.

The businessman who cashed his checks and signed his notes amidst such grandeur obviously expected no less when it came to the places where he dined and slept. Two hotels soon catered to this taste: the 1000-room LaSalle of 1908 by Holabird & Roche, and the 500-room Blackstone, built two years later by Marshall & Fox. The first, in the very heart of the Board of Trade district, was constructed in the Louis XIV style, because, as a brochure said, "of the French associations of LaSalle," a theme reiterated time and

OPPOSITE: *By the 1920s Chicago was famous for having "America's most beautiful ballrooms." Not a little of the credit for this was due to Andrew and William Karzas, who built two of the most splendid dance halls ever seen in the United States, the Aragon, on Lawrence Avenue on the North Side, and the Trianon, at 62nd Street and Cottage Grove Avenue on the South Side. The Trianon's 100- by140-foot dance floor was surrounded by marble columns with gilded Corinthian capitals that bore swags of crimson velvet. The constantly changing display of colored light on its domed ceiling anticipated that of New York's Rainbow Room by years. The Trianon opened on December 5, 1922, with a charity ball at which the music was supplied by Paul Whiteman and the Grand March was led by General John J. Pershing. Among the notable bands that played at the Aragon and the Trianon were Jimmy and Tommy Dorsey, Guy Lombardo, Eddy Howard, and Isham Jones. The Trianon closed in 1954 and in 1967 was demolished to clear the ground for an urban renewal project.*

again by the architects' liberal use of the emblems of the Sun King and the seventeenth-century explorer. The LaSalle's Blue Fountain Room became one of the city's most popular after-theater rendezvous; if the play was boring, one could always count on a lift from the Blue Fountain's famed Tango-Banjo Orchestra. On Michigan Avenue near the Congress Hotel and the Auditorium, the Blackstone not only attracted a clientele of successful bankers and lawyers, but also quickly became the preferred locale for Chicago debutante parties. Famed for its food—after World War I it scored a coup by obtaining Kaiser Wilhelm's chief steward as its maître d'hôtel—the Blackstone offered diners a choice of the airy Orangerie, the smart Cafe, or the regal Louis XVI–style dining room where, gazing out over the lake, one could savor champagne and blinis Romanoff.

The city's theaters were also affected by the new taste. And in the infancy of the twentieth century, Chicago was an important theater town, a close second to New York when it came to knowledgeable audiences, elaborate productions, and luxurious playhouses. As the center of the show-business "wheels" that brought drama and vaudeville to the middle third of the nation, it is estimated that there were no less than 10,000 theater people living in Chicago. When not on the road, they found ready employment in stock companies such as the Dearborn, one of the country's best; at theaters such as the Colonial, with its changing headliners like Eddie Cantor; at the Studebaker, where George Ade's plays *The Fair Co-ed,* starring Elsie Janis, and *Peggy from Paris* premiered; at Charles Frohman's Grand Opera House, with its presentations of Mrs. Fiske in *Becky Sharp* and George Arliss in *Disraeli;* at the Blackstone, where Mrs. Patrick Campbell captured the city's lasting affection by her performance in George Bernard Shaw's *Pygmalion.* Eleonora Duse had also accomplished that feat when, standing alone on the Auditorium's mammoth stage, she whispered the lines of her lover, the poet D'Annunzio. But there was one actress whom the city's playgoers cherished above all others. Sarah Bernhardt had won their undying devotion one night in 1891, when, after a performance of *Jeanne d'Arc,* she told the assembled reporters, "Chicago is the pulse of America." In the new century, when she played *L'Aiglon* at the Majestic, a sixty-year-old woman in the

role of Napoleon's teenage son, the crowds filled the theater night after night just to hear the timbre of "the divine Sarah's" magnificent voice.

A dozen new theaters were built in downtown Chicago in these years. Among the handsomest was the Princess on Clark Street, which reminded English visitors of London's Haymarket. The grandest of all, though, was the Illinois on Jackson Boulevard, which opened in January 1900 with Julia Marlowe in Clyde Fitch's patriotic drama, *Barbara Frietchie*. The work of the firm of Wilson & Marshall, the Illinois, with its limestone and granite exterior and a lobby of white Carrara marble set off by turquoise mosaics, was the epitome of the Beaux Arts style. Its rose, ivory, and gold auditorium featured a proscenium arch of genuine mother-of-pearl, and carried through the theme of the theater's name by having four grand boxes each honoring one of the state's famous sons: Stephen A. Douglas, Ulysses S. Grant, and John A. Logan, and—some thought this a bit insensitive—Abraham Lincoln.

Chicagoans desiring a residence in the new fashion could be certain of unfailing good taste from Howard Van Doren Shaw and David Adler. Shaw (1896–1926), who was born in Chicago and worked in the office of Jenney & Mundie, was a truly eclectic architect, designing a South Side Tudor palace for the Edward Morrises; an Arts and Crafts cottage, "Ragdale," for himself, in Lake Forest; an Adam-style residence for the William O. Goodmans on Astor Street; and a mansion echoing the Petit Trianon at Versailles for Eleanor Robinson Countiss on North Lake Shore Drive. Adler (1888–1949), upon graduation from Princeton, followed the prescribed architectural course in Paris and, after he came to Chicago in 1911, produced an *oeuvre* of striking houses in Georgian, Colonial Revival, and French and Italian Renaissance styles for some of Chicago's most prestigious personages: Stanley Field, Albert Lasker, William McCormick Blair, Robert Mandel, and Richard T. Crane. None of his houses surpassed the Louis XIV style *hôtel particulière* he designed for Mr. and Mrs. Joseph Ryerson on Astor Street. A perfectly scaled building, it was often paid the supreme compliment of having visitors ask from what Paris mansion its *boiseries* had come. They had been carved in Chicago.

Yet the city's most spectacular twentieth-century Beaux Arts gesture was not a building. Still enamored with the White City's formal grandeur, Daniel Burnham had, in 1895, begun drawing up a vast scheme which would transfer the concept of the Fair to Chicago itself. Using a phrase popular with Beaux Arts planners, Burnham called his idea "The City Beautiful," and was soon showing his drawings to any civic and business group willing to look. In 1902 he hired a young graduate of the École des Beaux-Arts, Edward H. Bennett, to help refine what Burnham now labeled the "Plan of Chicago." Daniel Burnham was an authentic genius when it came to public relations, and by 1907 he had persuaded the powerful Chicago Commercial Club to assume sponsorship of his plan. Within a year, Burnham had written the report and Bennett had prepared the drawings, which were superbly rendered in color by Gules Guerin. The "Plan of Chicago" was then beautifully bound and presented to the Commercial Club.

Burnham's vision may be summed up by his famed credo, "Make no little plans . . . ." One charge which could never be leveled against Daniel Burnham was that his plan was little. It took in the entire metropolitan area for a radius of sixty miles and swept along the lakefront for some twenty-three miles from the Midway to Wilmette in a dazzling sequence of harbors, piers, parks, lagoons, and man-made islands. Incorporated into Burnham's design was Grant Park, whose design, in 1903, had been awarded to Olmsted Brothers, the successor firm to Frederick Law Olmsted, the man responsible for the landscaping of the Columbian Exposition. Their concept for the Park incorporated elements drawn from André Le Nôtre's gardens at Versailles, as well as the Tuileries and the Place de la Concorde in Paris. Indeed, viewed from the old second-floor lobby of the Auditorium, Grant Park bears an uncanny similarity to the Place de la Concorde.

If Burnham's plan had a major fault it was its insensitivity to the importance of people in a city. Burnham longed to emulate the grand boulevards—St. Germain, Avenue de L'Opéra, Malesherbes—which Baron Georges Haussmann had in the 1850s and 1860s sliced through old Paris for the Emperor Napoleon III. But Burnham did not understand that above their first-floor shops most of the buildings lining Haussmann's boulevards contained apartments, and behind them was densely populated medieval Paris. In the evening, on holidays, the people of Paris became *boulevardiers,* using the broad thoroughfares as urban parks, to window shop, to chat, to stroll, or from the table of a café to enjoy the greatest city pleasure of all, watching the passing show. In contrast, when Burnham turned to the creation of his boulevards he envisioned them lined almost exclusively with commercial and civic structures. His plan helped empty the Loop of people. The lively Water Street Market along the river, Chicago's equivalent of Paris' Les Halles, was demolished to make way for the double-decked Wacker Drive. Thousands were evicted for the widening of Twelfth and other streets.

In some ways, Burnham was the precursor of New York's highway-obsessed Robert Moses, as is revealed in this proud account, by his friend and biographer Charles Moore, of what the Chicago Plan had accomplished in its first ten years:

> Of the improvements made in accordance with his plan, Mr. Burnham
> saw only the beginnings of the widening of Michigan Avenue. . . . During
> the past decade Roosevelt Road (Twelfth Street) has been widened for
> a distance of two miles. . . . A new diagonal, known as Ogden Avenue,
> is being cut from Ashland Avenue to Lincoln Park. . . . The congested
> market area along Water Street is being reconstructed . . . and bond
> issues for the widening of Western and Ashland Avenues and Robey
> Street at a cost of seventeen and a half millions have been voted. . . .

The three outer highway circuits and their connecting radials as recommended by the Plan are complete. . . .

While there can be no doubt that the new Michigan Avenue was a great achievement and that Burnham's scheme markedly improved vehicular circulation in the city, it is not surprising that the cry went up that the Chicago Plan was in reality a scheme to tax the poor to pay for the improvements desired by the rich.

Though the twentieth century witnessed the triumph of the Beaux Arts style, the First Chicago School of Architecture did not expire at once. Its dying was to take fifteen years and those years were to encompass some of its finest achievements. In the very last year of the nineteenth century, Louis Sullivan received one of his most important commissions, a building at the southeast corner of State and Madison streets for the Schlesinger & Mayer Department Store. (The original contact came in the early 1890s through Dankmar Adler, who was related by marriage to the Mayers; after he left the partnership in 1895, Schlesinger & Mayer turned to Sullivan.) The first unit on Madison Street was a mere 60 feet wide and nine stories tall, but in 1903 Sullivan was asked to extend the structure west to the corner and 150 feet south on State Street. (In 1904 while the building was still under construction, Schlesinger & Mayer sold out to Carson Pirie Scott & Co.) As Hugh Morrison in his *Louis Sullivan: Prophet of Modern Architecture* noted: "The Carson Pirie Scott store represents one of the most intelligent solutions of the problem of the large department store that has ever been made." The broad horizontal windows of the upper floors, stretching from one terra-cotta-clad steel column to another to permit as much of the all-important light as possible to penetrate the interior, give the structure a simple cellular elegance which has made it an icon of the proponents of the "International Style." But this restraint is abandoned in the two lower floors, which are sheathed in ornamental iron displaying Sullivanian designs of surpassing beauty. The ironwork—painted dark green over red—surrounds the ground-floor

Frank Lloyd Wright's Midway Gardens, which opened in June 1914 on Cottage Grove Avenue near the University of Chicago, was a handsome illustration of that "cleanly strength" the architect had called for in his famed Hull-House lecture, "The Art and Craft of the Machine." The Midway, whose winter garden is shown here, symbolized in its combination of avant-garde architecture and good music, food, and drink the urbanity of Chicago on the eve of the First World War. Among the musicians who, in the 1920s, made it a place of pilgrimage for devotees of jazz were the legendary "Bix" Beiderbecke and a young Chicagoan who played there in 1924, Benny Goodman. After being used as a garage and car wash, the Midway Gardens was destroyed in 1929. The site is now occupied by a public housing project.

display windows like the frames of precious paintings and vigorously wreathes the curved corner entrance, transforming it into a veritable doorway to Wonderland.

One reason for the splendid execution of the Schlesinger & Mayer decoration was the sure hand of Sullivan's chief designer, George Grant Elmslie, who in 1909 resigned to become a founding partner in the firm of Purcell, Feick & Elmslie. Its first important Chicago commission came in 1912 when it was asked to design a shop and sales office for the Edison Phonograph Company, one of the most advanced and attractive small buildings of its day. Two other disciples of Sullivan, Frank Lloyd Wright and George W. Maher, were building during this period striking, innovative houses. Maher, who had come to Chicago in the 1870s and who had worked with Wright and Elmslie in the 1880s, was a leading member of the Chicago Arts and Crafts Society, which encouraged fresh approaches to all aspects of design—furniture, stained glass, and fabrics, as well as architecture. In 1901 he designed for James A. Patten in Evanston an enormous granite house which, with its massive solidity, helped inaugurate a style which swept across the Midwest.

These were also the years when Wright designed some of his most accomplished houses, dwellings which in their emphatic horizontality, ground-hugging profile, and low roof lines emphasized by deep eaves were, in the words of the architectural critic Thomas Tallmadge, "an absolute result of the inspiration of the prairie." These were houses for civilized citizens of a republic, houses whose open plan emphasized the informality of the New World, houses with furniture of their own time, houses where Wright substituted the word "playroom" for "music room" because they were not chambers for concerts by visiting artists but rooms in which a family could make music together. The mature period of the Prairie House began in 1902, and after that Wright launched his structures like the perfectly crafted ships they so often resembled, their names being identification enough: the Heurtley, the Coonley, the Willitts, the Cheney, the Robie.

In 1913 Wright was asked to design a complex that in many ways symbolized the extraordinary level of urban life that existed in Chicago just before the First World War. The Midway Gardens, a pleasure ground near the University, was one of the Chicago School's most spectacular accomplishments, combining an open air cafe, a bandshell, and a large winter garden, all decorated with tradition-shattering Cubist sculptures. The caliber of entertainment at the Midway Gardens was high indeed: a sixty-member symphony orchestra under Theodore Thomas's associate Max Bendix, guest performers such as the Russian ballerina Anna Pavlova, and, in the winter garden, one of the city's leading dance bands. There was superb food prepared under the direction of John Vogelsang, whose restaurant on Madison Street had been celebrated by Eugene Field, a marvelous wine cellar, and no less than six brands of imported German beer. The Midway was a delightful expression of the Chicago School's commitment to public architecture for public pleasure. Henry-Russell Hitchcock states in his study *In the Nature of Materials* the essential intention of the Gardens' architect:

> Here Wright . . . aimed at public instead of private luxury, but not at the
> stodgy splendours of contemporary urban hotels and restaurants. Instead
> he sought a festive gaiety . . . a fresh open fantasia.

How well he succeeded is attested to by Edna Ferber, who used the Midway as a setting for her novel *The Girls:*

> It was deliciously cool there in that great unroofed space. There was
> even a breeze, miraculously caught within the four walls of the Garden.
> They ordered iced drinks. There was a revue between the general

> dancing numbers. . . . A row of slim trees showed a fairy frieze above
> the tiled balcony.

The Midway Gardens was just one of the places in which to find the writers who now sprouted in Chicago with the astonishing swiftness of skyscrapers in the '90s. Another spot was Maurice's on West Madison Street, affectionately mentioned by John Gunther in his first novel, *The Red Pavilion.* There was the Tip Top Inn atop the Pullman Building on Michigan Avenue, whose seafood dishes were a weakness of Floyd Dell. Dell, the literary editor of the *Evening Post,* was lionized after the appearance in 1920 of his novel *Moon-Calf,* a realistic semiautobiographical portrayal of the life of a young journalist who, as the story ends, decides to strike out from a small Illinois town for the Windy City: "But his tramping steps went to the rhythm of a word that said itself over and over again in his mind: 'Chicago! Chicago!'" The granddaddy of literary meeting places, however, was Schlogl's *weinstube* on North Wells Street. At its famed round table gathered the men who were giving America a new voice: Sherwood Anderson, Carl Sandburg, Robert Herrick, Edgar Lee Masters, Ben Hecht, Ring Lardner. So numerous did writers become in Chicago during these years that H. L. Mencken felt the city had annexed to itself the whole field of American letters:

> In Chicago there is the mysterious something that makes for individuality, personality, charm; in Chicago a spirit broods upon the face of the waters. Find a writer who is undubitably an American in every pulse-beat, an American who has something new and peculiarly American to say and who says it in an unmistakably American way, and nine times out of ten you will find that he has some sort of connection with the gargantuan abattoir by Lake Michigan — that he was bred there, or got his start there, or passed through there in the days when he was young and tender.

Most of the writers earned their daily bread as newspaper reporters, though Masters was, briefly, Clarence Darrow's law partner and Sherwood Anderson wrote advertising copy. But their creative lives, almost without exception, circled around two remarkable women: Harriet Monroe and Margaret Anderson. From a distinguished Chicago family — her father had been a close friend of Senator Douglas — Harriet Monroe had, by the turn of the century, carved out for herself an impressive career. She had written an excellent biography of John Wellborn Root, her brother-in-law, worked as an art critic on the *Tribune,* and composed the official odes for the opening of both the Auditorium and the Columbian Exposition. Poetry, though, was always her first love, and now, determined that poets should have a proper publication in which to display their talents, she set about raising money from people as diverse as Mrs. Potter Palmer and Samuel Insull, the utilities magnate, for a magazine which would print nothing but verse. The first issue of what she called simply *Poetry* appeared in October of 1912, and it soon numbered among its contributors William Butler Yeats, Rabindranath Tagore, and T. S. Eliot.

Harriet Monroe was particularly proud of *Poetry*'s encouragement of three poets from Illinois: Vachel Lindsay, Carl Sandburg, and Edgar Lee Masters. Lindsay became famous for his dramatic recitations, accompanied by drums, banjos, and tambourines, of his poems, including "General William Booth Enters Into Heaven," his paean to the founder of the Salvation Army. Among its lines:

The hosts were sandaled, and their wings were fire!
But their noise played havoc with the angel-choir.

Carl Sandburg's "Chicago" instantly became a kind of municipal anthem, the poem none dared omit when writing about the Windy City:

Hog Butcher for the World,
Tool Maker, Stacker of Wheat,
Player with Railroads and the Nation's Freight Handler;
Stormy, husky, brawling,
City of the Big Shoulders:

With *Spoon River Anthology,* Masters crafted one of the heartland's supreme epics, while his "Chicago" is a haunting evocation of the city:

Skyscrapers, helmeted, stand sentinel
Amid the obscuring fumes of coal and coke,
Raised by enchantment out of the sand and bog.
This sky-line, the Sierras of the lake . . .

Masters, Sandburg, and Lindsay also published in *The Little Review,* the magazine edited by the city's other phenomenal woman, Margaret Anderson. Beautiful and brilliant, Anderson swept into town from Columbus, Indiana, in 1912, and Chicago was never quite the same again. The description of her reaction to the city in her autobiography, *My Thirty Years' War,* echoes the excitement felt by Dreiser and Sullivan:

Chicago: enchanted ground to me from the moment Lake Michigan
entered the train windows. I would make my beautiful life here. A city
without a lake wouldn't have done.

After a stint as a reviewer for the *Evening Post* and clerking in the bookshop Frank Lloyd Wright had designed in the Fine Arts Building—as the Studebaker Building was now called—Margaret Anderson decided that she would found a magazine which would, in her words, "make no compromise with public taste." She undoubtedly got some pointers from her boss, Francis Brown, who in the back room of his bookshop was editing the distinguished literary publication, *The Dial.* That Margaret Anderson meant what she said became evident when the first issue of *The Little Review* appeared in March of 1914. Pulling no punches, she came out strongly in support of Margaret Sanger and birth control and defended the well-known anarchist Emma Goldman. Her literary taste was equally as bold, and she broke new ground by publishing Ezra Pound, Hart Crane, and some of the short stories of Sherwood Anderson's *Winesburg, Ohio.*

Strangely, at the very moment of its full flowering, there came a note of hesitation, as though the city's energy, its matchless vigor, was waning. No doubt this feeling was heightened by the awareness that hands so long at the helm were no longer there. George Pullman had died in 1897, P. D. Armour in 1901, Potter Palmer in 1902, Gustavus Swift in 1903, Marshall Field in 1906, Nelson Morris in 1907. In sharp contrast to the era when the old oligarchy took a hand in running Chicago and put up mayors like William Ogden, John Wentworth, and Joseph Medill, the new style was to turn over the city's political life to the Democratic and Republican machines. The mind of the new oligarchy is revealed in the story that Chicago was at this time offered the infant auto industry. After all, it was closer to the iron and coal, closer to the center of the country, than was Detroit. But its industrial barons said no. They didn't want the competition for workers from another giant. That is not the answer William Ogden or Potter Palmer would have given.

The changed atmosphere was felt severely by Chicago's architects. Though Sullivan lived until 1924, the Schlesinger & Mayer Store was his last important Chicago work. For the next quarter-century he found his patrons in towns such as Owatonna, Minnesota, and Grinnell, Iowa. The Edison Shop brought Purcell, Feick, & Elmslie not a single serious Chicago job; Minneapolis was the beneficiary of the firm's discerning eye. George Maher was to die in obscurity in 1926, and after the Midway Gardens, Frank Lloyd Wright built in the West, in the South, in the East, and in Japan, but never again in the city that had first nurtured his genius.

The power of New York, which Hamlin Garland had perceived at the beginning of the century, now became irresistible to Chicago's writers. It was made even more so by the fact that the spacious days of the Chicago press were ended by the cut-throat competition brought on by the "yellow journalism" of William Randolph Hearst's *Evening American* and *Herald & Examiner,* which ultimately absorbed many of the fine old papers. The city exported its best. Dreiser had already gone. Hemingway, born in suburban Oak Park, wouldn't pause long enough to use Chicago as the setting for a single story. Gunther and Ferber left; Sandburg and Masters; Floyd Dell and Ring Lardner. In 1917, Margaret Anderson decided that it was time to take *The Little Review* to New York:

This 1913 photograph shows Hamlin Garland (standing, right) at the Cliff Dwellers Club with, left to right, Chicago Tribune *"A Line o' Type or Two" columnist Bert Leston Taylor, Edwin Markham, and Theodore Dreiser.*

> I told everyone good-by—including the Fine Arts Building. I went
> to walk through its corridors which always seemed to me filled
> with flowers—its shops, which gave me the emotion of a perpetual
> Christmas. Last of all I went to a symphony concert. Coming back to
> the Fine Arts Building I met Ben Hecht.
>   After you have gone, he announced, I'm going to have an electric
> sign put across the building: WHERE IS ATHENS NOW?

Soon Hecht and MacArthur too would be in New York. Later, with *The Front Page,* they would preserve forever their Chicago salad days. In *Charlie,* his biography of MacArthur, Hecht remembered that his partner still pined for the Windy City, even though he was working for his old Chicago boss, the superb editor Walter Howey:

> "You've got to love a town to be a reporter in it," MacArthur said to the
> persistent Howey, "and baby, I don't love."
>   "For God's sake," said Howey. "Do you want to go back to Chicago?"
>   "No," said MacArthur. "That's over. But there's no place else."

─||| PLACES OF ENTERTAINMENT |||─

"A YEAR CAROL SPENT IN CHICAGO. . . . She reveled in the Art Institute, in symphonies and violin recitals and chamber music, in the theater and classic dancing."—Sinclair Lewis, *Main Street.* An unfailing test of whether a city is truly alive is the quality of public entertainment it offers its inhabitants. The forms that entertainment might take are myriad: an evening of theater or dancing, a well-served meal in an interesting setting, a film viewed in an opulent auditorium. A vast complex of buildings and people may call itself a city, but without these places of public entertainment, it is but that, a mere complex of buildings and people.

OPPOSITE: *After the 1857 McVicker's Theatre was destroyed in the Great Fire, McVicker raised a grander theater on the same site.*

ABOVE: *In 1884 and 1885 Adler and Sullivan extensively remodeled this house, but their work was destroyed when the theater was gutted by a fire in 1890. Adler and Sullivan were called in again to rebuild the structure. Sullivan designed magnificent interiors for the theatre and lobby, while Adler ingeniously added offices to the top and front of the building. This legitimate McVicker's Theatre was demolished in 1925 and replaced by a movie palace, also named McVicker's.*

LEFT: *As part of the 1884–1885 remodeling, Louis Sullivan covered the walls and ceiling of McVicker's vestibule with bright stenciling in a pattern which included lotuslike blossoms, seed pods, and leaves.*

Adler and Sullivan's first collaboration, the 1900-seat Central Music Hall, completed in 1879, stood at the southeast corner of State and Randolph streets. Among the tenants of the edifice's seventy offices was the Chicago Musical College, presided over by Dr. Florenz Ziegfeld, father of the glorifier of the American girl.

The vaguely ecclesiastical cast given to the hall by its stained glass windows and Gothic Revival seating was no accident. They had been suggested by the Reverend David Swing, a popular nondenominational minister who preached in the hall on Sundays. The Central Music Hall's marvelous acoustics made it nation-

ally famous. These were the result of Dankmar Adler giving the floor of the orchestra a greater rise than was required for good sight lines and by the carefully calculated lateral curve of the ceiling. This historic building was demolished in 1900 to make way for the expansion of Marshall Field's Department Store.

Randolph Street, Chicago's main theater thoroughfare, in 1900. On the right are the columns of James J. Egan's City and County Building. Starting on the left are Powers' Theatre, which opened as Hooley's the year after the Great Fire, and became Powers in 1898; the

Sherman House, the city's favorite stopping place for show people; Burnham & Root's round-bayed Ashland Block, which housed the law firm whose members included Governor John Peter Altgeld, Clarence Darrow, and Edgar Lee Masters. Just visible beyond the

Ashland Block is Adler & Sullivan's flat-topped Schiller Theatre Building, while in the distance is a pointed gable of the Masonic Temple, whose roof garden offered spectacular cabaret. All of these buildings have been razed.

ABOVE, LEFT: *The Schiller Building at 64 West Randolph Street was, after the Auditorium, the supreme example of Adler & Sullivan's brilliant response when called on to design a multiuse structure which included a large theater. The driving force behind the project was Anton Hesing, publisher of Chicago's preeminent German-language newspaper, the* Illinois Staats-Zeitung, *who convinced local German-Americans to back a German opera company and a downtown social and arts club. The presence of the 1300-seat auditorium, which occupied the first six stories*

of the structure, was proclaimed by a frieze of terra-cotta heads of famous German composers and playwrights modeled by Frederick Almenraeder. Above the theater were 342 offices, including the one where, in 1893, Frank Lloyd Wright began his private practice, and two floors of club rooms. The Schiller climaxed in a massive, richly decorated cornice which, in turn, was topped by a cupola. The office tower section of the seventeen-story building— the tallest ever constructed by Adler & Sullivan—eloquently declared Sullivan's conception of the tall building as "proud and soaring."

ABOVE, RIGHT: *The building's stairways and elevator cages were another example of Louis Sullivan's imaginative use of metal. In the early twentieth century the Schiller was bought by the Shubert organization and renamed the Garrick. Though a registered landmark, this gem of the city was smashed by the wrecker's ball in 1960.*

OPPOSITE: *Sullivan ornamented Adler's semicircular arches, which gave the theater its matchless acoustics, with subtle green and gold designs.*

194

OPPOSITE: *Two of the most elegant Beaux Arts theaters of the new century were the Illinois, on Jackson Boulevard between Michigan and Wabash avenues, and the Princess, on Clark Street. The $250,000 Illinois (TOP), which opened in 1900 with the backing of the powerful producer-manager Charles Frohman, was the work of H. R. Wilson and Benjamin Marshall. Later, as the partner of Charles Fox, Marshall was responsible for the Blackstone and the Drake Hotels. The Illinois, the Chicago home of the Ziegfeld Follies, was replaced by a parking*

lot in 1936. The Princess (BOTTOM), where the curtain first rose in 1906, was considered one of the city's best houses for straight drama. The handsome house was designed by the Milwaukee architects Charles Kirchoff and T. L. Rose. In 1941 it, too, gave way to a parking lot.

ABOVE: *One of Chicago's most pleasing and ingenious Beaux Arts designs was that of 1923 by Howard Crane and Kenneth Franzheim for a pair of theaters, the Selwyn and the Harris, on Dearborn Street, just north of Randolph. While the two theaters shared the same cornice*

line, their cream-colored terra-cotta façades subtly differentiated the two buildings. The Harris (LEFT), at 170 North Dearborn, had touches of Italian baroque decoration, while the Selwyn (RIGHT), at 186 North Dearborn, was in a more restrained English Palladian style. After the Second World War both theaters became movie houses. Despite studies in 1980 and 1985 which concluded that the structures were in reasonably good condition and could play a role in reintroducing round-the-clock activity to the Loop, in 1999 these intimate theaters were swept away.

ABOVE: *The auditorium of the Harris Theatre continued the Italian theme of the exterior. Inspired by fifteenth-century Florentine precedents, it possessed* *rich walnut paneling and a ceiling embellished with scarlet and gold. The Harris's interior, so different in feeling from those of Sullivan, reflected the influence* *of the restrained opulence that Beaux Arts architects such as John Carrère and Thomas Hastings had given to their New Theatre in New York in 1909.*

: DINING AND DANCING :

OPPOSITE: *One of Chicago's most romantic dining spots was the German Refectory in Jackson Park, which had been the German* *Government Building at the Columbian Exposition, notable for its 150-foot, onion-domed-crowned tower, romantic half-timbering,* *and bright exterior frescoes. The fairy-tale castle burned in 1920.*

ABOVE: *One of the prime ideals behind Chicago's park system was to give city residents the chance to escape, from time to time, the increasing tempo of urban life into what the great landscape architect Frederick Law Olmsted called places of "passive recreation." But he and Chicago landscape architects like Jens Jensen also recognized the need within the parks for refectories and other venues for inexpensive repasts. (There was, for instance, in Olmsted's Central Park in New York City, a milk bar.) This concept was given delightful concrete reality in the now-vanished High Victorian food stand in Lincoln Park, seen here in 1902.*

OPPOSITE: *"They were sitting at dinner in a private room at Kinsley's, and Aileen, whose color was high, and who was becomingly garbed in metallic-green silk, was looking especially handsome."*
— *Theodore Dreiser,* The Titan.

Kinsley's, one of the city's most fashionable restaurants, reveled in the exotic Moorish façade F. L. Charnley gave it in 1885. The Adams Street restaurant, owned and operated by Herbert M. Kinsley, was a favorite meeting place of Chicago's architects and its popular German Room was the scene of much of the preliminary planning for the Columbian Exposition. Kinsley's was demolished in 1894.

ABOVE: *Henrici's was, despite its Italian-sounding name, Chicago's preeminent German bakery-restaurant from the day Philip Henrici opened it in 1875. In 1895 it moved to 71 West Randolph Street and became the place where, late at night, one was most likely to see Lillian Russell, Ellen Terry, Eva Tanguay, John Barrymore, or other stars who were appearing at the nearby theaters. Though bought by the J. R. Thompson chain in 1929, Henrici's menu continued to be laden with sauerbraten, Wiener schnitzel, and Black Forest chocolate cake. Still flourishing, it was forced to close in August of 1962 to make way for the*

Civic Center. In the last three days Henrici's was open some 22,000 people stood in line to have one final meal in the grand old restaurant.

OPPOSITE, TOP: *Chicago had a penchant for restaurants with exotic architecture, whether it was the Middle European mode of the Old Heidelberg or the English village look of the Stock Yards Inn. Among the most picturesque was Ricketts at 103 East Chicago Avenue, seen here in 1954, which also took its architectural cues from the British Isles. Owned by a family that had begun feeding Chicagoans in 1898, Ricketts (which became*

Ballentines in the late 1950s) was knocked down in the ferocious redevelopment which swept the near North Side in the 1990s. The decade was not kind to the area's once lively dining and night life. Among its victims were the Club Alabam at 747 North Rush Street, where one could grab both a steak and a rambunctious floor show, and Ricardo's, 437 North Rush, with its intriguing paintings by local artists and its memories of Windy City journalists and writers like Ben Hecht and Studs Terkel.

LEFT: *If "beloved" ever applied to a restaurant, it applied to Le Petit Gourmet in the Italian Court on North Michigan Avenue. The original building had been constructed in 1919 by Chester and Raymond Cook, but in 1921, architect Robert DeGolyer imaginatively transformed a waste space into a Mediterranean courtyard. Passing through an arched entrance one entered an inviting complex of offices, apartments, and studios for artists, one of which was occupied by Irene Castle, the internationally famous dancer. Le Petit Gourmet, which had tables in the court in good weather, was established by the widow of poet William Vaughn Moody. The restaurant was often the setting for readings by the contributors to* Poetry Magazine. *The civilized enclave was superseded by an office building in 1969.*

ABOVE: *Chicago was indeed "that toddling town" and loved nothing better than a good dance band. Of them all, few could match King Oliver's Creole Jazz Band, shown here in Chicago in 1922. Its immortal members were, left to right, Johnny Dodds, Baby Dodds, Honoré Dutrey, Louis Armstrong, King Oliver, Lil Hardin (Mrs. Louis Armstrong), and Bill Johnson.*

OPPOSITE, TOP: *The Chez Paree at 610 North Fairbanks Court, operated by Joseph Jacobson* and Mike Fritzel, was Chicago's premier night club from the 1930s through the 1950s. Carved out of an unprepossessing warehouse near Ontario Street, the boite was decorated with a few Art Deco flourishes. In its halcyon days this was the place to catch performances by Lena Horne, Sophie Tucker, and Mae West, always backed by its chorus line of the Chez Paree Adorables. This shrine of an era when people stayed up late at night punishing the parquet to the beat of a Cole Porter tune fell before the onslaught of* television, which glued the former revelers to their couches.*

OPPOSITE, BOTTOM: *The outdoor summer garden of Frank Lloyd Wright's Midway Gardens provided the perfect ambience for dining, dancing, or listening to a concert. Working with Alfonso Iannelli and Richard Bock, Wright embellished the Gardens with striking modern sculpture and soaring standards composed of cubes.*

: MOVIE PALACES :

IN THE 1920S CHICAGO WAS, says Ben Hall, in *The Best Remaining Seats: The Golden Age of the Movie Palace,* "the jumpingest movie city in the world and had more plush elegant theatres than anywhere else." The theaters were divided into two types, the "hard top," which traced its ancestry back to the European opera house, and the "atmospheric," which projected clouds across a night-time sky of sparkling electric stars.

"He was on Cottage Grove . . . and before he knew it Mort was up to Sixty-third, and saw the blaze of the Tivoli lights. . . . Those Balaban and Katz boys were certainly going strong." — Meyer Levin, The Old Bunch.

The queen of the neighborhood houses that Cornelius W. and George Rapp built for Abe and Barney Balaban and Sam Katz was undoubtedly the South Side's Tivoli at Cottage Grove and 63rd Street. Their first movie theater for Balaban and Katz, the Central Park at 3535 West 12th Street, now Roosevelt Road, opened in 1917 and Rapp & Rapp went on to design innumerable opulent masterworks for the chain, including the Chicago, the Palace, and the Uptown.

To play the Tivoli's giant Wurlitzer for the theater's opening in 1921, Balaban and Katz hired Jesse Crawford, "The Poet of the Organ," away from Grauman's Theatre in Los Angeles. Crawford later played at the Chicago until 1928, when he moved on to the Paramount in New York. The Tivoli, a victim of television and a changing neighborhood, closed in 1963 and was torn down a few years later.

OPPOSITE: The six-story façade of the Tivoli in 1927, when Cottage Grove was an important entertainment artery in the Windy City.

ABOVE, LEFT: The theater's opulent marble lobby, which was modeled on Louis XIV's chapel at Versailles.

ABOVE, RIGHT: The Tivoli's auditorium, which could seat 3,414 theatergoers.

Rapp & Rapp's elegant 2999-seat
Norshore, which opened in 1927 on
Howard Street to serve the affluent

North Side, is recognized by movie
palace buffs as one of the finest cinema
theaters ever built. The Norshore's

outer lobby (ABOVE, LEFT) was
crowned by crystal chandeliers
suspended from a ceiling painted

with Pompeian motifs; the upper lobby (OPPOSITE, RIGHT) was a conscious escalation of grandeur, with gilded bronze, porcelain, and fine French antiques. The theater's richly decorated orchestra and loges (ABOVE) were the ultimate in elegant luxury. The Norshore closed in 1957 and was razed in 1960.

In the late 1920s Chicago's West Side was the site of two stunning new movie palaces, the 3931-seat Marbro and the 3612-seat Paradise. The Marbro (ABOVE)—the name reflected its ownership by the Marks Brothers, proprietors of an important chain of Chicago movie theaters—at 4110 West Madison Street opened in May of 1927. The opening bill featured The Loves of Sunya, starring Gloria Swanson. The designer of the Marbro was Edward Eichenbaum of the firm of Levy & Klein. In his invaluable study, The Four Major Works of Levy and Klein, *Joseph DuciBella says that Eichenbaum was a native of Cleveland, studied at the University of Pennsylvania, and, after working for, among others, Albert Kahn, came to Chicago in 1924. The Marbro's 122- by 124-foot hard-top auditorium was an elegant, classically*

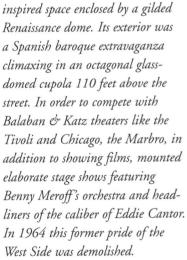

inspired space enclosed by a gilded Renaissance dome. Its exterior was a Spanish baroque extravaganza climaxing in an octagonal glass-domed cupola 110 feet above the street. In order to compete with Balaban & Katz theaters like the Tivoli and Chicago, the Marbro, in addition to showing films, mounted elaborate stage shows featuring Benny Meroff's orchestra and head-liners of the caliber of Eddie Cantor. In 1964 this former pride of the West Side was demolished.

The Paradise (ABOVE), at 231 North Crawford Avenue, now Pulaski, which opened in September 1928, was commissioned by the Guyon family, owners of the Paradise Ballroom and the Guyon Hotel across the street. A masterpiece of the atmospheric house, the Paradise was the creation of John Eberson. Born in Romania in 1875 and educated

in Vienna, Eberson, whose speciality was theater design, moved to Chicago in 1910. The Paradise's restrained Louis XVI exterior belied its interior, which was a fantasy version of an Imperial Roman villa open to a sky filled with twinkling electric stars. The villa's classical stat-ues, including the life-sized Apollo in his horse-drawn chariot atop the proscenium, were the work of Lorado Taft. This Paradise was lost in 1956.

OPPOSITE, BOTTOM: Another Edward Eichenbaum–designed theater was the Diversey, at 2830 North Clark Street, near Diversey Boulevard, seen here on July 31, 1925, the day after it opened. The 2966-seat movie palace was also an important stop on the vaudeville circuit. After the Diversey closed in 1973, its interior was converted into a multilevel shopping center.

ABOVE: One of Chicago's most attractive places of entertainment was the Apollo Theatre at the southeast corner of Randolph and Dearborn streets, originally built for the McCormick family as a legitimate house. The elegant Beaux Arts edifice was a 1921 work by Holabird & Roche. After it failed as a legitimate house in 1927, United Artists acquired the building and engaged C. Howard Crane to convert it into a movie theater. Crane made few changes to the exterior, but he replaced the restrained French interior by Will Hollingsworth and Winold Reiss with what one theater historian has described as "Persio-Stalactite."

In the 1980s the city bought the United Artists and in 1989 another palace on the Randolph Street Rialto vanished. This photograph shows the lobby in 1939.

X

Bad Times, Good Times

IT IS NOT FAR-FETCHED to compare the effect of World War I on Chicago with that of the Great Fire. Edgar Lee Masters in his memoirs charged "The World War destroyed the era out of which *Spoon River* came." Chicago had not wanted that war. Its foreign policy was well expressed by the noninterventionist position of Senator Robert La Follette from neighboring Wisconsin. It was a point of view shared by a broad spectrum of the city, from the Republican party and the conservative *Tribune,* through the German and Irish elements of the population, to humanitarians like Jane Addams, who headed the Women's International League for Peace, and the Socialists led by Eugene V. Debs. Chicago was dismayed by the vociferous bellicosity of its old Bull Moose hero, Theodore Roosevelt, laughed at the eastern socialites drilling at Plattsburgh, New York, distrusted the perpetual moralizing of the Princeton schoolmaster, Woodrow Wilson. Vachel Lindsay proclaimed in "Abraham Lincoln Walks at Midnight" that the war's legalized slaughter even awakened Illinois's supreme spirit:

> It breaks his heart that kings must murder still,
> That all his hours of travail here for men
> Seem yet in vain. And who will bring white peace
> That he may sleep upon his hill again?

The sanity of the heartland was not to prevail. While still piously protesting his reluctance to lead the United States into the conflict, Wilson was being pushed toward belligerence by those who, for various reasons, wanted the nation to become involved in the European conflict. Their task was facilitated by German diplomatic ineptness, such as the famed "Zimmermann telegram" offering to help Mexico regain its lost territories in the American Southwest in return for an alliance with the Central Powers. There was also the matter of United States credits to the Allies. By 1916 these had reached the level where American banks suddenly held an astonishing one-third of all the world's gold reserves. An Allied defeat, or even an indecisive resolution of the war, could have cost the country billions of dollars. Nineteen-sixteen was not a time to be sanguine about Allied prospects. It was the year in which an overconfident French general, Joseph Joffre, prepared the slaughter of half a million at Verdun, and Sir Douglas Haig, after announcing that the machine gun was a highly overrated weapon, sent thousands of British to die at the Somme. While the Midwest spoke for neutrality, American intervention was demanded by Wall Street bankers like the younger J. Pierpont Morgan, industrialists like steel king Charles Schwab, by the New York press, and by students of Harvard and Columbia.

The two most devastating losses of Chicago's interior spaces in the second half of the twentieth century were the rotunda of Henry Ives Cobb's Federal Building (a close-up of which appears on the front jacket) and the Diana Court in Holabird & Root's Michigan Square Building at 540 North Michigan Avenue, which opened in 1930. The exterior of the Michigan Square Building was a restrained Bedford limestone composition, but its lobby was a place of spectacular spatial effects filled with that sense of movement so dear to Art Deco designers. It unmistakably mirrored the sensational public rooms of the Ile-de-France, which the French Line had launched in 1926 to publicize the design concepts of the 1925 Paris exposition. In the Diana Court, white-metal-railed stairways zigzagged out of sight; floors bore brilliant terrazzo patterns; and marble piers, their corners sharply grooved, soared to a coved ceiling where hidden lights reflecting off gold leaf seemed part of the sky itself. At its center, the hub of this vibrant space, was a circular marble fountain topped by a lovely bronze statue of Diana by the Swedish sculptor Carl Milles.

"They talked of how they would come home in glory and victory, marching down Michigan Boulevard with their medals and souvenirs."—James T. Farrell, The Young Manhood of Studs Lonigan.

In this 1919 photograph, returning World War I soldiers parade along Michigan Avenue near the Art Institute.

Wilson had long been angered by the anti-interventionist stand of the heartland, and the Espionage Act, passed soon after America entered the war, gave him the weapon he needed to strike back. Its $10,000 fine and twenty-year jail sentence for disloyalty were ideal for silencing opposition. No midwestern city was more suspect than Chicago. With some 500,000 citizens of German descent in its population of two and a half million, it was, according to one official report, "the sixth largest German city in the world." Wilson's own statements against "hyphenated Americans" were soon echoed by his spy-hunting attorney general, A. Mitchell Palmer, who was capable of saying: "around sangerfests and sangerbunds and organizations of that kind . . . the young Germans who come to America are taught to remember, first, the fatherland, and second America." Suddenly, singing Schubert became incompatible with patriotism. German clubs and music societies were closed, the German language forbidden in the Chicago public schools, and German newspapers placed under censorship. It was not a surprising development in an atmosphere which found pretzels banned because they had a German name and doctors striving to rechristen German measles. The effect on Chicago, however, was far from humorous. The German beer gardens and singing societies and "Turners" (from *Turnvereine*, societies originally formed for physical education and exercise), with their active and independent political and intellectual life, had been among the most important influences in the city's neighborhoods. They had been civilizing centers, attracting not only Germans but Austrians, Scandinavians, Czechs, and even the city's French, who were mostly from Alsace-Lorraine.

The Germans were not Woodrow Wilson's only Chicago target. The city had for fifty years been the center of the nation's progressive political and social movements, and these too had no place in a country where every man, woman, and child was to be regimented into the war effort. The President, as the Chicago-born John Dos Passos observed in *Mr. Wilson's War,* ". . . saw Socialists, I.W.W.s [the Industrial Workers of the World], pacifists, anarchists of the Emma Goldman stripe all contributing in their separate ways to help enemy aliens and German agents impede the war effort." Wilson was quick to act. The Chicago leaders of the Non-Partisan League, which had backed La Follette, were arrested, Hull-House was investigated, William D. Haywood and one hundred members of the I.W.W. were indicted by the city's federal district attorneys, and Eugene V. Debs was sentenced to ten years in prison for sedition. (In 1920, while in jail, Debs received more than

900,000 votes as the Socialist candidate for president.) Looking about him, Clarence Darrow came close to despairing of American liberties.

Washington's attack cut out the heart of political movements that traced their lineage back to some of Chicago's most sacred moments: the nomination of Lincoln, the 1912 Progressive convention, the battle for the eight-hour day, the struggle for child labor laws. Smeared as subversive, after the war they would never re-emerge with their former bright confidence. They would be labeled "foreign," "alien," when in fact they were one of the most American things about Chicago.

The pro-war forces had still one more terrible weapon to unleash on Chicago. The Eighteenth Amendment prohibiting the manufacture, sale, or transportation of alcoholic liquors went into effect in January of 1920. For years the city had been the chief target of the Anti-Saloon League since its founding in Ohio in 1893. The League spoke for America's small-town Protestants, for Baptists and Methodists, and for the evangelicals, who saw in Chicago with its churches—Roman Catholic, Lutheran, Episcopalian, not to mention the synagogues, which used real wine in their sacraments—the depravity of Sodom and Gomorrah. The city was full of people who didn't speak English; it had beer halls; you could even get a drink on Sunday. New York was every bit as bad, but Chicago was closer to the League's midwestern base. In the battle against drink, the war was a godsend. Now it was possible to argue that the use of grain to make alcohol was not only sinful, it was unpatriotic as well. Beer drinking, in particular, was anathema, for it was perceived as a German custom and the profits went to the brewers, who were almost all "German-Americans." The Wisconsin superintendent of the Anti-Saloon League stated the argument bluntly:

> Pro-Germanism is only the froth from the German beer-saloon. Our
> German Socialist party and the German-American Alliance are the spawn
> of the saloon. Kaiser kultur was raised on beer. Prohibition is the infalli-
> ble submarine chaser we must launch by thousands.

Prohibition might be an effective submarine chaser, but in a city where more than half of the population paid a daily visit to a saloon it was difficult to enforce.

It did not take long for those willing to quench the city's thirst to get organized. By late 1920 the now-illegal breweries were producing at their pre–Eighteenth Amendment level, and beer-hustling was operating on a citywide scale, with the business divided among rival gangs along lines that followed Chicago's geographic divisions. In a matter of months Chicago became, in effect, a dozen states, each with its own military force. "Into the ranks of the several armies," reported Henry Justin Smith in *Chicago: The History of Its Reputation,* "rushed practically all the clever or athletic young hoodlums 'educated' during the last twenty years." Now, in place of the friendly corner saloon, of the gracious ambiance created by John Vogelsang at the Midway Gardens and Joseph Schlogl in his North Wells Street *weinstube,* instead of the strains of Strauss and Lehar, Chicago got Big Jim Colosimo and Scarface Al Capone and the rattle of machine guns in the alleys of the North and West sides. George Ade was filled with nostalgia for *The Old-Time Saloon:*

> During the nineties all of the alluring vices flaunted themselves in
> the open. Satan had all of his merchandise in the show-windows.
> The managers of the prolonged carnival did not kill one another.
> They cooperated, in the most friendly manner. . . .

The friendliness had departed. Big Jim Colosimo was cut down in his café; Dion O'Banion shot in his flower shop; Hymie Weiss slain on the steps of Holy Name Cathedral; and Angelo Genna, one of the six terrible Genna brothers, finished off by a shotgun blast in his sedan on Ogden Avenue. The profits from selling bootleg booze were enormous. The gang run by Johnny Torrio and Joseph Stenson netted an estimated $50 million between 1920 and 1924, while the kingfish, Al Capone, with headquarters in the Lexington Hotel at Michigan Avenue and 22nd Street, was pulling down $100 million a year. Capone felt that he was performing a kind of altruistic service. "I make my money by supplying a public demand," he told a reporter. "If I break the law, my customers, who number hundreds of the best people in Chicago, are as guilty as I am. The only difference between us is that I sell and they buy." And if one was buying it was wise to buy from Capone. In his mock autobiography, *The Story of a Wonder Man,* Ring Lardner defined "a Chicago caddy" as "a boy who carries your ordnance bag, retrieves sliced or hooked bullets and replaces divots in bystanders."

As though struggling desperately to forget the mayhem, Chicago became in the '20s a city devoted to the architecture of fantasy. Two pastimes attracted its pre-eminent efforts: moviegoing and dancing. Chicago had always been a toddling town, but as the '20s began to roar, dancing became a craze. The new beat had begun in the winter of 1915–1916 when Joseph K. Gorham began bringing New Orleans jazz bands to the city. The new music was a hit, but Chicagoans, not certain what steps to do to it, at first just sat around and listened. One night at Lamb's Café, where a group called Brown's Band was playing, the manager announced that it was all right to dance to the new music. After this invitation, the onetime wallflowers threw themselves onto the floor with such gusto that Brown's Band remained at Lamb's for thirty-three thronged weeks. Henry Osgood, the pioneer writer in the field, claimed in *So This Is Jazz* that Chicago introduced the white world to the new music: ". . . The craze for jazz in the North and East appears to have come out of New Orleans via Chicago."

Chicagoans quickly adapted the New Orleans music to something highly acceptable to white dancers, and, as the '20s got under way, Chicago hotels reverberated with music by the nation's premier orchestras. Typical was Marshall & Fox's posh new $8,500,000 Drake at the spot where Michigan Avenue becomes Lake Shore Drive. The Drake's glittering Silver Forest, a vast room running the whole length of the hotel's North Side, featured Fred Waring and Hal Kemp and first introduced Phil Spitalny and his All-Girl Orchestra. Chicago demanded the best. As the American popular music historian James T. Maher points out:

> Chicago was always a more sophisticated dancing city than New York. When Paul Whiteman was brought to Chicago with brassy fanfare the dancing Midwesterners turned their backs on his theatrical flair, his Wurlitzer-window display of instruments, and his symphonic arrangements.

Chicago's favorite dancing master was undoubtedly Isham Jones, an Ohioan who arrived in town just as the '20s began. In no time "Ish" was making the city swing and sway to his brilliant saxophone- and piano-playing at the Old Green Mill. But he found his true home at the Sherman House's College Inn, run by Chicago's premier restaurant impresario Ernie Byfield, who claimed, among other things, to have invented the club sandwich. The Sherman, in the midst of the Randolph Street rialto, was the favorite hotel of visiting show people, and they soon spread the word about Jones's music. During the six years he stayed at the College Inn, Isham Jones created some of the most subtle dance music in America. Soon orchestras were not only imitating his style, but playing the songs he wrote: "Swinging Down the Lane," "It Had to Be You," and "I'll See You in My Dreams."

The musicians in Chicago's fashionable hotels and clubs were almost all white. But a fresh wave of arrivals was adding a new element to the city's mix. Between 1890 and 1915 the black population had grown from about 15,000 to over 50,000. Most lived in the neighborhood north of 39th Street, between State and Federal streets, called for a time the "Black Belt." In the next four years, attracted by the jobs made available by World War I, Chicago's black population increased to 100,000. A bloody six-day race riot in the summer of 1919 that left 22 blacks and 18 whites dead and more than 500 people injured did not discourage the new arrivals. Settling in the decayed grandeur of the old South Side, they moved into houses vividly described in Richard Wright's *Native Son:* "That was the way most houses on the South Side were, ornate, old, stinking; homes once of rich white people, now inhabited by Negroes or standing dark and empty with yawning black windows."

The houses might be old and the winters cold, but life in Chicago was better than it was in Mississippi or Alabama or Louisiana. There was always work in the Stock Yards, and, between 47th and 48th streets, the lights were always bright. So they came on the Illinois Central, the "Green Diamond" as it was called, to the very spot where Lincoln's body had been brought home, to the Twelfth Street Depot, which became a kind of black Ellis Island. Chicago was mid-America's black capital, what Harlem was for the East, celebrated in a thousand songs such as Little Brother Montgomery's "Lake Front Blues":

> Chicago, Chicago, that is the town for me,
> Chicago, Chicago, that is the town for me,
> Drop me off by the lake front, that's where
> I'll be contented to be.

Now to the city that had welcomed McCormick and Pullman and Sullivan and Dreiser came another creative genius. Louis Armstrong arrived from Louisiana in the summer of 1921. He had been sent for by Joe "King" Oliver—who had created a sensation with his Creole Jazz Band at the Lincoln Gardens—to play cornet for an astounding $30 dollars a week. Armstrong had no hesitation about leaving New Orleans; he remembered the day of his departure as the greatest day of his life and wanted to shout to everyone he met that he was going to Chicago. Through the Romanesque arches of the old Illinois Central Station, Louis Armstrong, like thousands of other blacks, came to his new city. Robert Goffin, who worked closely with him on *Horn of Plenty,* described Armstrong's feelings this way:

> The train arrived in Chicago at twilight of a blistering hot day. Louis was
> wearing his best black suit, his derby and a wing collar that was anything
> but spotless after the long trip. As he followed the hurrying crowd toward
> the nearest station exit, a sense of power surged in him. . . .

The power was soon displayed at the Lincoln Gardens and the Royal Gardens and the Plantation Café, where Armstrong revealed to Chicago a new musical structure as astonishing in its way as the city's skyscrapers. Along with that architecture, this black jazz was one of America's truly original gifts to the world's arts.

Places to dance were not limited to the city's hotels and clubs. In 1922, Andrew and William Karzas unveiled a whole new concept with a $1,500,000 South Side ballroom of marble columns, crystal chandeliers, and gilt which could trace its ancestry back to

London's eighteenth-century pleasure grounds and the sumptuous dance halls of Second Empire Paris. Appropriately named the Trianon in honor of its Versailles-inspired splendor, it was, as the first-night program said, "truly a palace dedicated to dancing." Over the years the palace would make a place in the musical world for Ted Weems, Jan Garber, Kay Kyser, and the "Old Maestro," Ben Bernie. When, on February 18, 1923, Rudolph Valentino danced the tango at the Trianon, 6000 enthusiastic fans followed in his footsteps. The appearance of Valentino was prophetic. America's taste for fantasy was growing increasingly exotic, and when the Karzas brothers inaugurated a new North Side ballroom in 1926 it was named the Aragon and was all Spanish-Moorish. There might be three feet of snow in the streets outside, but as the dancers whirled to the music of Wayne King or Dick Jurgens or Freddy Martin, inside it was sunny Spain. The Windy City was still a mecca for musicians when Jack Kerouac hit it in the 1950s. As he remembered in *On the Road:* "At nine o'clock in the morning everybody—musicians, girls in slacks, bartenders, and the one little skinny, unhappy trombonist—staggered out of the club into the great roar of Chicago."

The architectural fantasy of the Trianon and the Aragon was surpassed only by the city's cinemas. Three men will always be associated with the Chicago movie theater—Abe and Barney Balaban and Sam Katz. When the Balabans and Katz decided in 1916 to build the Midwest's first motion picture palace, the 2400-seat Central Park, they were fortunate in finding two architect brothers, Cornelius W. and George Rapp, who could give them exactly what they wanted. Along with Chicago's John Eberson, the master of the atmospheric stars-and-clouds house, and New York's John Lamb, Rapp & Rapp made up a triumvirate of sensational movie-theater fabricators. But the Rapps were unequaled when it came to the presentation of stunning opulence without vulgarity. Among the dozens of Chicago theaters they built, two stand out as masterpieces of cinematographic architecture: the Tivoli on Cottage Grove Avenue, whose main lobby suggested the chapel Jules Hardouin Mansart had built for Louis XIV at Versailles, and the 3000-seat Norshore on Howard Street. The Norshore's restrained yet sumptuous Louis XVI interior was unquestionably one of America's finest classical compositions. It reminded theatergoers of the palaces of France and Russia, and in a 1925 interview George Rapp said that was exactly what he intended:

> Watch the eyes of a child as it enters the portals of our great theaters
> and treads the pathway into fairyland. Watch the bright light in the eyes
> of the tired shopgirl who hurries noiselessly over carpets and sighs with
> satisfaction as she walks amid furnishings that once delighted the hearts
> of queens. See the toil-worn father whose dreams have never come true,
> and look inside his heart as he finds strength and rest within the theater.
> There you have the answer to why motion picture theaters are so palatial.

Not all of Chicago's architectural fantasy was in its ballrooms and cinemas. Between 1919 and 1924, on a spectacular site on Michigan Avenue just north of the Chicago River, Charles G. Beersman and Ernest R. Graham, of the firm of Graham, Anderson, Probst & White, created for William Wrigley, Jr., head of the chewing gum company, a gleaming white terra-cotta structure which brilliantly combined the verticality of the modern skyscraper with the beauty of Renaissance design. The Wrigley Building was a proclamation of the opening of the North Side to commerce made possible by the inauguration of the Michigan Avenue Bridge in 1920. In 1922, the *Chicago Tribune* marked the celebration of its 75th anniversary by announcing an international competition for "the most beautiful building in the world." The site was just across Michigan Avenue from the Wrigley Building. The commission's importance and the $10,000 prize attracted 264 entries from around the world. The preliminary decision of the judges gave first place to the restrained, very modern skyscraper designed by Finland's Eliel Saarinen, but the *Tribune's* management reversed the decision and awarded first prize to New York's Raymond M. Hood and John Mead Howells. Louis Sullivan, old and ill with heart trouble and living in the modest Warner Hotel, was astonished when Howells & Hood's structure turned out to be a Gothic tower replete with flying buttresses and niches for statues. "It is an imaginary structure—not imaginative," he wrote in *The Architectural Record.* Sullivan went on to praise Saarinen's entry and to express his surprise that a foreigner had so perfectly captured what he considered to be the ideals of a true American architecture. Sullivan should not have been surprised, for his own work, and the work of Burnham & Root, of Holabird & Roche, and of Wright, was known and admired by contemporary European architects. Despite Sullivan's censure, time has been on the side of the Howells & Hood building, and few would now say that the thirty-six-story limestone-clad edifice was not "beautiful." Together the Tribune Tower and the Wrigley Building constituted a resplendent monumental gateway to North Michigan Avenue.

While the Wrigley Building was under construction in Chicago, in Germany the leader of a new imperialism, Adolf Hitler, was beginning his rise to power. Hitler, who was to proclaim that "Never was humanity in its appearance and in its feelings closer to classical antiquity than today," would ban modern architecture, close the schools that taught it, and ask his favorite architect, Albert Speer, to raise a becolumned Berlin. Ironically, the aesthetics of Adler & Sullivan and of Holabird & Root, which had fallen out of favor when Chicago had turned to an American classicism, would be carried back to the shores of Lake Michigan by architects who were refugees from Germany's National Socialism.

The events which brought a number of these admirers from Europe to the American heartland were, to say the least, historic. In 1919, in the wake of Germany's defeat in World War I, the architect Walter Gropius (1833–1969) founded at Weimer a school of design, the Bauhaus, literally the "building house." Before the war Gropius had received international recognition for the Fagus Boot-Last Factory at Alfeld of 1911, designed with Adolph Meyer. The Fagus Factory was heralded as a revolutionarily "honest" building because it unreservedly revealed the realities of its industrial age construction. Since its steel frame made load-bearing walls unnecessary, Gropius had created walls of glass with corners which had no visual supports. His aesthetic ideals, grounded in the realities of the industrial world and also in his philosophical desire for a classless society, were at the center of the Bauhaus's curriculum. The school attempted in its teaching to abolish the distinction between the fine arts, such as painting and sculpture, and the crafts, such as ceramics and weaving. In addition, students were to be trained to design everything from tableware to entire houses for mass production. Gropius's ideology was strikingly stated in his famous "Manifesto" of 1919:

> Let us create a new guild of craftsmen, without the class distinctions
> which raise an arrogant barrier between craftsman and artist. Together
> let us conceive and create the new building of the future, which will
> embrace architecture and sculpture and painting in one unity and which
> will rise one day towards heaven from the hands of a million workers
> like the crystal symbol of a new faith.

The faculty of the Bauhaus reflected the broad scope of Gropius's vision for the institution. Among its most famous teachers were painters Joseph Albers, Paul Klee, Lyonel

Bertram Goldberg's gasoline station of 1940 at the northeast corner of La Salle and Maple streets was a beguiling combination of technical prowess and daring design. Goldberg, the architect of, among other projects, Marina City, was born in Chicago in 1913, and after attending Harvard and the Bauhaus in Berlin, began private practice in Chicago in 1937. "I tried in the gasoline station to relate the excitement of driving a car to the excitement of making a car, which for me has always been a rather pleasurable part of American engineering," he wrote. The station was essentially a cable-suspended structure erected on two towers with "GAS" inescapably spelled out in neon tubing. The whimsical pavilion for car servicing disappeared in 1965.

Feininger, and Wassily Kandinsky; architects Ludwig Mies van der Rohe, Marcel Breuer, and Gropius himself; and photographer and graphic artist Laszlo Moholy-Nagy.

By 1925 political opposition in Weimar to what some deemed the "un-German" character of the school had grown to the point that the Bauhaus moved to Dessau, where, in 1930, Mies became its head. In 1932 the Bauhaus was forced out of Dessau and began holding classes in a Berlin factory, and a year later, in April 1933, the Nazi government ordered the police to close the school on the grounds that it was an exponent of "degenerate art" and a "hotbed of cultural bolshevism."

The Bauhaus was already well known in Chicago, and some local architects, including Bertram Goldberg, had studied there. As a consequence, Moholy-Nagy was invited to Chicago, and with the backing of the Association of Arts and Industries, set up a New Bauhaus in 1937 in the Marshall Field mansion on Prairie Avenue. This New Bauhaus lasted scarcely a year, and after its demise, Moholy-Nagy founded his Institute of Design. Moholy-Nagy was not the only Bauhaus luminary to emigrate to Chicago. Mies van der Rohe arrived in the city in 1938 to head the architecture department of what eventually became the Illinois Institute of Technology, which later merged with Moholy-Nagy's Institute of Design. Through his teachings and his buildings, Mies became the father of what was to be called the Second Chicago School of Architecture. One of that school's heroes was Louis Sullivan, although the architect would not live to savor the recognition. His last commission, which came in 1922, was for the façade of a small music store on Lincoln Avenue for William P. Krause. Sullivan enriched the modest two-story structure with a lush, foliate cartouche, which in a bold flourish, like a final farewell, rises three feet above the building's cornice. In the end he possessed little more than a suit of clothes and his drawing board. The one bright element of his last years was his work on *The Autobiography of an Idea*, written in 1922 and 1923 at the Cliff Dwellers Club atop Orchestra Hall or, when weather permitted, in Washington Park. Sullivan died in his sleep on April 14, 1924. He was buried, through the charity of a few faithful friends, including Frank Lloyd Wright, who never forgot the heady days of the Auditorium, in Graceland Cemetery, in a lot that he had purchased for his parents. A few days before his death a copy of the just-published *Autobiography* was placed in his hands. One of the final passages in the book reaffirmed Sullivan's faith in democracy and his belief that one day America would have an architecture worthy of a great nation: "That dream has never ceased. That faith has never wearied."

By the time Franklin Delano Roosevelt stood at the podium of the Chicago Stadium in 1932 and pledged a New Deal for the American people, none needed it more than the citizens of the Windy City. The prohibition wars had reached a climax in 1929 with the machine-gunning by Al Capone's boys of seven of rival George "Bugs" Moran's hoods in a North Clark Street garage. After that, St. Valentine's Day had a very special meaning in Chicago. The mobs had strong-armed their way into the city's cleaners and dyers trades, into the bakers and barbers, into the electrical workers and the garage repairmen, into the plumbers and the garbage haulers, the window cleaners, confectionery manufacturers, and the undertakers. The profits were estimated at $6 million a week. And nothing was done. Ferdinand Lundberg, a Chicago newspaperman in the '20s, who was later to write *The Rich and the Super-Rich*, remembered:

> Nobody was ever convicted of murder in any of the gang wars that chalked up several thousand killed. Actually, all the gangs were politically connected and were paying off someone from the mayor down through the alderman, judges and others. Had the politicians wanted to squelch the gangs they could have easily done so. But the money lay in cooperating with them.

The 1929 Illinois Crime Survey reported that hoodlums had control of most of Chicago's voter lists and election boards. It was rumored that when Mayor "Big Bill" Thompson's safety deposit box was opened, it contained $1 million in cash.

The stock-market crash left Chicago with an unemployment rate of more than 25 percent, a devastated banking system, and most of its hotels in receivership. This last was not a very serious matter for the hundreds sleeping under the Michigan Avenue bridge. Policemen and schoolteachers were paid in scrip, and in the Black Belt men were without the carfare to look for work. The disaster was compounded by the collapse of Samuel Insull's giant Commonwealth Edison Company, which hit middle- and upper-income Chicagoans particularly hard. It was even difficult to escape the gloom momentarily, for Louis Armstrong and many of the city's best musicians had taken the train for New York.

As a final insult, desperate Chicagoans now meekly stood in line outside the kitchen Al Capone had set up near police headquarters. The sign read: "FREE SOUP, COFFEE, AND DOUGHNUTS FOR THE UNEMPLOYED."

Indeed, Capone became a kind of local folk hero. After a visit to Chicago in 1930, the novelist Mary Borden reported in *Harper's* that he had pre-empted the conversation of a city which had once talked of Louis Sullivan and Theodore Dreiser and Jane Addams:

> I went to a dinner dance. . . . I met a lovely member of Chicago's four hundred who spoke to me with tears in her eyes of Capone. I was already getting rather sick of the Scarface, but this suddenly made me feel quite ill, this sentimentality frightened me.

Chicago made one gallant effort to dispel the gray clouds hanging over the metropolis. To celebrate its one-hundredth birthday the Windy City staged in 1933 on the lake front a Century of Progress Exposition. (The Fair would last seventeen months.) The difference between its architecture and that of the Columbian Exposition held forty years earlier was staggering. Because of its impermanence and the necessity to attract the most attention at the lowest cost, the Century of Progress became a dynamic laboratory for new design and innovative structural forms. It most certainly drew inspiration from Paris's 1925 Exposition Internationale des Arts Décoratifs et Industriels Modernes, but it moved forward into a streamlined 1930s modernism which would have an impact across the United States from New York's 1939 World's Fair to the hotels of Miami Beach. Among its outstanding structures was Bennett, Burnham & Holabird's massive rectangular midnight blue, white, gray, light blue, and red Administration Building; Alfonso Iannelli's Havoline Thermometer Building in the form of a giant thermometer; and Raymond Hood's Electrical Building, whose cubistic massing made it a striking contrast to his *Tribune* tower. Nothing better illustrated the aesthetic distance between the 1893 and 1933 fairs than their sculpture. The sculpture and architectural ornamentation for the Century of Progress was coordinated by Lee Lawrie, the sculptor later responsible for the Atlas and other works in New York's Rockefeller Center. Lawrie brilliantly employed modern artists such as Leo Friedlander, Alfonso Iannelli, Gaston Lachaise, and Carl Milles to illustrate the Fair's central theme, "Science in Industry." For example, on the Lake Michigan side of the Electrical Building, Lawrie created his own sensational Water Gate consisting of two high pylons adorned with bas-reliefs representing atomic and stellar energy. It was a world apart from MacMonnies' Columbian Fountain.

While the Century of Progress itself was a financial success, its concomitant purpose—bringing some desperately needed cash to Chicago's businesses—was a failure. Sally Rand, the Century of Progress' answer to the Columbian Exposition's Little Egypt, vividly articulated the dismal results in an interview she gave Studs Terkel for *Hard Times: An Oral History of the Great Depression:*

Along with the Stock Yards, the manufacturing of farm machinery, and the retail business, one of the engines which drove Chicago's economy was the Board of Trade. In 1885 William W. Boyington provided it with an appropriately grandiose room, 174 by 155 feet and more than five stories high, in which to conduct the deadly serious game of buying and selling grain. The hall is vividly described in Frank Norris's powerful Chicago novel, The Pit: "It was a vast enclosure, lighted on either side by great windows of colored glass, the roof supported by thin iron pillars elaborately decorated. To the left were the bulletin blackboards and beyond those, in the northwest angle of the floor, a great railed-in space where the Western Union Telegraph was installed. To the right, on the other side of the room, a row of tables, laden with neatly arranged paper bags half full of samples of grains, stretched along the east wall. . . ." In the distance is the corn pit, while the large pit in the foreground is the wheat pit. Boyington's building was replaced by the present Chicago Board of Trade in 1929.

They planned this Fair to bring business to Chicago, into the Loop. But you could have fired a cannon down State Street and hit nobody, because everybody was out at the Fair sleeping in their Fords.

There was indeed a certain stillness in Chicago. The glamorous Art Deco masterpieces of Holabird & Root, of Thielbar & Fugard, of Philip B. Maher, those buoyant expressions of the 1920s economic boom, the Board of Trade, the McGraw-Hill Building, the Diana Court, the Woman's Athletic Club, were poignant reminders of a lost, better world. For more than two decades, as all significant construction halted, they would be the final expression of the Windy City's unparalleled architectural cavalcade.

In 1935, in the darkest depths of the Great Depression, Willa Cather published a novel, *Lucy Gayheart,* whose heroine is a girl from Nebraska who comes to Chicago in the first years of the twentieth century to study music. There is a passage in the book which celebrates Lucy's feeling for the city:

> The next afternoon Lucy was walking slowly over toward Michigan Avenue. She had never loved the city so much; the city which gave one the freedom to spend one's youth as one pleased, to have one's secret, to choose one's master and serve him in one's own way. Yesterday's rain had left a bitter, springlike smell in the air; the vehemence that beat against her in the street and hummed above her had something a little wistful in it tonight, like a plaintive hand-organ tune. All the lovely things in the shop windows, the furs and jewels, roses and orchids, seemed to belong to her as she passed them. Not to have wrapped up and sent home, certainly; where would she put them? But they were hers to live among.

That was what Chicago had given the millions who had come to it, lovely things to live among: hotels and restaurants, department stores and shops, mansions and apartment towers, concert halls and movie palaces, stadiums and skyscrapers. For a hundred years the city had given and the gift had been glorious.

"GOD MADE THE COUNTRY," the English poet William Cowper wrote, "and man the town." Because the city is indeed man's handiwork, it is, at its best, one of the noblest expressions of the human spirit. One thinks immediately of Athens's temple-topped Acropolis, the semicircular colonnades of Rome's Piazza San Pietro, and Paris's obelisk-centered Place de la Concorde. But the creation need not be on such a grand scale. It can be a well-wrought shop front, a commercial structure bearing the precious gift of wit, an exhilarating racetrack, or a welcoming clubhouse. The one criterion is that the edifice be, in art historian Bernard Berenson's term, "life enhancing," a thing that lifts the heart and brings joy.

COMMERCIAL GRACE

ABOVE: *The inviting iron-framed windows on the State Street side of the Field & Leiter Store, later Marshall Field's, clearly reflected precedents such as those of Paris's Au Bon Marché department store. Erected in 1878 at the northeast corner of State and Washington streets, the structure was replaced by the present Field's building in 1907.*

OPPOSITE, ABOVE: *At the center of Daniel Burnham's classical Illinois Trust and Savings Bank on La Salle Street at Jackson Boulevard was a skylit Roman Renaissance court of dazzling green, white, and purple marble. After its opening in 1897, Charles F. McKim wrote Burnham: "It will remain a monument long after you are gone." The temple did not long survive its architect, who died in 1912, and was demolished in 1924.*

LEFT: *If the Illinois Trust conjured up images of Borghese princes, the Howard Avenue Trust and Savings Bank, at 1737 West Howard Street, vibrated with the sounds of the Jazz Age. Designed by Jens Jensen, not the famed designer of parks who bore the same name but the architect responsible for structures such as the Guyon Hotel, the bank was constructed between 1929 and 1930 for the Ure family. Its glamorous interior, notable for its metal furnishings, silvered plasterwork, and silver and mauve art glass skylight, revealed the influence of French Art Deco designers, particularly the renowned metalworker Edgar Brandt. The sensational banking room was obliterated in 1978 and the building itself came down in 1999.*

The character of cities can almost be determined by their leading jeweler: Tiffany in New York, Cartier's in Paris, and Garrard's in London are examples which come quickly to mind. In Chicago the most dazzling jeweler was without doubt Peacock's. Founded in 1837, the firm's apotheosis came in 1927 with the opening of its opulent shop at the southeast corner of State and Monroe streets in Holabird & Roche's new Palmer House. Its combination of rich green Verde Antico marble, Italian walnut fittings, and crystal chandeliers suspended from a Florentine-inspired ceiling made it one of Chicago's most palatial commercial interiors. By the 1980s, though the store still bore the Peacock name, it had passed out of the hands of the family. Now the store is closed and the space stands empty, stripped of its dazzling merchandise and elegant ambience.

ABOVE: *Holabird & Root's Michigan Square Building was one of the structures which made Chicagoans begin calling North Michigan Avenue "Boul. Mich.," in tribute to its Paris-like elegance.*

LEFT: *View of the corridor leading from Michigan Avenue to the Michigan Square Building's Diana Court. The visitor walked across a splendid terrazzo floor, designed by Helmuth Bartsch, to a Moderne metal balustrade where, suddenly and unexpectedly, the bedazzling sweep of the inner Court was dramatically revealed.*

The Michigan Square Building was originally planned in 1928 to be twenty-three stories high, but the stock market crash of 1929 forced its backers to halt construction at the eighth floor. Thus the hotel which now occupies the site could have been built atop the original structure and had the Diana Court for its lobby. The building, alas, together with the unforgettable space over which the goddess of the hunt presided, was lost in a cloud of wrecker's dust in 1973.

RIGHT: *In its use of planting and its open, welcoming entrance, Purcell, Feick and Elmslie's Edison Phonograph Shop, built at 229 South Wabash Avenue in 1912, was a stellar example of how a small store can humanize a busy street. Its bold, geometric design in buff brick relieved only by touches of formal floral ornamentation was also a notable example of the influence of the Vienna Secession movement on Chicago design. In 1957 the Commission on Chicago Landmarks described the shop as "a place of dignity and beauty." These qualities were evidently expendable, for the Edison shop was destroyed in 1967.*

OPPOSITE, BOTTOM:
Among the varied shop fronts on the Michigan Avenue side of the Michigan Square Building the most eye-catching was the harlequin pattern of artificial marble which Holabird & Root designed for Socatch's Bakery. Both façade and bakery disappeared in 1935.

226

ABOVE: *This 1957 photograph looking south on Michigan Avenue from Oak Street, with the 900 North Michigan Avenue Building in the distance, dramatically illustrates the lamentable loss of the charming human-scaled structures which made this one of the city's most agreeable neighborhoods. On the near right is a pioneer in creating the Upper Avenue's urbane ambiance, the Palmer Shops Building at the southwest corner of Michigan and Oak Street. Designed in 1921 by Holabird & Roche for Honoré and Potter Palmer, Jr., its elegant classical detailing—it was originally capped with urns— helped set the tone for design on the Upper Avenue. The Palmer Building was also a trend-setter when it came to attracting the type of business which metamorphosed Michigan Avenue from the Chicago River to Oak Street into "The Magnificent Mile." The building's tenants included the Martha Weathered Shop, selling women's apparel, and the Women's Exchange. All of the structures in this photograph have now vanished. The Palmer Shops Building came down in 1971.*

One of the landmarks of "the Magnificent Mile" was the 900 North Michigan Avenue Building at the northwest corner of Michigan and Delaware Place, completed in 1927. Its architect, Jarvis Hunt, a nephew of Richard Morris Hunt, was born in Vermont in 1869 and educated at Harvard and the Massachusetts Institute of Technology. After working on the 1893 Columbian Exposition, Hunt chose to remain in Chicago. The exterior of the structure, with its street level facing of Florentine marble, its second and third floors covered with limestone, and six stories of red brick, exemplified the Beaux Arts principle that while a building should be handsome, its design should never be obtrusive or out-of-scale with its urban environment. The 900 building incorporated a brilliant mixed-use plan of ground-floor commercial space, two floors of small rental pied-à-terres, and six floors of co-op apartments individually tailored to the owner's specification. Among the owners were Joseph L. Cudahy, Cyrus McCormick, Jr. and Jarvis Hunt. The building quickly attracted prestigious retail establishments, including the Dorothy Gray shop for fine cosmetics; Grande Maison de Blanc for linens; and Syrie, Ltd., an interior decorating firm owned by Mrs. Somerset Maugham. In 1938, Jacques, a popular French restaurant, moved into 900 and transformed the spacious courtyard into an oasis where one could enjoy omelets and crepes suzette. In the late 1980s this distinguished structure, seen here in 1971, was replaced by the titanic Bloomingdale's building.

"THE CHICAGO CLUB, which up to now Ned had known only in its rushed midday aspect, all cigar smoke and munching millionaires, was a desert this hot Sunday night" —Arthur Meeker, *Prairie Avenue.*

By the second half of the nineteenth century Chicago possessed private clubs, including the Chicago, the Standard, and the Calumet, which, in the power and wealth of their members, equaled anything to be found in New York or Boston. But Chicago also became home to private clubs whose members were involved in the arts, like The Cliff Dwellers and The Arts Club, or whose primary objective was to have a rip-snorting good time, like the Casino.

One of the first of the famous clubs that were founded after the turn of the century was The Cliff Dwellers. In 1907, Hamlin Garland approached his brother-in-law, the sculptor Lorado Taft, and others to form a club which would be, in Garland's words, "a home for all workers in the fine arts." Its model was the National Arts Club in New York. In 1909 the club took the name Cliff Dwellers from the title of Chicago novelist Henry B. Fuller's precedent-shattering study of urban life. Perched atop Orchestra Hall at 220 South Michigan Avenue, The Cliff Dwellers Club's so-called "Kiva" was a restrained arts and crafts penthouse designed by member Howard Van Doren Shaw. In this photograph, taken at the Cliff Dweller's Club on March 11, 1915, Louis Sullivan is second from the left. On the far right is the architect Irving K. Pond, who was associated with Solon S. Beman in designing houses for Pullman. In 1997 the Cliff Dwellers were evicted from their historic Orchestra Hall club rooms and moved to new quarters nearby.

The roots of the Casino, a Chicago club whose raison d'être had always been gaiety, reach back to 1914. The idea for a club which would include both men and women and be a venue for dining and dancing originated with Lucy McCormick Blair (Mrs. Howard Linn), but the forces that made the club a reality were Mrs. Joseph Coleman and Rue Winterbotham (Mrs. John Alden Carpenter).

If the Casino had a historical precedent it was the Casino in Newport, Rhode Island, designed by McKim, Mead & White, which opened in 1880. In 1914 a lease was taken on land belonging to the Palmer family on what is now Michigan Avenue between Chestnut Street and East Delaware Place and architects Arthur Heun and Ernest Walker were brought in to help with plans for a clubhouse. But the real designer was undoubtedly Rue Winterbotham, one of Chicago's great interior decorators. The resulting building, at 167 East Delaware Place, was a pale pink stucco structure, with Spanish and Italianate touches, and long French windows opening onto balconies. The interiors, also by Rue Winterbotham, were in a crisp Directoire style. When it opened on December 12, 1914, A History of the Casino Club reports: "[T]here were present eleven Blairs, eleven McCormicks, seven Cudahys, six Armours, five Carpenters, five Palmers. . . ."

In 1926 the Palmers sold the land out from under the Casino and the club was forced to move eastward to the corner of East Delaware Place and Seneca. In the summer of 1928, shortly before the new clubhouse was finished, the original Casino burned. It is seen here that very year amid the empty lots which still dotted Streeterville.

No club has had more profound influence on Chicago's cultural life than has the Arts Club. The club began in 1916 in, appropriately, the Fine Arts Building, with a dual mission: to forge links between artists and patrons and to mount exhibitions. In 1918, Rue Winterbotham, who had already left her mark on the Casino, became president and expanded the club's scope to include musicians, architects, and writers. She was superbly qualified for the task, for not only was she well known as a designer in Chicago, but she had worked on Elizabeth Arden's salon in New York and created the sets for her husband John Alden Carpenter's opera, Skyscraper, at the Metropolitan Opera. She received invaluable assistance from Alice Roullier, the daughter of an important art dealer.

In 1947 the Arts Club, then located in the Wrigley Building, lost its lease and rented space in a newly constructed building at 109 East Ontario Street (LEFT, TOP). In a move consistent with the Club's avant-garde bent, it asked Ludwig Mies van der Rohe to take charge of the design of its new space. The gallery, restaurant, and lounge Mies completed in 1951 proved to be subtle masterpieces of form elegantly on the trail of function. His steel stairway became an icon of modern design, carrying architecture into the realm of sculpture. In 1995 the building housing the Arts Club was demolished to make way for another North Michigan Avenue high rise. Fortunately Mies's staircase (LEFT, BOTTOM) was moved to the new home John Vinci designed for the Arts Club at 201 East Ontario Street.

RIGHT, TOP: *Library of the demolished Arts Club.*

RIGHT, BOTTOM: *The Salon, with bold sofas chosen by Rue Winterbotham in the 1920s and some of the Club's superb art collection, including* Tete de femme *by Picasso and a torso by Antoine Bourdelle.*

BELOW: *A 1919 watercolor by Paul Thévanaz of Rue Winterbotham.*

The Tavern, on the 25th floor of 333 North Michigan Avenue, was, like the Cliff Dwellers, another Chicago social club high in the sky. Conceived by artist William P. Welsh in 1926 and popular with architects and painters, including John Wellborn Root, Jr., Philip Maher, and John Norton, the Tavern Club moved into its skyscraper home in 1929. Root was chairman of the club's decorating committee, but much of the actual work was by Johns Hopkins of Holabird & Root and Winold Reiss, a New York designer responsible for, among other projects, the Art Deco Longchamps Restaurant in the Empire State Building. Art Deco was the essence of the Tavern's ultramodern club rooms.

The club's main lounge (LEFT, ABOVE AND BELOW) featured exuberant copper Deco grillework, a salmon-colored ceiling, fireplace mantels picked out in gold, and draperies and wall coverings with bold geometric patterns in browns and beige. The lounge's leather coverings ranged from violet to blue-red.

The Tavern Club's refreshment room (ABOVE) *was decorated with posters, including a 1927 Deco one advertising the French Railways crack train,* Star of the North, *by the famous artist Cassandre. The chairs in the dining room* (RIGHT), *designed by Winold Reiss, were painted gray with blue upholstery, while the ceiling was blue with silver beams.*

The Tavern Club was sensitively refurbished by member Samuel Marx in the late 1930s, but remodeling in the 1960s eradicated its rare Art Deco spaces.

ABOVE: *Chicago's first presidential convention was that of the new Republican Party held May 16–18, 1860, in the Wigwam, located at the southeast corner of Lake and Market streets. Built in five weeks especially for the convention, the two-story pine structure could hold 10,000 people. Here on May 18, the Republicans nominated for President of the United States Abraham Lincoln of Illinois and for Vice- President, Senator Hannibal Hamlin of Maine.*

The 51-year-old Lincoln remained in Springfield throughout the proceedings. The Wigwam, seen here in a photograph taken during the convention by the noted Chicago photographer Alexander Hesler, was dismantled shortly afterward.

LEFT: *This 1860 lithograph of the candidate by local lithographer and engraver Edward Mendel was based on a photograph of Lincoln taken in Chicago in October 1859.*

It would be difficult to imagine a structure with a more historic and picturesque past than the Chicago Coliseum on the east side of South Wabash Avenue at 14th Place. In 1888 Charles F. Gunther, a Chicago candy manufacturer and a major

collector of Civil War memorabilia, had the Libby Prison, in which Union officers had been held during the Civil War, transported from Richmond, Virginia, to Chicago. He used the reconstructed prison to house his collection and charged

admission to view, among other things, the bed in which Abraham Lincoln died. But the structure, originally a warehouse, was an unprepossessing brick building. To make it more attractive, in 1889 Gunther commissioned Charles M.

Palmer to surround it with a crenelated castle wall.

By 1900, with interest in the museum waning, the Libby Prison was demolished and the 14,000-capacity Coliseum, designed by Frost & Granger, constructed within Palmer's walls. For two decades the Coliseum was the venue of choice for Republican conventions, the site where in 1904 Theodore Roosevelt was nominated, in 1908 William Howard Taft was nominated, in 1916 Charles Evans Hughes was nominated, and in 1920 Warren G. Harding was nominated. But none of these conventions matched the drama of the convention held in the Coliseum June 18–22, 1912, when Teddy Roosevelt, convinced that his chosen successor, Taft, had betrayed the party's progressive principles, challenged the sitting President for the Republican nomination. After wild scenes with 600 police present,

the pro-Roosevelt forces stalked out of the Coliseum claiming that Taft had gotten the nomination only because of fraud in the selection of delegates. Roosevelt bolted the party and in August the "Bull Moose" Progressive Republicans held their own convention at the Coliseum. Roosevelt spoke on August sixth before an adoring throng. The next day he became the Progressive nominee. Jane Addams made a seconding speech.

These two photographs were both taken during the 1912 Republican convention. In the exterior view on the opposite page, the utilitarian Coliseum rises behind Charles Gunther's fanciful castle. The Coliseum was knocked down in 1983. For a time fragments of the castle's Lemont limestone walls survived, but now they too have disappeared.

ABOVE AND LEFT: *With the construction in 1929 of the Chicago Stadium at 1800 West Madison Street—seen here during the 1932 Democratic convention—the Coliseum fell out of favor as a location for major political gatherings. Designed by Hall, Lawrence & Ratcliffe, its sleek Art Deco limestone and tan brick elevations were embellished with spirited bas-reliefs of athletes. The vast hall, which could effortlessly hold 25,000, was billed as the largest indoor arena in the world. It also had the world's largest organ and splendid accoustics. The Chicago Stadium received national attention when the Democrats met*

there from June 27 to July 2, 1932, with the fullest radio coverage ever given to such an event. On July 1, Franklin Delano Roosevelt was nominated for President and the next day electrified the country by flying from New York to Chicago through stormy skies to address the convention. He is seen here on the podium, with Mrs. Roosevelt on the left, the evening of July 2. His speech contained the historic line: "I pledge you, I pledge myself, to a New Deal for the American people." This majestic hall, which witnessed the nomination of Herbert Hoover in 1932, of Roosevelt and Wallace in 1940, of Thomas Dewey in 1944, and of Roosevelt and Truman in 1944, and had also been the home of the Chicago Bulls basketball team and the Blackhawks hockey team, was demolished in 1994 and replaced by the United Center across Madison Street.

ABOVE, LEFT AND RIGHT: Another site where political history was made in Chicago was the International Amphitheatre at 42nd and Halsted streets, part of the Stock Yards complex. Built in seven months in 1934 after a fire destroyed the Yards' exposition hall, the 16,000-capacity Amphitheatre was a straightforward red brick structure, designed by Abraham Epstein. It was the site of the Stock Yards famed annual International Livestock Show and Rodeo. It is seen here during the 1952 Republican convention held at the Amphitheatre July 6–11. This was another famous Grand Old Party fight which featured General Douglas MacArthur giving the keynote address, Illinois Senator Everett McKinley Dirksen wagging his finger at Thomas E. Dewey while accusing the New York governor of leading the party "down the path to defeat," and Dwight David Eisenhower finally snatching the nomination away from the conservatives' hero, Senator Robert

A. Taft of Ohio. Shortly afterward the Democrats convened at the Amphitheatre to nominate Illinois governor Adlai E. Stevenson. Stevenson would be nominated there again in 1956 and the Amphitheatre would be the arena for the tumultuous August 1968 Democratic convention which selected Hubert H. Humphrey to be the party's standard bearer.

In 1960, to commemorate the nomination of Lincoln in Chicago a century earlier, the GOP gathered at the Amphitheatre July 25–28. The party's Presidential nominee, Richard Nixon, with Mrs. Nixon behind him, is shown delivering his acceptance speech on July 28. The speech included these prophetic words: "when Mr. Khrushchev says our grandchildren will live under communism, let us say his grand-children will live under freedom." The International Amphitheatre was demolished in 1999.

ABOVE: *The most historic of Chicago's thoroughbred racetracks was Washington Park, located between Cottage Grove Avenue and South Park, a continuation of Grand Boulevard, now Martin Luther King, Jr. Drive, and 61st and 62nd streets. Though it was privately owned, the track took its name from the public park just to the north. Beginning in 1884 it was the site of the annual running of the American Derby, the Chicago equivalent of Louisville's Kentucky Derby and New York's Belmont Stakes. Shown here is Washington Park's magnificent clubhouse, the work of Solon S. Beman in 1896.*

RIGHT: *A view of the grandstand with a crowd gathered for the 1903 American Derby.*

ABOVE: *The old Washington Park closed in 1904 and was later demolished. Four years later, in 1908, a new Washington Park opened some 20 miles south of the city, in Homewood. This view from the new Washington Park's clubhouse in July, 1939, looks east toward its main entrance at Halsted and 179th streets.*

LEFT: *Lucky bettors line up to cash winning tickets.*

ABOVE, RIGHT: *One of the memorable events in the annals of American racing took place at Washington Park on August 31, 1955, when Nashua, the champion three-year-old of the East, owned by William Woodward, Jr. of New York, and Swaps, the champion of the West, owned by Rex Ellsworth of California, met there in a match race before a crowd of 33,000. The genius behind the event was Benjamin F. Lindheimer, who made his Washington and Arlington Park tracks centers of American thoroughbred sport in the 1940s and 1950s. Shown here is William Woodward, Jr.'s wife, Ann, with Nashua—Eddie Arcaro is the jockey—after winning the $100,000 purse. Some two months later, Mrs. Woodward killed her husband with a shotgun blast, claiming that she thought he was an intruder. Dominick Dunne would turn the tale into a bestseller,* The Two Mrs. Grenvilles. *In the winter of 1977 Washington Park burned to the ground. The site is now occupied by offices.*

241

TOP: *The University of Chicago's Stagg Field, named for famed football coach Amos Alonzo Stagg, was the site of an indisputably earthshaking event. Constructed in 1903 from designs by James Gamble Rogers, the stadium later had alterations and additions by Shepley, Rutan & Coolidge and Holabird & Root. Beneath its Gothic West Stand, shown here, Enrico Fermi and a group of colleagues, on December 1, 1942,* engineered the world's first self-sustained nuclear fission chain reaction, ushering in the Atomic Age. The West Stand was demolished in the summer of 1957.

BOTTOM: *The South Side celebrated the arrival of the American League White Stockings—later the White Sox—in a variety of ways. The whimsical baseball player in living flowers grew on Drexel Boulevard at the turn of the century.*

ABOVE: *Old Comiskey Park was Chicago's field of dreams. Designed by Zachary Taylor Davis, who also designed Wrigley Field, it was the home of the South Side's beloved White Sox. Rising at 35th Street and Shields Avenue, the stadium— seen here in 1913—drew crowds from the nearby neighborhoods of McKinley Park, Canaryville, and Bridgeport. When it opened in July 1910, it was swathed in red, white, and blue bunting, and five bands*

played "Hail to the Chief" for owner Charles Comiskey, whose box was decorated to resemble the coliseum in Rome. The park was home to the team that broke the hearts of Chicago fans, the 1919 White Sox, one of the strongest teams in baseball, who threw the World Series to the underdog Cincinnati Reds. After being implicated in taking bribes from gamblers, eight members of the team—labeled forever thereafter "The Black Sox"—were banned

from baseball for life. Among them was the legendary "Shoeless Joe" Jackson, one of the greatest natural hitters in the history of the game. The old park was embedded in the childhood memories of Chicagoans. In Chicago: City on the Make, Nelson Algren recalled: "Yet that was a time of several treasures: one sun-bright-yellow beer cork with a blood-red owl engraved upon it, a Louisville slugger bat autographed by Swede Risberg, and a Comiskey

Park program from one hot and magic Sunday afternoon." The comfortable old ballpark gave way in 1991 to a new Comiskey Park, a stadium long on skyboxes and restaurants but short on dreams.

Coda

THE GREAT DEPRESSION and World War II, poverty and the shortage of materials, preserved Chicago's architecture for two decades. Virtually nothing of significance was constructed between Graham, Anderson, Probst & White's Field Building on South La Salle Street, completed in 1934 , and Naess & Murphy's Prudential Building of 1955. America's entry into the war in December of 1941 revived the city's industries. Inland Steel, International Harvester, Pullman, and Sears, Roebuck & Company, among others, became essential suppliers of materiel for the war effort and they were joined by new industries such as the Douglas Aircraft Corporation, which made frames for the C-54 transport.

This new prosperity and the embargo on nonessential civilian construction kept intact Chicago's neighborhoods with their variegated mix of apartment houses, one- and two-family homes, movie theaters, retail establishments, restaurants, and bars. A case in point was the West Side neighborhood centered on Madison Street and Crawford Avenue, now Pulaski Road. A rich, ethnic mix of Italians, Poles, Irish, and others, many of whom worked in the vast Sears plant on South Homan Avenue, it boasted luxury apartment hotels like the Guyon on Washington Boulevard, the Graemere at Homan and Washington, and the Midwest Athletic Club on Hamlin Boulevard; a quality department store, Madigan's; famous restaurants, like Little Jack's; and two of the city's supreme movie palaces, the Marbro and the Paradise. Washington Boulevard was lined with impressive single-family homes such as the one owned by Patrick Nash, who with his brother, Richard, was half of the Kelly-Nash Democratic Machine, which from the 1930s to the 1950s dominated politics in the Windy City. It had for its centerpiece Garfield Park, 185 acres beautifully planned by William Le Baron Jenney and Jens Jensen. Among Garfield Park's attractions were a 15-acre lagoon, a spectacular conservatory, and a golden domed Administration Building by Michaelsen & Rognstad, which transported the Spanish Revival style of California to the Illinois prairie. The neighborhood had easy access to the Loop by means of buses on Washington Boulevard and Madison Street and the Lake Street Elevated.

The advent of peace in 1945 did not lead to an immediate building boom in Chicago. There were several reasons for this. Following World War I the nation had experienced a brief, but painful, financial crisis, and the nightmare of the Great Depression of the 1930s, which left Chicago with 700,000 unemployed and some 2000 sleeping under the Michigan Avenue Bridge, was a still vivid memory. There were also more concrete reasons for the hesitation on the part of the business community. The city which for a century

The Tree Studios at 603-621 North State Street, designed by the Parfitt Brothers with Bauer & Hill, occupied land just behind Judge Lambert Tree's mansion, which stood on what is now Wabash Avenue, since 1910 the site of the Medinah Temple, headquarters of Chicago's Shriners. The idea of a complex of artists' studios undoubtedly came, in part, from Judge Tree's wife, Anna, who was a painter. Tree, a distinguished jurist, was the American ambassador to Russia. The Trees' son, Arthur, married Marshall Field's daughter, Ethel. The buff-colored Roman brick State Street façade, with its multiplicity of gables, bears a marked resemblance to McKim, Mead & White's Casino in Newport, Rhode Island, completed in 1880. In 1912 and 1913 additions were made to the Tree Studios on Ohio and Ontario Streets. This colored charcoal drawing on paper of 1997 by Barton Faist shows the Studios' charming courtyard. Developers have long coveted the block occupied by the Tree Studios and the adjacent Medinah Temple. In 1999 the World Monuments Fund placed the block and its buildings on its list of One Hundred Most Endangered sites.

had the reputation for being the place where, if you wanted to work, you could find a job, a city which had gloried in its blue-collar, factory worker ethos, was suddenly aware that its industrial base was eroding. Symbolically, in the 1950s, International Harvester, whose plant along the South Branch of the Chicago River had been a mainstay of the Lower West Side, moved its operations out of the city. Other historic industries, ranging from Western Electric's Hawthorne Works in Cicero to packers like Swift and Armour, also departed.

In a parallel development, the children and grandchildren of those who had worked in Chicago's traditional industries, the new middle class, began deserting their old neighborhoods. This was the result of ethnic change, the desire to own a house surrounded by grass and trees, as well as the job opportunities offered by a variety of industries locating outside the city in campus-like industrial parks. This trend was exemplified by Sara Lee Bakeries, which, in 1964, opened an attractive new half-million-square-foot plant in Deerfield, north of Chicago. This flight was facilitated by the spectacular growth in automobile ownership in the United States, which jumped from 25,800,000 in 1945 to 54,300,000 in 1956 (in Chicago the change was from 428,000 to 765,000) and by the $24 billion for new superhighways authorized by the Federal Aid Highway Act. In their invaluable study *Chicago: Growth of a Metropolis,* Harold M. Mayer and Richard C. Wade spelled out the startling statistical reality: "By 1950 the metropolitan population reached nearly 5,600,000; yet Chicago's 3,521,000 represented only a 6.6 per cent gain over 1940. By 1960 the figures of 6,794,461 and 3,550,404 indicated a further relative city decline and an absolute drop over the previous count."

The emigrants settled first in the outer edges of Cook County, but soon spilled over into Lake, DuPage, Kane, and Will counties. Some opted for new developments like Park Forest, a town created on 3000 acres 30 miles south of the Loop, which welcomed its first residents in 1948 and grew in a dozen years to more than 30,000. Others transformed old towns such as Arlington Heights, northwest of the city, which in 1950 was a compact village of 8768 surrounded by farmland. By 1990 Arlington's population had burgeoned to 75,460 and the farmland had disappeared.

In the midst of this population hemorrhage major areas of the city remained remarkably unchanged. There were indeed aspects of Chicago in the 1940s and 1950s which were reminiscent of Venice or of Charleston, South Carolina, two other cities kept intact by lack of money and a loss of nerve. Strolling up Lake Shore Drive past Edith Rockefeller McCormick's Romanesque palazzo with its astonishing iron gates brought from the 1893 Fair, one would not have been surprised to see the grande dame's ghost, as was her wont in life, step into a Rolls Royce for the two-minute trip across Bellevue Place to the Fortnightly Club. Further north on the Drive, the Potter Palmer castle, gone gray with age, its tall Norman tower and crenelated parapets jagged against the sky, at once thrilled and threatened. Though Bertha Honoré Palmer had in 1918 moved on to a Greek temple in Graceland Cemetery, it was not difficult to imagine that a face in one of the dark windows was the castle's chatelaine regally attired in her diamond tiara, high dog collar, and rope of perfectly matched Oriental pearls. On the South Side, on once-fashionable boulevards like Drexel, immense mansions which had taken their architectural cues from English Tudor palaces and required, at a minimum, a staff of thirteen to run, stood empty within their spacious untended gardens, conjuring up images of Miss Haversham in Charles Dickens's *Great Expectations.*

The Loop in these years was a still vibrant mix of thoroughfares devoted to special functions and side streets brimming with life, a mix found only in great urban complexes. State Street, with its vitality not yet drained away by suburban malls, was both a mart proffering a matchless array of merchandise and a Baedeker of splendid commercial architecture. The spectrum of its offerings was unabashedly democratic, ranging as they did from modestly priced children's clothing at the Boston Store to costly pastel cashmere sweater sets at Field's. This reality had been noted, with acuity, in a late nineteenth-century ditty:

> All the girls who wear high heels
> They trade down at Marshall Field's,
> All the girls who scrub the floor
> They trade at the Boston Store.

Undoubtedly State Street's *dernier cri* in the first decades after the Second World War was Marshall Field & Co.'s "28 Shop," named for its private elevator entrance at 28 East Washington Street. Designed by Joseph Platt, who conceived the sets for *Gone With the Wind,* the "28 Shop" specialized in the latest creations of designers such as Adrian and Hattie Carnegie.

The architecture of the State Street bazaars was a tribute to the merchants who had created the emporiums and to the city which had such outstanding talent on tap. Side by side stood William Le Baron Jenney's Fair Store, magnificent with its richly crowned pilasters; Holabird & Roche's Mandel Brothers, whose second-floor façade, extraordinary for 1905, was a ribbon of glass; D. H. Burnham & Co.'s noble limestone-fronted Field's; and Louis Sullivan's Carson Pirie Scott & Co., whose curved entrance at State and Madison streets was festooned with iron foliage which visually echoed the architect's words in *The Autobiography of an Idea:* "Was there to be no end to the sweet, clamorous joy of all living things?"

If State Street was redolent with the scent of Elizabeth Arden's "Blue Grass" wafting out of its department store's revolving doors, La Salle Street reeked of stocks and bonds. This magnificent financial furrow terminated at its southern end beneath the 30-foot-high aluminum statue of Ceres, Roman goddess of grain, by Chicagoan John Storrs, which had for a pedestal Holabird & Root's forty-five-story Deco Chicago Board of Trade Building. Just behind it, as essential to the economic well-being of the city as the Board itself, was the La Salle Street Station. Here a red carpet was rolled out daily for the passengers arriving on the New York Central's crack *Twentieth Century Limited,* which, practically and symbolically, linked La Salle Street to Wall Street. La Salle was still graced by Adler & Sullivan's sublime Stock Exchange and by the LaSalle Hotel, whose elaborate mansard roof brought a touch of Parisian glamour to this hive of commerce. The LaSalle's nineteenth-floor ballroom, a bit Louis XIV and a bit Louis XV, was one of the handsomest in the city, while its wood-paneled Blue Fountain Room was a spot where top newspaper reporters rubbed shoulders with Windy City financiers.

The mention of the LaSalle summons up those other hotels which helped to energize the Loop in the 1940s and 1950s, providing not only rooms for sleeping, but marvelous venues for a joyous and sophisticated nightlife. This is no trivial matter, for as William H. Whyte noted in *Are Cities Un-American?* "a city deserted at night by its leading citizens is only half a city." There was the Joseph Urban Room in the Congress, whose décor exemplified Urban's brilliant gift for lighting effects and whose music was supplied by Vincent Lopez; the Sherman's Bal Tabarin, with a "black tie" dress code; The Boulevard Room in the Conrad Hilton—by many still called the Stevens—which featured an "ice extravaganza"; and the Palmer House's stately green and gold Empire Room, where, in addition to fox trots and rumbas provided by the house orchestra, one might catch Dorothy Shay or George Gobel.

A great city offers its citizens a variety of urban precincts, "Provides," in the words of the theologian Paul Tillich, "what otherwise could be given only by traveling." The contrast between the Loop and North Michigan Avenue in the twenty years after World War II was a vivid case in point. Crossing the Chicago River and heading north was to leave behind the behemoth buildings of a metropolitan downtown and step onto a thoroughfare which suggested a suburban main street or Palm Beach's Worth Avenue. After the imperial scale of Field's and Carson's, the sky opened up and the architectural note was set by low-rise structures, a mix of old houses converted to commercial uses and new buildings, predominately in a French Art Deco or English Palladian style. These charming structures, many by Philip B. Maher, Robert S. DeGolyer, Holabird & Root, and Jarvis Hunt, were humanly scaled and beautifully detailed. The shops of North Michigan Avenue, with the exception of a comparatively small Saks Fifth Avenue at 661 and Bonwit Teller at Michigan and Pearson, were almost all Chicago establishments: Stanley Korshak, Bes-Ben Hats, Sally Greenbaum, the Town Shop for Men, and Spaulding & Company, jewelers. The restaurants, too, were marked by a subtle combination of big city worldliness and small town intimacy. The Carnegie Drugstore in the Drake served dishes prepared in the same kitchen used by the hotel's opulent Oak Room and at a quarter of the price; Le Petit Gourmet, at 619 North Michigan, still featured specialities using the recipes of its founder, Harriet Tilden, who had helped Field's begin its restaurants in the 1890s; and the Normandy House, which occupied a tall gray stone mansion at 800 North Michigan, which had rooms embellished with murals depicting that French province by the fine Chicago painter Edgar Miller.

Yet there were stirrings in the city, harbingers of coming change. Undoubtedly the most important aesthetically took place at the Illinois Institute of Technology, a university created in 1940 by the merger of the Armour Institute of Technology and a West Side technical school, the Lewis Institute. Mies van der Rohe's carefully ordered plan for the ITT campus, lying between 31st and 35th streets and South Michigan Avenue and the Illinois Central tracks, was in the great tradition of Thomas Jefferson's University of Virginia and Charles F. McKim's Columbia University in New York. All of the twenty buildings in the plan were to be designed by Mies and all were to be constructed with welded steel frames, painted black, with an infill of either glass or tan-colored brick. The masterpiece of the campus was Crown Hall, completed in 1956, the home of the College of Architecture headed by Mies himself. Crown Hall's elegantly-attenuated, evenly-spaced steel beams, separated by tall sheets of glass, gave the structure the serenity and nobility of a Greek temple, thus constructing out of the most modern materials a new classicism. Here truly less is more.

The unmistakable signal that Chicago's business community had exorcised the demons of the Great Depression came in 1955 with the construction of the Prudential Building at 130 East Randolph Street. While the forty-two-story aluminum and limestone skyscraper's design was banal, its location over the Illinois Central Railroad yards at the northern end of Grant Park made it a bold affirmation of urban optimism. For while old smokestack industries vanished and large numbers of the middle class fled to the suburbs, while the passenger portion of the rail lines dwindled and the stock-yards closed their gates, the essential importance of the metropolis of the Midwest was reasserted in the 1950s and 1960s. It was a place for, among other things, company head-quarters, law firms, banks, and hundreds of other business enterprises. O'Hare International Airport, which had been constructed earlier in the 1960s at Orchard Place, northwest of the city, was, by 1967, serving 27 million passengers annually. And between 800,000 and 900,000 people were daily entering and leaving the central business district.

In the boom which followed in the wake of the Prudential Building—between 1955 and 1965 more than a billion dollars was spent on new construction in the Loop—there were projects which strikingly exemplified Chicago's historic tradition of excellence in architecture and others which were inescapably execrable. Among the former was Skidmore, Owings & Merrill's Inland Steel Building on West Monroe Street of 1958. A structure which engagingly flaunted the bifurcation of functions, it enclosed the company offices in a crystalline glass and stainless steel envelope while segregating service functions, including elevators, in a nontransparent adjacent tower. Some of the new edifices, such as Skidmore's 110-story Sears Tower on South Wacker Drive, which was constructed between 1968 and 1974 and was for a time the world's tallest building, were triumphant feats of engineering. Some, alas, like 150 North Michigan Avenue, completed in 1984, were design disasters. Indeed this forty-one-story office building at the northwest corner of Michigan and Randolph, on the site of the superb Crerar Library, presented to the world an angled, sliced-off top which resembled nothing so much as a wedding cake after it had been cut by an inebriated groom.

Accompanying the striking upturn in commercial construction was a spate of new residential buildings. On the South Side these were often urban renewal projects. Sometimes, as in the case of Prairie Courts on South Prairie Avenue of 1956 by George Fred Keck and William Keck, the results were impressive. But by far the most spectacular consequence of the resurgence in residential construction appeared along the lake on the North Side. These new postwar high-rise apartments of metal, marble, brick, and glass shouldered one another like thirsty pachyderms trying to get to water. The resulting mix of sand and steel, of the flat expanse of the inland sea and the soaring silhouette of the buildings, made Studs Terkel feel a bit, as he admitted in *Chicago,* "chesty":

> No other city in the world has a neighborhood like this. Visitors, no
> matter how weary-of-it-all and jaded, are always overawed. You feel
> pretty good; and like a spoiled debutante, you wave a limp hand and
> murmur: It *is* rather impressive, isn't it?

In addition to Mies, with his translucent prisms on Lake Shore Drive between Chestnut Street and Delaware Place, other architects succeeded in shaping splendid residential additions to the Windy City skyline. Among the handsomest was Schipporeit & Heinrich's Lake Point Tower of 1968. Perched on a podium containing parking facilities and shops, the Tower, in its isolated site east of Lake Shore Drive, manages, with its fluid, curved glass walls, to look as good in reality as it did on the drawing board. A more hard-edged aesthetic is exemplified by the metallic structuralism of the John Hancock Center on North Michigan Avenue, erected in 1969. Internally, Skidmore, Owings & Merrill's 100-story tapered behemoth subtly combines commercial and residential functions. Externally, its boldly revealed vertical columns and horizontal beams, visually unified by its gargantuan cross bracing, makes the Hancock a worthy successor to Holabird & Roche's Tacoma Building and other icons of the First Chicago School. Chicago's residential building boom also produced aesthetic disasters. The sixty-one-story North Pier Apartment Tower at 474 North Lake Shore Drive, for instance, combined a façade of ineptly detailed precast concrete with a color scheme focused on rust to achieve the awesomely ugly.

Away from the lakefront, architects such as Stanley Tigerman, Larry Booth, and Jim Nagle were designing noteworthy apartment houses and individual residences. A number of these played a significant role in reviving aging neighborhoods by replacing desolate lots with new housing. Typical was Booth & Nagle's Grant Place Portals on West Grand of 1972, a row of townhouses with walled gardens smoothly slipped into the context of the surrounding structures.

·) Coda (·

The building boom, whose pace accelerated in the 1980s and 1990s, had an indisputedly sinister side. To make way for new buildings and modern expressways, older structures were often callously bulldozed and streets and entire neighborhoods obliterated with a brutal disregard for Chicago's urban fabric. The losses included unquestionable masterworks, such as Adler & Sullivan's Stock Exchange, fragments of which are now displayed in museums in Paris, New York, and Chicago like sculptures from the Parthenon, and the Potter Palmer castle, which would have admirably served as a much-needed official residence for the Chicago mayor, a majestic setting for receptions and ceremonies. Along with these monuments were obliterated special places that played an essential role in Windy City urbanity: the Stop & Shop on West Washington Street, an establishment whose marrons glacés, English biscuits, and freshly ground coffees made it the Fauchon of Chicago, and the Woods theater, whose departure, along with the neighboring United Artists, Schiller, Harris, and Selwyn, transformed Randolph Street from a sparkling rialto to a dull gray street of bureaucrats toiling at the Civic Center.

There was an element of conscious animosity in this destruction. As William H. Whyte observed in 1958: "Most of the rebuilding underway and in prospect is being designed by people who don't like cities. They do not merely dislike the noise and the dirt and the congestion. They dislike the city's variety and concentration, its tension, its hustle and bustle." This bias against cities has a long history in America. No less a person than Thomas Jefferson, in his *Notes on Virginia* published in 1784, warned of the corrupting influences of urban life: "The mobs of great cities add just so much to the support of pure government, as sores do to the strength of the human body." These sentiments were endorsed in the nineteenth and early twentieth centuries by Sir Ebenezer Howard and other advocates of the Garden City movement, who envisioned an arcadian America, a nation ensconced in neat white cottages embowered with roses. The conception was given a modern form by both Frank Lloyd Wright and Le Corbusier, who merely stacked the cottages on top of one another to form a mile-high skyscraper surrounded by bucolic green space. Thus the free-spirited jazz clubs of the Loop, the late night corner bar, and even the local drugstore became little more than structural vermin to be eradicated in the name of order, neatness, and eternal tranquility.

The consequences of such thinking are graphically illustrated by River North, a district west of Michigan Avenue stretching from the Chicago River to Elm Street. In the 1940s, '50s, and '60s, this was a kinetic mix of warehouses, industrial buildings, venerable mansions, and pre–World War II apartment houses. The variety of places to eat was dazzling, ranging from the elegant Kungsholm on East Ontario with a uniformed doorman, puppets who sang opera arias, and the most Lucullan smorgasbord west of the Scandinavian peninsula, to Charmets at Michigan and Chicago, a winning example of that vanishing American institution, the unfranchised coffee shop. Late-night entertainment was available in a dozen raffish watering holes like the Club Alabam and also at the Happy Medium, which mounted shows of the caliber of the memorable *Shoestring Review*. The old buildings of River North provided space for art galleries, rehearsal studios, and photographers, as well as affordable housing for writers and others starting out in the Windy City. Some of the edifices, such as the seven-story buff brick and terra-cotta Cass-Superior Building of 1921 by Walter Anschlager, architect of New York's Roxy Theatre, were of a high quality. The area's quintessential structures, though, were the Tree Studios on North State Street between Ohio and Ontario, constructed in 1894 by Judge Lambert Tree to entice artists who had worked at the 1893 Columbia Exposition to remain in Chicago. Numbered among the Tree Studios' tenants over the years have been J. Allen St. John, the illustrator of the Tarzan books, muralist John Warner Norton, and John Singer Sergeant. With their high windows and large skylights, the Tree Studios bring an unexpected touch of Paris's La Vie Bohème to the City of Big Shoulders.

In the 1980s and 1990s River North, because of its potpourri of galleries and shops, restaurants, and nightlife, as well as its proximity to the Loop, became a highly desirable neighborhood. It attracted, in particular, both newcomers brought to Chicago by the flourishing economy and returnees from suburbia. Ironically, these arrivals were, for the most part, housed in just-constructed faceless, high-rise towers whose very presence vanquished the ambiance which had made the neighborhood so attractive. Everywhere, the old was replaced by the new. This exchange can be, for metropolises, a dangerous thing. In *The Death and Life of Great American Cities,* Jane Jacobs warns, "Newness, and its superficial gloss of well-being, is a very perishable commodity." A telling testimony to the value of the old is evident in those neighborhoods, once dismissed as passé, decrepit, and even undesirable, which survived and are now among Chicago's most vital, attractive, and expensive. These include the Printing House District of the South Loop, Old Town, the neighborhoods west of Lincoln Park, and the area of the Near West Side between Halsted and Damen Avenue, where abandoned warehouses and factories have been converted into lots, townhouses, shops, and restaurants.

Great cities require tender care. The special quality of Chicago is fragile, the consequence of all the generations who have dwelt within it, of cultures carried to Illinois from the four corners of the earth, and of a few rare geniuses. That special quality can be as mundane as the aroma of sauerbraten in the vanished Henrici's or in the still-extant Berghoff, as heart-stoppingly beautiful as the demolished Michigan Square Building's Deco Diana Court or the bronze peacock feather doors on State Street still proclaiming the entrance to the defunct jewelers which bore the bird's name, as uplifting as a daily double on a perfect July day at the burned-out Washington Park or the sight of St. Stanislaus Kostka's single surviving baroque tower. In his memoir *A Movable Feast* that Oak Park native Ernest Hemingway wrote: "There is never any ending to Paris and the memory of each person who has lived in it differs from that of any other." The memory of which Hemingway writes is inseparable from the buildings which fuel the recollection. There will never be an ending to Chicago either, unless its precious architectural legacy is lost.

: SOURCES OF ILLUSTRATIONS :

vii Detail of photo by Andreas Feininger on page 35. *Centre Canadien d'Architecture/ Canadian Centre for Architecture, Montreal.*

1 *Private Collection.*

3, 6 Engravings from Alfred T. Andreas, *History of Chicago, 1884–1886. Private Collection.*

5 *Private Collection.*

7 Top and bottom: *Private Collection.*

8 *Chicago Historical Society.*

9 Top: *Chicago Historical Society.* Bottom: Photo by Harold Allen.

10 *Chicago Historical Society.*

11 Top: *Chicago Herald-American.* Bottom: *Chicago Historical Society.*

12 Top: *Chicago Historical Society.* Bottom: *Art Institute of Chicago.*

13 Top: Photo by Sigmund J. Osty. *Chicago Historical Society.* Bottom: Photo by Harold Allen.

14 Photo by Alexander Hessler. *Chicago Historical Society.*

16 *Private Collection.*

18 *Private Collection.*

21 *Chicago Historical Society.*

22 *The Art Institute of Chicago.*

23, 24, 25, 26 *Chicago Historical Society.*

27 Top: *The Art Institute of Chicago.* Bottom: *Chicago Historical Society.*

28, 29, 30 *Chicago Historical Society.*

31 *Private Collection.*

32, 33 (top) From a McCormick family album, "The Old Home." *State Historical Society of Wisconsin.*

33 Bottom: Photo by Frederick O. Bemm.

34 *Chicago Historical Society.*

35 Photo by Andreas Feininger. *Centre Canadien d'Architecture/Canadian Centre for Architecture, Montreal.*

36 Top: *Chicago Historical Society.* Bottom: *Private Collection.* Floor plan: *Illinois Society of Architects.*

37 *Chicago Historical Society.*

38 Top: *Chicago Historical Society.* Bottom: *Art Institute of Chicago.*

39, 40, 41 *Private Collection.*

42 Top: *Private Collection.* Bottom: *Chicago Historical Society.*

43, 44 *Chicago Historical Society.*

45 *Chicago Historical Society.*

46 *Private Collections.*

47 Photo by Harold Allen.

48 Photo by Philip A. Weibler.

50 *Chicago & North Western Railway.*

53 *Private Collection.*

54 *Chicago Historical Society.* Inset: *Art Institute of Chicago.*

55 Top and bottom: *Chicago Historical Society.*

56 Top: *Library of Congress.* Bottom: *Private Collection.*

57 Top: *The Atchison, Topeka & Santa Fe.* Bottom: *Chicago Historical Society.*

58 *Penn Central Railroad*

59 Top: *Chicago-American.* Bottom: Photo by Ed Nowak. *Penn-Central Railroad.*

60, 61 *Chicago Historical Society.*

62 Top: *Penn-Central Railroad.* Bottom left: *Southern Pacific.* Bottom right: *Lucius Beebe collection.*

63 *Private Collection.*

64, 69, 73, 74 (top and bottom) *Chicago Historical Society.*

75 Left: *Private Collection.* Right: *Chicago Historical Society.*

76 Top: *Centre Canadien d'Architecture/Canadian Centre for Architecture, Montreal.* Bottom: *Herald and Examiner.*

77 Top and bottom: *Chicago Historical Society.*

78 Top: *David R. Phillips Collection, Chicago Architectural Photographing Company.* Bottom: *The Copelin Album; Chicago Historical Society.*

79 Top: Photo from A. Wittmann, *Select Chicago,* 1889. *Chicago Historical Society.* Bottom: *Chicago Historical Society.*

80 *Chicago Historical Society.*

81 *Library of Congress.*

82 *Chicago Historical Society.*

83 Top and bottom: Photos by J. Sherwin Murphy. *Chicago Historical Society.*

84 *David R. Phillips Collection, Chicago Architectural Photographing Company.*

85 Top: Photo by F. S. Dauwalter. *Chicago Historical Society.* Bottom: *Hedrich-Blessing.*

86 *Chicago Historical Society.*

88, 90 *Private Collection.*

93 Photograph from *The Lakeside Memorial of the Burning of Chicago,* 1872. *Private Collection.*

94 Top: From the Rev. Edgar J. Goodspeed, *History of the Great Fires in Chicago and the West,* 1871. *Private Collection.* Bottom: Photograph from *The Lakeside Memorial of the Burning of Chicago,* 1872. *Private Collection.*

95 Top: *Chicago Historical Society.* Bottom: Photograph from *The Lakeside Memorial of the Burning of Chicago,* 1872. *Private Collection.*

96 *Private Collection.*s

97 Top: *Chicago Historical Society.* Bottom: *Private Collection.*

98 *Chicago Historical Society.*

102 *Brown Brothers.*

103 Top: *Chicago Historical Society.* Bottom: *Private Collection.*

105 *Private Collection.*

106 *Chicago Historical Society.*

107 Top and bottom: *The Chicago Historical Society.*

108 (top and bottom), 109: *Chicago Historical Society.*

110 *David R. Phillips Collection.*

111 Top: *Chicago Historical Society.* Bottom: *Private Collection.*

112 Top: *Chicago Historical Society.* Bottom: *Private Collection.*

113 Top: *Hedrich-Blessing.* Bottom: *Library of Congress.*

114 *Hedrich-Blessing.*

115 *Private Collection.*

116 *Private Collection.*

117 Top and bottom: *Hedrich-Blessing.*

118 *Library of Congress.*

121 Photo by Ralph Marlowe Line.

122 *The Art Institute of Chicago.*

125, 126 *Private Collection.*

128 *Private Collection.*

129 *Private Collection..*

130 Top: *Private Collection.* Bottom left: Photo by Harold Allen.

131 Photo by Harold Allen.

132 Top: *Chicago Historical Society.* Bottom: Photo by Ralph Marlowe Line.

133, 134 (top and bottom) *Chicago Historical Society.*

135 *David R. Phillips Collection. Chicago Architectural Photographing Company.*

136 *Chicago Historical Society.*

137 *Roosevelt University.*

138 Photo by Richard Nickel. *Chicago Historical and Architectural Landmarks Commission.*

139 Photo by Roget-Viollet.

140 Top: Photo by Ralph Marlowe Line. Bottom: Photo by Richard Nickel. *Chicago Historical and Architectural Landmarks Commission.*

141 *Chicago Historical Society.*

142, 143, 144 *Chicago Historical Society.*

145 Top: Photo by Glenn E. Dahlby. *Chicago Historical Society.*

146 *Montgomery Ward.*

147 Left and right: *Chicago Historical Society.*

148 *Private Collection.*

149 *Private Collection.*

151 *Private Collection.*

152 *Private Collection.*

155 Courtesy of the New-York Historical Society.

157 Photo by Harold Allen.

158 From *The Columbian Portfolio,* 1893. *Private Collection.*

159 Top: *Chicago Historical Society.* Bottom: *Private Collection.*

160,161 *Chicago Historical Society.*

162 Top and bottom: *Private Collection.*

163 *Private Collection.*

164 *Chicago Historical Society.*

165 Top: *Chicago Historical Society.* Bottom: *Private Collection.*

166 *Chicago Historical Society.*

167 (top and bottom) From *The Columbian Portfolio,* 1893. *Private Collection.*

168, 169 *Private Collection.*

170, 171, 172 *New York Public Library.*

173, 174 *Hedrich-Blessing.*

175 *New York Public Library.*

176 Top: *Culver Pictures.* Bottom: *Hedrich-Blessing.*

177 Top: *Hedrich-Blessing.* Bottom: *Private Collection.*

178 Photo by Byron C. Karzas.

180 *Chicago Historical Society.*

181 *David R. Phillips Collection. Chicago Architectural Photographing Company.*

183 *David R. Phillips Collection. Chicago Architectural Photographing Company.*

187 *Private Collection.*

188 From the *Copelin Album, Chicago Historical Society.*

189 Top: *Chicago Historical Society.* Bottom: *Private Collection.*

190 Top: Photo by J. W. Taylor. *Chicago Historical Society.* Bottom: *The Art Institute of Chicago.*

191 *Library of Congress.*

192 Left and right: *Private Collection.*

193 Photo by Richard Nickel.

194 Top: *Hedrich-Blessing.* Bottom: *Chicago Historical Society.*

195, 196 *Private Collection.*

197–200 *Chicago Historical Society.*

201 Top: Photo by J. Johnson, Jr. *Chicago Historical Society.* Bottom: *Private Collection.*

202 *Frank Driggs Photo Files.*

203 Top: *Hedrich-Blessing.* Bottom: *Private Collection.*

204 *Chicago Historical Society.*

205, 207 *Private Collection.*

208 Top: *Chicago Historical Society.* Bottom: *Private Collection.*

209 Left and right: *Chicago Historical Society.*

210 *Hedrich-Blessing.*

212 *Chicago Historical Society.*

218 *Private Collection.*

220 Top: *Brown Bros. Photo.* Bottom: *Private Collection.*

222 *Chicago Historical Society.*

223 Top: *Private Collection.* Bottom: Photo by Hedrich-Blessing. *Chicago Historical Society.*

224 Top and bottom: *Private Collection.*

225 Top and bottom: *Hedrich-Blessing.*

226 *The Art Institute of Chicago.*

227 Top: *Chicago Historical Society.* Bottom: *Private Collection.*

228 *Chicago Historical Society.*

229 *Private Collection.*

230 *Private Collection.*

231 Top and bottom : *The Arts Club of Chicago.*

232 Top and bottom right: Hedrich-Blessing. *The Arts Club of Chicago.* Bottom left: *The Arts Club of Chicago.*

233 Top and bottom: *Tebbs and Knell, Inc.*

234 Top and bottom: *Tebbs and Knell, Inc.*

235 Top and bottom: *Chicago Historical Society.*

236, 237 *Chicago Historical Society.*

238 Top and bottom: *Chicago Historical Society.*

239 Left: *Library of Congress.* Right: *Chicago Historical Society.*

240 Top and bottom: *Chicago Historical Society.*

241 Top left: *Max F. Kolin Press Photography.* Top right and bottom: *Private Collection.*

242 Top left: *Private Collection.* Bottom left: *Chicago Historical Society.*

243 *Chicago Historical Society.*

244 *Private Collection.*

INDEX